FHM PRESENTS...

THE BIGGEST BOOK OF

BAR-ROOM
JOKES

THIS IS A CARLTON BOOK

Text copyright © Emap Elan Network 2001, 2004
Design copyright © Carlton Books Limited 2004
This edition published by Carlton Books Limited 2004
20 Mortimer Street
London W1T 3JW

A CIP catalogue record for this book is available from the British Library.

ISBN-10: 1-84442-681-5
ISBN-13: 978-1-84442-681-2

The material in this book was previously published as *The Best of Bar-Room Jokes*
and *The Best of Bar-Room Jokes 2*

Typeset by e-type, Liverpool
Printed in the UK

Thanks to FHM's readers for all their jokes

www.fhm.com/jokes

FHM PRESENTS...

THE BIGGEST BOOK OF

BAR-ROOM
JOKES

CARLTON

The Ordeal of Fruit

Two men shipwrecked on an island are captured by cannibals. The chief informs them the only way to avoid becoming dinner is to undergo the 'Ordeal of Fruit'. The men accept at once, and the chief sends them into the jungle to collect 100 pieces of fruit and bring them back to him. The first man comes back with 100 grapes. The chief says that if he can shove all the grapes up his arse without giggling then he will be free. But no sooner has the first grape reached his butt than the man bursts out laughing. 'What's so funny?' the chief asks. 'Don't you realize we're going to kill you now?' 'I'm sorry,' the sailor replies. 'It's just that my friend is collecting pineapples.'

The Amish go to town

An Amish boy and his father rode into town to visit a new shopping mall. All that they saw had them reeling in amazement, but the one thing that really caught their eye was a pair of shiny 'walls' that could slide open and close effortlessly shut again. The boy looked at his father and asked,

'What is this thing, father?'

Having never seen an elevator before, the old man responded:

'Son, I have never seen anything like this in my life. I don't know what it is.'

At that moment, a fat lady in a wheelchair rolled up to the moving walls and pressed a button. The walls opened and the lady moved between them into a small room. The walls then closed, and the boy and his father watched in awe as a series of semi-circular numbers above the walls lit up sequentially. They continued to stare as the numbers lit in reverse order. Finally the walls opened again and a gorgeous, voluptuous blonde woman stepped out. Without taking his eyes off the young woman, the father said quietly: 'Son, go get your mother ...'

Drunk driving (i)

A man is driving happily along when he is pulled over by the police. The copper approaches him and politely asks, 'Have you been drinking, sir?'

'Why?' snorts the man. 'Is there a fat bird in my car?'

A fisherman's mistake

A fisherman is sorting through his catch on the edge of a lake when a man sprints up to him, obviously in some distress. 'Help me please,' he gasps. 'My wife is drowning and I can't swim.' He points out to a distant figure, splashing around pathetically 100 m from the shore. 'Please save her. I'll give you a hundred quid if you do.' Nodding, the fisherman dives into the water. In a few powerful strokes, he reached the woman, puts his arm around her, and swims back to shore. Depositing her at the feet of the man, he looks up at him.

'Okay,' he says, regaining his breath, 'where's my hundred?' The man frowns back at him. 'Look,' he says. 'When I saw her going down for the third time, I thought it was my wife. But this is my mother-in-law.' The fisherman reached into his pocket. 'Just my luck,' he says. 'How much do I owe you?'

Q: Why did the woman cross the road?

A: Never mind that – what is she doing out of the kitchen?

Never gamble with a chemist

This deaf mute strolls into a chemist's shop to buy a packet of condoms. Unfortunately, the mute cannot see any of his required brand on the shelves, and the chemist, unable to decipher sign language, fails to understand what the man wants.

Frustrated, the deaf mute decides to take drastic action: he unzips his trousers and drops his cock on the counter, before placing a £5 note next to it. Nodding, the chemist unzips his own trousers, performs the same manoeuvres as the mute, then picks up both notes and stuffs them in his pocket.

Exasperated, the deaf mute begins to curse the chemist with a wild gesturing of his arms. 'Sorry,' the chemist says, shrugging his shoulders. 'But if you can't afford to lose, you shouldn't gamble.'

He said she'd be sorry ...

From the day of their wedding, Sarah has been nagging her husband about his past.

'Come on, tell me,' she asks again, 'how many women have you slept with?'

'Honey, ' he says, 'if I told you, you'd just get angry.'

'No, I promise I won't,' she begs.

'Well, If you insist. Let's see. One ... two ... three ... four ... you ... six ... seven ...'

The accommodating wife

A woman complains to her friend that her husband is losing interest in sex, and he prefers nights out with the lads to the joys of copulation. Her friend tells her that to win his love she must make more effort. She advises her to cook a slap-up meal and then send him drinking with his pals down the pub. When he returns she must be dressed in her naughtiest lingerie and look her most beautiful.

The following evening, she does exactly as instructed and is dressed to kill by the time her husband returns. When he sees her lying on the bed in all her gear, he tells her to stand up and take it all off. He then tells her to do a handstand against the bathroom mirror and open her legs. This excites the woman immensely, as her husband has never been this erotic before. She does as instructed, and then he puts his face between her legs, faces the mirror and says, 'No, no ... Maybe the lads are right. A beard wouldn't suit me.'

One for Beatles fans

What would it take to reunite the Beatles?

Two bullets.

Mistaken diagnosis

A woman is lying in the road after being run over. The driver of the vehicle that knocked her down comes to her help. 'Are you all right, love?' he asks.

'You're just a blur,' she says. 'So my sight is clearly affected.'

Very concerned, the driver leans over the woman in order to test her eyesight. 'How many fingers have I got up?' he asks her.

'Oh shit!' she replies. 'I must be paralysed from the waist down as well.'

Booby prize

After a woman meets a man in a bar, they talk and end up leaving together. They get back to his flat, and as he's showing her around, she notices that his bedroom is completely packed with teddy bears. Hundreds of them – all arranged in size, from the smallest on the shelves along the floor, to the huge Daddy bears on the very top shelf.

Surprised, the woman still decides not to mention this to him. After an intense night of passion, as they are lying there together in the afterglow, the woman rolls over and asks, smiling, 'Well, how was it?'

'Well,' says the man, frowning. 'You can have any prize from the bottom shelf.'

It's that old playground favourite

How do you confuse a dickhead?

Forty-two.

All fingers and thumbs

While cutting wood in his workshop, Jim the carpenter slips and manages to slice all his fingers off on his powerful electric saw. He screams and runs out of the workshop, sprinting in considerable pain to the nearest hospital. After he has been waiting half an hour, a nurse emerges.

'I'm sorry, sir,' she says, 'but without your fingers, we can't do anything except stop the bleeding. Go back and get our fingers so we can sew them back on.'

Nodding forlornly, Jim wanders out of casualty. An hour later, he returns.

'Did you recover your fingers, sir?' asks the nurse.

'No,' he replied. 'I couldn't pick them up off the floor.'

Is that a frog in your pocket ...?

A man surveys the women in a nightclub, picks out the most attractive, and takes a seat next to her at the bar. He uses all his best lines, but gets nowhere. Finally, he reaches into his pocket, takes out a small box, and pulls a frog out of it.

'Cute,' says the woman. 'Is that a pet?'

The man smiled. 'Yes, and he's good at doing tricks too.'

'Like what?'

'He eats pussy. Come back to my place and I'll prove it to you ...'

Once in the bedroom, the girl strips off and puts the frog between her legs. The frog doesn't move. After a couple of minutes the woman looks at the immobile frog, and finally demands, 'Well?'

The man shakes his head sorrowfully, picks up the frog, and says, 'Okay, you idiot, I'm only going to show you one more time.'

The power of drugs

Enid sat at her husband's hospital bedside, watching him slowly regain consciousness as the effects of a particularly powerful anaesthetic wore off. Slowly the man's eyes fluttered open, and, seeing his wife's anxious face looming over him, he murmured, 'You're beautiful.'

An hour later the man's eyes once again opened, and he said, 'You look nice.'

'What happened to beautiful, then?' Enid enquired.

'The drugs are wearing off,' came the frail reply.

Q: What type of bees produce milk?

A: Boobees!

The flute player

While out on a hunting expedition, a man is climbing over a fallen tree when his shotgun goes off, hitting him straight in the groin.

Rushed to hospital, he awakes from the anaesthetic to find the surgeon has done a marvellous job repairing his damaged member. As he dresses to go home, the surgeon wanders over and hands him a business card.

'This is my brother's card. I'll make an appointment for you to see him.'

The guy is shocked. 'But it says here that he's a professional flute player,' he says. 'How can he help me?'

The doctor smiles. 'Well,' he says, 'he's going to show you where to put your fingers so you don't piss in your eye.'

Circus kills

How do you kill an entire circus at once?

Go for the Jugguler.

Knickers!

After ten loyal years working at the local factory, Nigel and Trevor were laid off, so first thing Monday morning they made their way to the DSS. When asked his occupation, Nigel said, 'I'm a panty stitcher. I sew the elastic into cotton knickers.'

The clerk looked up 'panty stitcher' and, finding it to be classed as unskilled labour, gave Nigel £100 a week benefit money.

Trevor then approached the counter and explained that he was a diesel fitter. As diesel fitting was considered to be a skilled occupation, Trevor was awarded £200 a week.

When Nigel learned how much his friend was being given he was furious, and went storming up to the clerk, demanding to know why his mate was collecting double his own pay.

'It says on my list that diesel fitters are an intrinsic part of the skilled labour force,' explained the clerk, patiently.

'What skill?' screamed Nigel. 'I sew in the elastic, he pulls the knickers on and says, "Yup – diesel fitter!"'

He's armless

A man with no arms or legs is sunbathing on the beach. He is approached by three beautiful young women who take pity on him. The first says to him, 'Have you ever been hugged?'

The man shakes his head, and she leans down and gives him a big hug.

The second says to him, 'Have you ever been kissed?'

He shakes his head. She kisses him.

Rather abruptly, the third girl asks, 'Have you ever been fucked?'

'No,' says the man, his eyes lighting up.

'Well, you are now. The tide's coming in.'

A medical request

A senior lecturer at a London medical college is rather surprised one afternoon when one of his most promising students breaks through the door in a clear state of distress. Sitting the lad down, the kindly old-timer waits for him to compose himself before asking, 'What on earth is the matter?'

'I can't take it anymore, doc,' wails the distressed student. 'I need to find somewhere else to live!'

'But our student digs are the best in the land,' protests the lecturer.

'No, doctor – it's this new policy of mixed living quarters. Every night when I'm trying to study, I have to push away beautiful young nurses, who have come in drunk from a night on the town and are hungry for sex.'

'I see,' says the quack. 'So how do you think I can help?'

'Oh doc,' says the desperate young man, quietly. 'You're going to have to break my arms.'

Divine wisdom

Why did God create Adam before Eve?

To give him a chance to speak.

The Legion take anyone

A captain in the Foreign Legion was transferred to a desert outpost. On his first day there he noticed a very old, seedy-looking camel tied up at the back of the barracks. He asked his sergeant what this animal was for.

The sergeant replied, 'Well, sir, we're a fair distance from anywhere, and the men have natural sexual urges, so when they do, uh, we have the camel.'

The captain thinks about this, and says, 'Well, if it's good for morale, then I suppose it's all right with me.'

After he has been at the fort for about six months, the captain became very frustrated himself. Finally he could stand it no longer and so he told his sergeant, 'Bring in the camel!'

The sarge shrugged his shoulders and led the camel into the captain's quarters. The captain then got a footstool and began to have vigorous sex with the camel. As he stepped down, satisfied, and was buttoning his pants up, he asked the sergeant, 'Is that how the enlisted men do it?'

The sergeant replied, 'Well, no sir, they usually just use it to ride to the brothel in town.'

The tell-tale fingers

'I'm baffled by your yellow penis,' the doctor told his patient. 'Does anyone else in your family have this condition?'

The concerned fellow shook his head.

'Do you handle any chemicals at work?'

'I don't work. I'm unemployed.'

Well, what do you do all day?'

'Oh, I mostly sit around watching porno movies, eating Quavers.'

Mistaken identity

Two Irishmen are walking through Calcutta when an old woman wanders past. 'Hey, Seamus,' one says. 'I think that's Mother Teresa.'

'Rubbish,' says the other.

'I'm telling you it was.'

To settle the argument, they approach the lady and ask her.

'Are you Mother Teresa?'

The old woman eyes them scornfully.

'Piss off, you perverts,' she hisses.

'Jeez,' Seamus says, watching her disappear into the crowd. 'Now we'll never know.'

Saving the species

There's a very rare breed of orang-utan, and one of the few left is Daisy, who lives in a zoo. The problem is that Daisy is getting older and her fertility rate is dropping. Scientists in the field can't find a suitable mate for Daisy – but suddenly a report comes out which proves that, for the first time, man can mate with orang-utan.

But who would ever attempt to impregnate a fully grown ape? Well, who better than Paddy? For 17 years, he has been Daisy's zookeeper and if any man has built a bond of trust with her, then it's him. So the scientists call him in and put the proposal to him.

They say, 'Look, Paddy, we know Daisy's really close to you.'

'She's like a partner to me,' Paddy agrees.

'Well, we need someone to mate with the orang-utan and reproduce the species. Time is running out, and we think you're the guy to carry it off.'

Paddy thinks about this for a minute, then says, 'I understand what you're saying, but I'm not interested.'

So they say, 'Look, Paddy, it's a £500 deal and there's a cloak of secrecy wrapped around it. Believe us, it's for Daisy's benefit and the continuation of the species. That's why we're asking you.'

Paddy says, 'Okay. I understand, but let me sleep on it and I'll let you know tomorrow.'

Next day, all the boffins are sitting there. Paddy comes in, very emotional, and says, tears welling in his eyes, 'I'm going to do it, but there are three conditions. One: no kissing on the lips, because it's too intimate.'

The scientists agree.

Paddy continues, 'Two: any child born of this project will be a strict Catholic.' The scientists say it's no problem.

'And three,' says Paddy, 'you'll need to give me at least a week to get the £500 together.'

Not for sale in Scotland

Two Scotsmen are walking down a country lane.

'Och, Duncan,' says Jimmy all of a sudden, 'I dinnae half need a shit.'

'Well, just go behind a bush and do it, then,' replies his mate.

So Jimmy goes behind a bush, and after a while he shouts, 'Have you got any paper?'

To which Duncan replies, 'Och, don't be such a tight bastard. Leave it.'

What a wanker

Worried about his failing eyesight, a man goes to his optician – who tells him he must stop masturbating.

'Why?' asks the man, worriedly, 'Am I going blind?'

'No, your eyesight is fine,' says the optician, 'But it upsets the other patients in the waiting room.'

The old ones are the best

A man walks into a pub with a lump of tarmac under his arm.

'A pint please, landlord,' he says, 'and one for the road.'

Ask a stupid question ...

At 7am, a lone wife hears a key in the front door. She wanders down, bleary eyed, to find her husband in the kitchen – drunk, with ruffled hair and lipstick on his collar.

'I assume,' she snarls, 'that there is a very good reason for you to come waltzing in here at seven in the morning?'

'There is,' he replies. 'Breakfast.'

It's all in the phrasing

An Essex girl is out driving one day when her car skids at a roundabout and hits the car in front. As she's injured, an ambulance is called and a paramedic quickly arrives. 'What's your name, love?' he asks.

'Sharon,' she replies.

Looking around, the medic sees there's a lot of blood.
'Sharon,' he asks, 'where are you bleeding from?'
'Romford,' she replies.

Drunk driving (ii)

While patrolling country lanes around his local village, a young
policeman notices a car being driven erratically. With a quick burst
of the siren he pulls the driver over, and sternly walks up to the car
to ask the gentleman whether he's been drinking.

'Oh aye,' says the man, quite proudly. 'It's Friday, so a few of the
lads and I went straight to the pub after work, and I must have had
about six or seven there. Then we went to the bar next door for
happy hour, and they were serving these great cocktails for a
pound, so I had three or four of those. Then my cousin Mick asked
for a lift home – his sister's sick, you see – so I drove him back. Of
course, he asked me in, so I had a Murphy's – lovely stuff it is, too
– and took a bottle for the road.'

With that, the man reaches into his coat, pulls out a bottle of
scotch, waves it at the policeman, and beams happily.

'Sir, would you exit the vehicle immediately for a breathalyser
test,' the officer says as calmly as he can.

'Why?' asks the man. 'Don't you believe me?'

Twin controls

Two Siamese twins go on holiday to the same resort in southern
France every year. Unsurprisingly, the head waiter recognizes the
conjoined brothers, and asks if they keep coming back for the weather.

'Oh no,' replies one of the twins, 'Actually we burn quite easily.'
'Perhaps you are wine connoisseurs, then?' wonders the waiter.
'Again, no,' says the other twin. 'We're both beer drinkers'
'I know!' cries the waiter. 'It must be the fine French food?'
'Actually,' they say, shaking their heads, 'We prefer English fish
and chips.'

The waiter is astounded. 'So what makes you come back year
after year?'

'Well,' says one twins, pointing to his brother. 'It's the only
chance our kid gets to drive.'

Caught short

A girl takes her new boyfriend back home after the dance. She tells him to be very, very quiet as her parents are asleep upstairs and if they wake up, she would be in big trouble as she's not allowed to bring boys home.

They settle down to business on the sofa, but after a while, he stops and says, 'Where's the toilet, I need to go.'

She says, 'It's next to my parents' bedroom. You can't go there, you might wake them up. Use the sink in the kitchen instead.'

He goes into the kitchen then, after a short while, he pops his head round the door and says to his girlfriend, 'Have you got any paper?'

Q: What do you call a lesbian with thick fingers?

A: Well hung.

Sand trap

Pinocchio complains to his father saying 'Whenever I attempt to make love to a woman, she complains of splinters.' His father shows pity and gives Pinocchio a piece of sandpaper to smooth his knob down whenever he needs to. A few days later during dinner his father asks, 'How are the girls?' Pinocchio replies, 'Girls? Who needs girls?'

Laughter is the best medicine

What's grey, sits at the end of your bed and takes the piss?
A kidney dialysis machine.

Chinese takeaway

A man goes to a disco and starts chatting up a very attractive-looking Chinese girl. After a night of cavorting, she asks him back to her place 'for a coffee'. They get to her flat, and she tells him to help himself to a drink while she slips into something more comfortable. Just as he finishes his drink, the sexy Chinese seductress returns wearing only a see-through negligée.

'I am your sex slave!' she says. 'I will do absolutely ANYTHING you want.'

The man can't believe his luck. 'Hmm,' he says, grinning from ear-to-ear.

'I really fancy a 69.'

'Fuck off!' replies the girl. 'I'm not cooking at this time of night.'

Shhh!

A blonde walks into a library.

'Excuse me – can I have a burger and large fries, please?' she demands.

Tutting, the librarian looks back at her. 'Miss,' he says, 'this is a library.'

The blonde leans over the counter.

'I'm sorry,' she whispers. 'Can I have a burger and large fries, please?'

The interpretation of dreams

Waking after a long night's sleep, a wife begins recounting her dream to her husband. 'I dreamt I was at an auction for cocks,' she began. 'The long ones went for a tenner, and the meaty ones for £20.'

'How about the ones like mine?' asked her husband.

'Oh, they gave those away,' she replied, grinning slyly.

Miffed, the husband responds: 'Well I had a dream too – where they were auctioning off pussies. The pretty ones cost £1,000 and the little tight ones went for double that.'

'And how much for the ones like mine?' inquired his wife.

The man grinned. 'Oh, that's where they held the auction.'

Are they related?

What have Kermit the Frog and Henry the VIII got in common?

They both have the same middle name.

At least someone's happy

A doctor walks into his office, where a patient is anxiously awaiting results from a blood test. 'Mr Stirling, I'm not going to mess you around,' the medic announces. 'There's good news and bad news. Which do you want?'

'Give me the bad stuff,' replies the man.

Calmly, the doc says, 'You've got 48 hours to live.'

His patient howls, claws his hair and moans, 'Oh my God, what am I going to do? Surely there must be a cure!'

'Of course not,' says the doctor, gruffly.

'But I thought you said there was some good news,' sobs the man.

'Oh yes, that's right – there is,' replies the quack, cheerfully. 'Remember the beautiful nurse at reception when you came in?'

'Yes,' replies the puzzled patient.

'The blonde with the tight, white uniform?'

'Yeah! With the big tits!' says the patient, brightening up somewhat.

'Well,' says the doctor, leaning over to whisper. 'I'm shagging her.'

Q: Where would you find a duck with no legs?

A: Where you left it.

Dispute Down Under

The Australian Prime Minister flies to England for a meeting with the Queen. Over a cup of tea, the PM brings up his grand new plan for his country.

'Your Majesty, mate,' he begins. 'Can we turn Australia into a kingdom, in order to increase our role in the global economy?'

The Queen shakes her head and replies, 'One needs a king for a kingdom, and unfortunately you are most certainly not a king.'

Not to be dissuaded, the politician asks, 'Would it be possible to transform Australia into an empire, then?'

'No,' replies the Queen. 'For an empire you need an emperor, and you are most certainly not an emperor.' The PM thinks for a moment and then asks if it's possible to turn Australia into a principality.

The Queen replies, 'For a principality, you need a prince – and you are not a prince.' Pausing for a sip of her tea, Her Majesty then adds: 'I don't mean to appear rude, but having met both you and several other Australians, I think Australia is perfectly suited as a country.'

Transfer of guilt

Liverpool Football Club are on the look out for some new talent and send a scout to Bosnia where they find a fantastic new player and bring him back with them. In his first game, he scores a hat-trick and the fans love him. When he gets home he decides to phone his mum and give her the good news, but when she answers she immediately starts crying.

When he asks what the matter is, she replies, 'Well, this morning your sister was raped by a street gang, then your little brother was savaged by wild dogs while playing football in the street. After that your dad was shot by a sniper and I was mugged and beaten up while shopping.'

The guy is gobsmacked. 'Mum, what can I say? I'm so sorry.'

'Sorry?!' she shouts. 'It's your fault we moved to Liverpool!'

Open and shut case

After a long marriage and nine children, a woman's husband dies. Devastated, she nevertheless remarries and has seven more children – before her second husband passes away. Undaunted, she marries for a third time – and has another six children before finally kicking the bucket herself.

At her funeral, the vicar stands next to her coffin and prays for her soul.

'Oh Lord,' says the preacher, 'Protect this woman, who fulfilled your commandment to go forth and multiply. And we thank you, Lord, that they're finally together.'

Leaning over to his neighbour, one of the mourners asks, 'Do you think he means her first, second or third husband?'

The other mourner frowns. 'I think,' he replies, 'that he means her legs.'

The power of spinach

What happened when Jesus went to Mount Olive?

Popeye kicked the shit out of him.

Lucky dog

Three guys are comparing their drunkenness from the night before. The first guy says, 'I was so drunk I don't even know how I got home ... I just woke up in my bed in a pool of sweat.'

'Oh yeah?' brags the second guy. 'I was so wasted I took home a strange woman and was having sex with her when my wife walked in.'

'That's nothing,' says the third guy. 'I was so pissed I was blowing chunks all night.'

'Big deal,' scoff the other two.

The third guy says, 'I don't think you understand – Chunks is the name of my dog.'

Countdown

After months of ill-health, a man goes to his doctor for a complete check-up. Afterward, the doctor comes out with the results.

'I'm afraid I have some very bad news,' says the physician. 'You're dying, and you don't have much time left.'

'Oh, that's terrible!' says the man. 'How long have I got?'

'Ten,' the doctor replies, shaking his head.

'Ten?' the man asks. 'Ten what? Months? Weeks? What do you mean?'

The doctor looks at him sadly. 'Nine ...'

Dearth of a princess

Princess Diana and the Queen are being driven around the grounds of Balmoral, when the Land Rover is stopped by a robber. He tells the Queen to wind down her window and hand over all her money.

'I'm the richest woman in the world,' replies the Queen. 'I have no need for money.'

So the robber turns to Diana and demands she hands over all her jewellery.

'I'm the most beautiful woman in the world,' replies Di. 'I have no need for jewellery.'

The robber decides to cut his losses and so steals the Land Rover instead. When he's gone, the Queen asks Diana where she hid all her jewellery.

'Well,' says Diana, 'when I saw him approaching, I stuffed it all up my fanny. Why, what did you do with all the money you were carrying?'

'Same thing,' says the Queen. 'When I saw him approaching, I stuffed all the cash up my fanny.'

'It's a pity Fergie wasn't here,' says Diana. 'Otherwise we could have saved the Land Rover as well.'

Size does matter

Three men are marooned on a desert island desperately seeking a way to get off. A cannibal approaches them and flops his penis out. 'If the length of your three penises put together is as big as mine, then I'll show you a way to get off the island,' he says. 'But otherwise you'll be killed and eaten.'

The native's love muscle was a staggering 20 inches. The first man got his out, and it was 10 inches. The second man then produced a 9-inch knob. Realizing they only needed 1 inch to go, the first two men were quietly confident. The third got his penis out, and it was only 1 inch long.

After some tense calculations, the native says, 'Okay, you've equalled the length of my penis. I have a boat which you can use to escape.'

While sailing away on the boat, the first man says to the other two, 'You're lucky I've got a 10-inch penis.'

And the second says, 'You're lucky I've got a 9-inch penis.'

To which the third man replies, 'And you're lucky I had an erection.'

A fishy tale

Two parrots are sitting on a perch. One says to the other, 'Can you smell fish?'

Happy meal?

One cold winter evening, an elderly couple wander into a fast-food restaurant. As the young families look on, the old gent walks up to the counter, orders a meal and then pays. Taking a seat next to his wife, he slowly unwraps the plain burger and cuts it in two – placing one half in front of his beloved. Then, he carefully divides the fries into two piles: one for him, one for her.

As the man takes a few bites of hamburger, the crowd began to get restless – this is obviously a couple who've been together for decades, and all they can afford is a single meal. Eventually, a young onlooker wanders over and offers to buy another meal.

'We're just fine, thanks,' says the pensioner. 'After 50 years, we're used to sharing everything.'

Then the young man notices that the little old lady hasn't eaten a bite of her portion. Instead, while her husband wolfs down his half, she sits and occasionally sips the drink.

'Ma'am,' says the young chap. 'Why aren't you eating? Your husband says you share everything. What are you waiting for?'

Over horn-rimmed glasses, she looks back at him. 'The teeth,' she says.

Marital economics

Little Johnny walks past his parents room one night and sees them making love. Puzzled, he asks his father about it in the morning. 'Why were you doing that to mummy last night?'

His father replies, 'Because mummy wants a baby.'

The next night, Johnny spots mummy giving daddy a blow job and the next morning he asks his father, 'Why was mummy doing that to you last night?'

His father replies, 'Because mummy wants a BMW.'

Q: What do Essex girls use for protection during sex?

A: Bus shelters.

Two countries separated by a common language

A tourist walks into a drug store in Los Angeles, and asks for a packet of condoms. 'Rubbers, eh?' says the chemist, recognizing his customer is English. 'That'll be five dollars – including the tax.'

'Is that necessary?' cries the man. 'Back home, we roll them on.'

The taxman cometh

A Yuletide meal at an expensive restaurant is disturbed when a woman starts screaming. 'My son's choking! ' she cries. 'He's swallowed the sixpence in the Christmas pudding! Please, anyone – help!'

Without speaking, a man stands up at a nearby table, and walks over nonchalantly. Smiling pleasantly, he grips the boy by the gonads and squeezes: the boy coughs, and out pops the coin.

'Thank you so much!' beams the relieved mother. 'Are you a paramedic?'

'No,' replied the man, 'I work for the Inland Revenue.'

Builders' arse

One day a construction crew arrives next door to a young family to build another house. The family's six-year-old daughter naturally takes an interest, and begins hanging around the site. Eventually the brickies adopt her as a kind of mascot – chatting to her and giving her errands to run. Then, at the end of the week, they present her with a pay envelope containing a fiver.

Excitedly, the little girl runs home to her mother, who suggests they take it to the bank. Running straight up to the pay-in desk, the little girl thrusts her wages over the counter.

'I earned this building a house,' she beams, proudly. 'For a whole week.'

'Goodness!' smiles the teller. 'And will you be building it next week, too?'

'Yes,' trills the little girl. 'If the fucking bricks ever get delivered.'

Calling all cars ...

A burglary was recently committed at Manchester City's ground and the entire contents of the trophy room were stolen. Police are looking for a man with a pale blue carpet.

Know your own strength

Sven-Goran Eriksson arrives for his first training session as England manager, and wanders into the changing room – only to spot a massive, steaming turd nestling in the middle of the shower room. Fuming, he returns to his players in the main changing area.

'Who's shit on the floor?' he screams.

'Me, boss,' cries Emil Heskey, 'but I'm not bad in the air.'

Can I get some privacy?

Little Red Riding Hood is walking through the woods one day, when she spies the wolf crouched down behind a bush. Thinking that it would be a laugh and make a bit of a change to sneak up on him for once, she creeps over and taps the wolf on his shoulder.

'My, mister wolf,' she says with a smirk, 'what big eyes you have. Don't you want to play?'

'Leave me alone!' the wolf cries, and runs off. Riding Hood trails him for a way, and finds him behind an old oak tree.

'My, mister wolf,' she says, 'what big ears you have. Don't you want to play?'

'For God's sake, please leave me alone!' the beast howls, and runs off into the woods. Riding Hood strikes out after him, and discovers him in a patch of old stinging nettles.

'My, mister wolf,' she says, 'what big teeth you have. Don't you want to play?'

'For Christ's sake, leave me alone!' the wolf barks in fury. 'I'm trying to have a shit!'

It's obvious, really

What do you call an Italian with a rubber toe?
  Roberto.

The awkward customer

Cursed with a bald head and a wooden leg, a man is surprised to learn that he's been invited to a fancy dress party. Deciding that he might pull it off if he wears a costume to hide his head and leg, he writes to a theatrical outfitters asking them for advice. A few days later, he receives a parcel from the company with a note that says, 'Dear sir. Please find enclosed a pirate's outfit. The spotted handkerchief will cover your bald head, and with your wooden leg you will be just right as a buccaneer.'

Unfortunately, the man finds this deeply insulting, as they have so clearly emphasized his wooden leg, so he fires off a letter of complaint. A week passes before the postman delivers another parcel with a note that reads, 'Dear sir, sorry about our previous suggestion – please find enclosed a monk's habit. The long robe will cover your wooden leg and with your bald head you will really look the part.'

This infuriates the man again, because they have simply switched from emphasizing his wooden leg to his balding head, so he writes the company another letter of complaint. The next day he receives a tiny parcel and a hastily scrawled note, which reads:

'Dear sir, please find enclosed a tin of treacle. Pour it over your head, stick your wooden leg up your arse and go as a toffee apple, you grumpy twat.'

Justice, South African style

Three men in a prison in South Africa; two white, one black. The first white guy says, 'I'm in for six years for robbery. The judge said I was lucky. If it had been armed robbery, I would have got ten.'

The second white man says, 'I'm in for 15 years for manslaughter. The judge said I was lucky. If it had been first degree murder, I would have got more than 20.'

The black man says, 'I got 20 years for riding without my bicycle lights on. The judge says I was lucky. If it had been dark at the time, he would have given me life.'

Q: What's long, thin and smells of piss?

A: Pensioners doing the conga.

Holiday dilemma

The Good Lord is up in Heaven, moaning about the pressures and stresses of omnipotence and being Number One. He decides it's time to go on holiday.

He summons all his superbeing mates and they pop round with a few suggestions. 'What about Mars?' says one.

'Nah,' replies God. 'I went there 15,000 years ago, and it was awful – no atmosphere and too dusty.'

'Pluto?' suggests another.

'No way,' God pipes up. 'I went there 10,000 years ago. Freezing. Awful place.'

'Well,' says another of God's protegés. 'How about Mercury?'

God turns the suggestion down. 'Been there. Nearly burnt my nuts off – never again.'

'Okay,' says another of God's favourite cronies. 'How about Earth?'

'Woah!' God exclaims. 'Not a chance! I went there about 2,000 years ago, knocked up some bird and they're still bloody talking about it!'

The numbers game

A man is strolling past a lunatic asylum when he hears a loud chanting. 'Thirteen! Thirteen! Thirteen!' goes the noise from within the mental hospital's wards.

The man's curiosity gets the better of him and he searches for a hole in the security fence. It's not long before he finds a small crack, so he leans forward and peers in. Instantly, someone jabs him in the eye.

As he reels back in agony, the chanting continues:

'Fourteen! Fourteen! Fourteen!'

Load of balls

While holidaying in southern Spain a man visits a local restaurant –
where he sees a diner happily wolfing down two large pink objects.
'I'll have those, please,' he tells the waiter.

'I'm sorry, Senor,' comes the reply, 'but they are cojones – the
testicles of the bull killed in the local bullfight. We won't have any
more until after the next fight.'

Disappointed, the man returns after the next fight. The waiter
remembers him and brings out a plate of two steaming balls. 'Just a
minute,' says the man. 'These are tiny. The ones the man had were
four times as big.'

The waiter shrugs. 'Senor – sometimes the bull, he win.'

Good dog!

There were three rottweilers in the waiting room at the vet's
surgery, and after a while they got talking.

'I was out walking with my master,' says the first one, 'when
a thug attacked him, so I chased the guy, caught him by the
throat and savaged him to death. That's why I'm here to be
put down.'

'I was in the house,' began the second dog, 'when a burglar
broke in and tried to nick the TV. So I pinned him to the floor, bit
his arm off, and now I'm here to be put down.'

The third rottweiler then started his story. 'I was patrolling the
house one evening, and I wandered into the bathroom to see my
master's wife naked, bending over the tub, so I leapt up and gave
her a good seeing-to from behind.'

'What, and you're being put down for that?'

Oh, no. I'm just here to get my claws clipped.'

Who can blame her?

What's the difference between a penis and a bonus?

Your wife will always blow your bonus.

Short tempered

The supervisor of a local firm is somewhat startled when his secretary bursts into his office and demands to file a complaint of sexual harassment against a man who works in the same department.

'What on earth did he do?' asks the concerned boss.

'It's not what he did, it's what he said!' she shrieks. 'He said that my hair smelt nice!'

'And what's so wrong with telling you that?' asks the supervisor, confused.

'He's a midget,' huffs the woman.

Going bats

Two bats are out searching for a midnight feed. After a while they reunite at the belfry. Boris is still starving, not having found a thing to eat. But Brian comes in licking his lips, fresh blood oozing from his mouth and fangs.

'Wow,' exclaims Boris. 'I couldn't even find a mouse to eat. Where on earth did you get all that from?'

'Come on, I'll show you,' replies Brian, and off they venture into the night. After a few moments, Brian slows to a hover and whispers, 'Right. See that tree?'

'Uh-huh,' murmurs Boris.

'I didn't,' says Brian.

Loaded for bear

An extremely wealthy 80-year-old man arrived for his annual check-up and smiled when the doctor enquired about his health.

'Never better,' he announced proudly. 'I've taken an 18-year-old bride, and she's pregnant. What do you think of that?'

The doctor considered this for a moment, then said, 'I once knew a guy who was an avid hunter. One day he slept late and in the subsequent rush, he dashed out with his umbrella instead of his rifle.'

'Go on, doc,' says the old-timer.

'Deep in the woods, he faced a huge, angry bear, raised his umbrella, pointed it at the animal and squeezed the handle. And do you know what happened?'

Dumbfounded, the old codger shook his head.

'The bear fell dead in front of him.'

'That's impossible,' exclaimed the old man. 'Someone else must have been doing the shooting.'

Sighing, the doctor gave his patient a friendly pat on the back.

'That's what I'm getting at.'

I dream of genie

Bill is sitting in a pub and pulls out a tiny piano and a little guy about a foot tall. The little guy sits down and starts playing the piano quite beautifully. The fellow on the next bar stool, Joe, says, 'That's amazing. Where did you get him?'

Bill says, 'Well, I got this magic lamp with a genie inside. He granted me one wish.'

'That's great, could I use it?'

Bill agrees, and hands him the lamp. Joe rubs it and out pops the genie who offers him anything he wants. He says, 'I want a million bucks.'

Suddenly the room is entirely filled with quacking ducks. Joe exclaims, 'Hey! I asked for a million BUCKS! Not DUCKS!'

Bill explains, 'Yes, he's a bit deaf, isn't he? You don't think I asked for a 12-inch pianist do you?'

Right-winger

After a heavy night in his local pub, a worse-for-wear lout rises to his feet, determined to start up a fight.

'Right,' he hollers, 'everybody on the left side of the pub is a bastard!'

The drinkers look across at him briefly, then resume their drinking.

'No takers, eh?' shouts the piss-head. 'Right then – everyone on the right side is a poofter!'

Suddenly, an old man on the left-hand side of the pub stands up. 'You want some, then?' screams the lout.

'Not really,' replies the man, sheepishly. 'It's just that I appear to be sitting on the wrong side of the pub.'

Farmer in the dock

A well-known farmer is caught in a mindless act of bestiality with an ox on his farm, and – after much public humiliation and ridicule from the police – looks up both the village lawyers. He finds himself faced with two choices. The first lawyer has a brilliant reputation of finding a sympathetic jury, but has a history of making ludicrous statements and summing up in a disastrous fashion. The second is a fantastic debater and a real case-winner, but is always plagued by juries that want to lynch him. The farmer eventually settles on the first lawyer.

A week later, sitting in court, his lawyer stands, adjusts his tie and turns to the jury. 'My client,' he says confidently, 'approached the ox from behind, took it by surprise, grabbed it hard by its flanks, and went at it hell for leather. When he had finished, he casually walked round to the front of the beast, who proceeded to lick his penis clean.'

The farmer stares at his lawyer in disbelief, cursing himself for hiring such an obvious simpleton, when suddenly the jury nod enthusiastically and the foreman whispers, 'Mmm, yes – a good ox will do that.'

Feeding time

What do elephants have for dinner?
An hour – just like the rest of the animals.

Mistaken identity

Feeling rather daring, a grey-haired old woman goes to a tattoo parlour. 'I want a picture of Frank Bruno on my left inner thigh and a picture of Mike Tyson on my right inner thigh,' she says to the tattooist.

When he's finished, she looks at her new tattoos. Disgusted, she says, 'These are rubbish! I want to see the manager.'

The manager comes out, 'What seems to be the problem, madam?' he asks.

'I wanted a tattoo of Frank Bruno and Mike Tyson and they don't look like either of them!'

The manager steps back to take a look. 'You're right, they don't. But the one in the middle is definitely Don King.'

Sticky wicket

The Lone Ranger and his faithful red Indian chum, Tonto, are riding down a hillside in the Wild West, when Tonto suddenly stops, gets off his horse and puts his head to the ground.

'Buffalo come,' Tonto said.

'Amazing! How do you know?' asks the Lone Ranger.

'Ear stuck to ground,' replies Tonto.

Sweet chastity

A brave knight has to go off to fight in the Crusades and leaves his sexy wife at home. As he can't trust his wife to be left on her own, he fits her with a very special chastity belt made out of razor blades. On his victorious return, he lines up all his male staff, and makes them drop their trousers. He is greeted by a whole line of shredded todgers, apart from one. He goes up to that man and said, 'I trusted you and, unlike all the others, you have not betrayed my trust. In return I shall give you half my land.'

To which the man replies, 'Ugg ou gery muk.'

What do you expect from a horse?

Roy Rogers is riding through the Wild West on his trusty horse, Trigger, when he happens upon Apache Indians. Not best pleased at having trespassers in their territory, the Indians capture Roy and bury him up to his chin in the sand. Before leaving him to die in the scorching heat, the Indians grant him one last wish. 'Could I say a parting farewell to my trusty steed?' comes the request. The Indians seem to understand, and agree, so Roy beckons Trigger to come closer then whispers in his ear. The horse bolts off at once in the direction of the nearest town.

Half an hour later, the horse returns bearing a scantily clad, gorgeous prostitute. The prostitute jumps down off the horse and gently removes the small, frilly knickers she's wearing. Sitting astride Roy Rogers' face, she proceeds to give him firsts, seconds and thirds of her fanny, almost suffocating him in the process.

Well, the Indians think this is magic and decide that he deserves another wish. So Roy beckons his horse again and whispers in his ear.

'I said fetch a posse, you stupid git!'

Smells funny

After years of flirting, a man and woman in an old people's home agree to make love – and one day, when the residents go on a day trip, they both stay behind. Impatient for his first action in decades, the man quickly goes to the woman's room and asks her if there's anything she prefers. She replies she loves it when men perform cunnilingus on her – and grinning widely, the man goes down.

After a few seconds, however, he reappears. 'I'm sorry,' he says, 'but I'm afraid the smell is just too bad.'

'Hmmm,' she replies, thinking for a moment. 'It must be the arthritis.

He looks at her confused. 'Surely you can't get arthritis down there,' he cries, 'And even if you could, it wouldn't cause that smell.'

'No, the arthritis is in my shoulder,' she bleats. 'I can't wipe my arse.'

Surprise package

At the end of the primary school term, a kindergarten teacher is receiving gifts from her departing pupils. First up is the local florist's son, whose gift is a well-wrapped cone. 'I bet I know what it is,' she says, after shaking it and inhaling deeply. 'Have you got me flowers?'

'That's right!' cries the boy. 'But how did you know?'

'Just a wild guess,' she said, grinning.

The next pupil was the daughter of the local sweetshop owner. Again, the teacher held her box over her head, shook it, and heard the soft rattle.

'Thank you,' she says, 'I love chocolates!'

'That's right! But how did you know?' asked the girl.

'Just a lucky guess,' laughs the teacher.

Finally, the son of the local off-licence owner shyly approaches. Again, the teacher holds his box above her head and shakes it side to side – only to find it leaking.

'Mmmm,' she says, tasting a drop of the leakage with her finger. 'Is it wine?'

Open-mouthed, the youngster shakes his head – and the teacher repeats the process. 'Oh. Is it a nice vintage champagne, perhaps?' she asks.

Again, the boy shakes his head excitedly.

'OK,' admits the teacher, 'I give up. What is it?'

The boy laughs in delight. 'A puppy!'

The Mexican bandit

Two young travellers are braving their way across Mexico behind the wheel of an old van, when they come across a group of bandits standing behind a roadblock. The head honcho walks around to the door, sticks a gun into their faces and says, 'Start masturbating, gringos!'

Shocked, but fearing for their lives, the pair duly oblige – and, despite the stress, manage to perform.

As soon as they finish, the bandit chief leans in and demands: 'Again!' They manage a repeat performance, but are then told to continue until, tired and sore, the pair are physically incapable of another erection.

'Good work,' smiles the toothless Mexican as a dark figure emerges from the trees. 'Now drive my sister to the nearest town.'

Desert island dicks

A man who has been shipwrecked on a desert island for several years is beginning to feel the effects of being starved of sex for so long. However, the only living creatures on the island are a pig and a dog. One day, the man decides he's had enough and thinks to himself that it has to be the pig. But when he approaches the sow for his moment of passion, the dog bites the man's backside. This continues for several days, and the man is beginning to get very frustrated.

But one morning, the man's luck changes: out to sea, he notices a beautiful young woman on the point of drowning. He swims over, drags her out on to the beach and proceeds to give her the kiss of life. The woman comes to and is very grateful.

'Thank you so much,' she says. 'I will do anything for you, and I mean absolutely anything.'

The man can't believe his luck and quickly replies, 'You wouldn't mind taking that bloody dog for a walk, would you?'

Are you local?

Hopelessly lost, a businessman approaches a local in a village.
'Excuse me,' he says, 'but what's the quickest way to York?'
The local scratches his head. 'Are you walking or driving?' he asks.
'I'm driving,' comes the reply.
'Hmm,' mulls the local. 'I'd say that's definitely the quickest way.'

Q: What CAN a lawyer do that a duck can't?

A: Stick its bill up its arse.

The mumbling midget

One morning, a stud farm owner receives a visit from a midget wanting to buy a horse. It soon becomes obvious that the dwarf has a bad speech impediment. 'Can I view a female horth?' he asks.

Dutifully, the owner leads one out, and shows the midget the hoofs and legs. 'That'th a thtrong looking beatht, for thure,' says the gnomic breeder, nodding his head. 'Can I thee her mouf?'

Confused as to how the tiny man will ride the animal, the farmer still picks up the midget by his braces and shows him the horse's mouth.

'Nith, healthy-looking horth,' agrees the midget. 'Now move me awownd to her eerth ...'

Now getting annoyed, the owner lifts up the midget one more time to look at the ears.

'Finally,' says the Lilliputian, 'can I see her twat?'

With that, the owner picks up the midget and shoves his head into the horse's vagina. He pulls him out after a minute, and the tiny man stumbles around, dazed.

'Perhapth I thould rephrathe that,' says the midget, shaking his head. 'Can I thee her wun awownd?'

Never satisfied

Two rabbits, who have spent their whole lives in a laboratory, are set free one night by an animal activist. They run off into the countryside and come across a field of carrots. Instinct takes over: they get stuck in and start to eat all the carrots they can, until they fall asleep.

The following night, they go into a field of cabbages. Again, they eat all they can and fall asleep. The night after that, they find a field full of lettuce, which, as before, they proceed to chomp through until they fall asleep.

The next night they find themselves in a field full of lady rabbits, all of whom are willing partners. They do what comes naturally and embark upon an all-night shagging session. In the morning, the older rabbit decides he wants to return to the lab.

'What the hell for?' asks his pal. 'We've had carrots, cabbages, lettuce and, best of all, those ladies last night. What's your problem?'

'Life is sweet, I agree,' says the older chap. 'But the thing is, I'm dying for a fag!'

The fearless firemen

During a particularly dry summer, a chemical plant bursts into flames, and the alarm goes out to all available fire departments. Twenty engines duly arrive, and spend the next three hours battling the inferno. Eventually, with little sign of the fire being put out, the company director runs over and says: 'All of our industrial secrets are still in there. I'll offer £50,000 to any team that can salvage them.'

With renewed vigour, the firemen try to quench the flames, but to no avail. Suddenly, a dilapidated old engine with a volunteer crew of geriatrics comes screaming down the street, straight into the middle of the inferno. The other firefighters can only watch in awe as the old fellas hop out and bring the flames under control in ten minutes.

As he writes out the cheque, the company director says to the chief fireman: 'You old boys have done a great job. But tell me, what will you do with the money?'

The smoke-addled elderly gent peers at him, coughs, and says:
'Well, the first thing is to get some fucking brakes for that truck.'

Undercover story

What's pink and hangs out your pants?
  Your mum.

Be gentle with me

A bloke walks into the doctor's surgery looking very sheepish. The doctor asks him what the problem is and he explains that it's a rather delicate matter to do with his back passage, which he finds a bit difficult to talk about.

The doctor says, 'Look, I've been in this profession for 26 years and there isn't much I haven't seen. I understand you're embarrassed about it, but it would save us both a lot of time if you just told me.'

'I think I'd find it a lot easier if I just showed you,' the man replied. The doctor agrees, so the man drops his trousers and bends over. The sight of the guy's arsehole renders the doctor speechless; it has been torn to the size of a football and is badly bruised.

'Jesus Christ!' said the doctor, 'What the hell happened to you?'

'Well,' the bloke says, 'I was on Safari in Kenya and I got raped by a bull elephant.'

The doctor considers this for a second and says, 'Well, with my rather limited knowledge of veterinary science, I thought elephants' penises were very long and very thin.'

'That's right, doctor,' the guy agrees, 'but he fingered me first.'

They grow up so fast

Desperate for a Sunday afternoon quickie, Bill and Marla decide that the only way to distract their ten-year-old son long enough is send him out onto the balcony of their flat to report on all the neighbourhood activities.

The boy began his commentary as his parents put their plan into operation. 'There's a car being towed from the parking lot,' he says, after few minutes. 'And now an ambulance is driving past.'

There's a moment's quiet, before the amorous couple hear his narration again: 'Looks like the Andersons have company,' he calls out. 'Matt from no.8 is riding a new bike ... and the Coopers are having sex.'

Mum and Dad shoot up in bed. 'How do you know that?' asks Bill, startled.

'Their kid is standing out on the balcony, too,' his son replied.

Bringing them round

Two young guys are picked up by the cops for smoking dope and appear in court before the judge. The judge tells them, 'You seem like nice young men, and I'd like to give you a second chance rather than jail time. I want you to go out this weekend and show others the evils of drug use and get them to give up drugs forever. I'll see you back in court on Monday.'

When the two guys return to court, the judge asks the first one, 'So, how did you do over the weekend?'

'Well, your Honour, I managed to persuade 17 people to give up drugs forever.'

'Seventeen people? That's wonderful. What did you tell them?'

'I used a diagram, Your Honour. I drew two circles like this – O o – and explained to them that the big circle is your brain before drugs and that the small circle is your brain after drugs.'

'That's admirable,' said the judge, turning to the second guy. 'And you, how did you do?'

'Well, Your Honour, I managed to persuade 156 people to give up drugs forever.'

'156 people! That's amazing! How did you manage to do that!'

'Well, I used the same diagram, only I pointed to the small circle first and said this is your arsehole before prison ...'

Moo!

Two cows in a field. One says to the other,

'What do you make of this mad cow disease?'

The other one says, 'Doesn't affect me, mate.'

'Oh, yeah? Why's that?'

'I'm a helicopter.'

The perils of gambling

An old man and his grandson went into a betting shop, and the boy asked his grandfather if he could put a bet on. The old man asked his young grandson if he could touch his arse with his dick.

'No,' replied the boy.

'Well then, you're not old enough,' remarked his grandfather.

So the boy went next door to the paper shop to buy a scratch card, which he immediately scratched, to find he had won £50,000. He ran back to his grandpa, who suggested that they split it 50:50.

The boy said, 'Grandfather, can you touch your arse with your dick?'

'Yes, of course. I'm a grown man,' he replied.

'Well then, go fuck yourself.'

In the bakers

A Glaswegian walks into a bakers, and looks at the array of cakes on offer. 'Scuse me,' he barks at the assistant, in his thick Scottish brogue. 'But is that a macaroon, or a meringue?'

'No, you're right,' says the woman behind the counter. 'It is a macaroon.'

The city of love

A young Australian is enjoying his first night in Rome. He's drinking cappuccino at a pavement cafe when a pretty girl sat herself beside him. 'Hello,' he says, 'do you understand English?'

'Only a little,' she replies.

'How much?' he asks.

'Fifty dollars,' she replies.

Sex education

Young Judith runs out to the backyard, where her father is chopping wood. She looks up at the hard-working parent, smiles, and asks: 'Daddy, what is 'sex'?'

Laying down his axe, the old-timer sits beside his daughter and starts to explain about the birds and the bees. Then he tells her about conception, sperm and eggs. Next he thinks, 'What the hell

– I might as well explain the whole works,' and goes into great detail about puberty, menstruation, erections and wet dreams. Judith's eyes bulge as her old man continues his lesson, moving on to masturbation, oral, anal and group sex, pornography, bestiality, dildos and homosexuality.

Realizing he has probably gone too far, the father pauses and asks,

'So, Judith, why do you want to know about sex?'

'Well,' says the fresh-faced youngster. 'Mummy said to tell you that lunch will be ready in a couple of secs.'

Q: What's the definition of "making love"?

A: It's what a woman does while a man's screwing her.

For you, the war is over

At the start of World War One, a father approaches his son to explain he has to go to fight for his country. Nodding, his son asks that on his return could he bring back a souvenir from the battlefields – perhaps a German helmet. 'You know,' says the boy, 'One with a spike on top.'

And so, weeks later the man is out on the mud-soaked fields of Flanders, when he spies a German helmet lying in the mud. Bending down to pick it up, he finds it stuck fast; as he grasps the spike for a better grip, he realizes there is a German soldier still attached underneath.

'If you pull me out of ze dirt, you can tek me prisoner,' says the soldier, through the grime.

'If I pull you out,' says the Brit, 'can I have your helmet for my son?'

'Ja – be my guest!' comes the German's cheerful reply.

And so, with great effort, he begins to pull the soldier from the ground. But, after half an hour, he's still only managed to get him up to his waist.

'I'm bloody knackered,' he says, catching his breath.

'Vud it help,' replies the German soldier, 'Iff I took my feet out of ze stirrups?'

Slip of the tongue

A guy is talking to his friend and says, 'Man, I made the most embarrassing mistake yesterday. I went to the airport and the woman behind the counter had these beautiful big breasts, and I asked her for two pickets to Tittsburgh!'

'Yeah, I know what you mean,' his friend replied. 'Just this morning I meant to ask my wife to pass the salt and I said "BITCH, YOU RUINED MY LIFE!"'

www.oj.com

Where would you find OJ Simpson's website on the Internet?
Slash, slash, backslash, escape.

Open question

A couple of newlyweds are strolling along the beach one morning on honeymoon in Australia. Suddenly the husband spots a fat woman, stark naked, sitting legs akimbo, gorging herself on a fresh watermelon. Excited, he imagines his wife in the same position, and asks her if she would like to feel the sea breeze wafting between her legs? The wife looks at him in disgust.

The next day, they take the same walk, and sure enough the naked woman is there again slobbering over a slice of watermelon. Unperturbed by his wife's earlier refusal, the husband asks again if his bride would like to adopt the large woman's stance and feel the cool air circulate against her fanny? Again, she declines.

This happens everyday for two weeks, until the very last day, when yet again they spot the naked, fat woman.

'Don't you want to know how it feels to have your privates cooled by the salty air?' the husband enquires. And again his missus gets the hump.

'Well, if you're not prepared to try it, why don't you ask her how it feels and see if she can persuade you?' Reluctantly his wife agrees and walks over to the open-legged bloater.

'Er, excuse me, but my husband and I were wondering how it must feel to have the sea breeze wafting over your vagina?' she asked nervously.

'Ah, strewth, I don't know,' says the woman. 'But it sure keeps the flies off my watermelon.'

Good reception

A woman rushes into the foyer of a large hotel and sprints up to the reception desk. Seeing that the only member of staff is talking on the phone, she hammers on the bell for service.

The receptionist slowly puts down the phone. 'Yes?' he says, wearily.

'Excuse me,' says the woman, 'But I'm in a frightful hurry. Could you check me out, please?'

The clerk stares at her for a second and looks her up and down.

'Not bad,' he smiles. 'Not bad at all.'

Lucky motorist

On holiday in Ireland, an American is happily driving through Donegal in the Cadillac he has shipped over from home. But on the third day, his car breaks down, leaving him stranded in the country. He opens the hood but just stands there, staring, not knowing how to fix it.

Then from nowhere he hears a voice saying: 'Check the battery connections.' He turns around but there is no one there. He checks the battery connections and finds them loose, so tightens them up; the car starts and he drives off.

A couple of yards down the road he spots a nice pub and goes in for lunch. He ends up chatting to the barman and tells him of the incident.

'Ah, you must have been at O'Conner's farm,' says the barman.

'I was near a farm – but how do you know it was O'Conner's?' asks the Yank.

'Was there a little bridge?'

'Yes, there was' the man replies.

'And to your left was there a grey mare and a black stallion in the bottom field?' the barman probes.

'Gee, there was,' the holidaymaker retorts.

'Ahh, you're a lucky man,' laughs the publican. 'The grey mare knows nothing about engines.'

Drunk driving (iii)

While walking his beat, a policeman is bemused to find a young man, clearly drunk, staggering about with a key in his hand.

'They've stolen my car,' the drunk shouts. 'It was right here earlier on the end of this key.'

'More importantly, sir,' says the policeman. 'Do you know your penis is hanging out?'

'Oh my God,' wails the drunk. 'They've got my girlfriend as well.'

Getting the hump

Quasimodo asks Esmerelda one day if he really is the ugliest man alive. Esmerelda says, 'Go upstairs and ask the magic mirror who is the ugliest man alive and the magic mirror will tell you.'

Five minutes later, Quasimodo comes back and sits down.

After a while, Esmerelda says, 'Well?'

To which Quasimodo says, 'Who's Iain Dowie?'

Fleas take a break

Two fleas are planning a holiday at the other end of the house. One flea turns to the other and says: 'Should we hop or take the cat?'

Ye Gods!

Thor, the Viking God of Thunder, and Odin, the King Of The Gods, are enjoying a flagon of mead in Valhalla, the Norse heaven. Suddenly, Thor turns to Odin.

'You know, my Lord,' he says, thoughtfully thumbing his mystical hammer. 'Being a god is brilliant, but it's been millennia since I had any sex.'

Odin nodded and pondered for a while. Raising his mighty head, he took pity on his subordinate.

'Go to Earth, Thor,' he replied. 'Find thyself there what they call a "lady of the night". Treat her to your manly pleasures.'

Bowing gracefully, Thor retired and followed Odin's advice, before returning the next night.

'My Lord,' he said, grinning from ear to ear, 'You were right – it was wonderful. We had passionate sex 37 times!'

'Thirty-seven times?' exclaimed Odin. 'That poor woman! Mere mortals cannot endure such treatment. You must go and apologize this instant!'

Humbled, Thor went back down to earth and found the prostitute.

'I'm sorry about last night,' he apologized. 'But you see, I'm Thor.'

'You're Thor?' shouted the girl, 'What about me? I can't even pith.'

Cowboy bluffs it out

A cowboy rode into town and stopped at a saloon. Unfortunately, the locals had a habit of picking on strangers, and when he finished his drink, he found his horse had been stolen. He went back into the bar, flipped his gun in the air, caught it above his head without looking and fired a shot into the ceiling.

'Which one of you sidewinders stole my horse?' he bellowed, making the glasses on the bar shake.

No one answered. The cowboy squinted around the room then, without looking, shot the tops off three bottles of whisky on the bar.

'All right,' he snarled at the room in general. 'I'm gonna have another beer, and if my horse ain't back outside by the time I finish, I'm gonna have to do what I done in Texas.'

The locals shifted uneasily in their seats as the cowboy swivelled around suddenly. 'And let me tell you – I really don't want to do what I done in Texas.'

Chairs creaked restlessly, and the cowboy sat at the bar again, and quickly downed another beer. The locals watched as he got up, paid the bill and walked outside – to find his horse back where he'd left it. As the cowboy saddled-up and started to ride out of town, the bartender wandered out of the bar. Unable to contain his curiosity, he approached the lone wanderer.

'Say partner, before you go – what happened in Texas?'

The cowboy turned back, sadly. 'I had to walk home.'

Lonely this Christmas ...

What weighs 8 lbs and won't be plucked next Christmas?

John Denver's guitar.

Wrong number

A rich man is away on a business trip and phones home. The maid answers and he asks if he can speak to his wife.

'She's upstairs having sex with her lover,' the undiplomatic home-help replies.

'Right,' says the man, 'go upstairs. Take out my shotgun and shoot them both.'

The maid leaves, and the man hears two loud shots, then the maid returns. 'What shall I do with the bodies?' she asks.

'Take them out the back,' the man says. 'And dump them in the swimming pool.'

'What swimming pool?' the maid asks.

'That is 849 9698, isn't it?' asks the man.

One thing at a time

Old Mrs Harris goes to the doctor with an embarrassing problem.

'I pass wind all the time,' she says. 'It doesn't smell, and it's completely silent, but it's very uncomfortable. In fact, I've done it 20 times since coming in.'

The quack thinks for a minute then gives her a prescription.

'Try taking these pills for a week and come back and see me then,' he tells her.

The next week, an even more embarrassed Mrs Harris marches in.

'Doctor, I don't know what was in the pills, but my problem is worse! My wind is as bad as ever, but now it stinks too!'

'Calm down,' says the doc. 'Now we've sorted out your sinuses, we'll see to your hearing ...'

Q: Why was the blonde sacked from the sperm bank?

A: She was caught drinking on the job.

Bad news for new father

A man is waiting nervously for news of his new-born baby when a nurse walks in. 'It's bad news,' she says. 'Your baby is badly deformed.'

Naturally the man tells himself that he will love the baby whatever it looks like. The midwife then leads the man out to the incubators. Passing a baby that is no more than a head, the midwife says 'Brace yourself, dear – your baby is a lot worse than this.'

Finally they arrive at the incubator and the father stares open-mouthed at his child. For there, sitting on the blanket, is a pair of eyeballs blinking away. 'I'm sorry,' offers the midwife.

The man, holding back tears, says, 'It's my baby and I'll look after it the best I can.'

He gives the little eyes a tender wave.

'I wouldn't bother doing that,' says the midwife. 'It's blind.'

The DIY expert

A wife, frustrated by her husband's bone-idleness around the house, especially in the DIY department, sees cause for concern one day when the toilet clogs up. She decides to ask him if he'd mind seeing to it, and is greeted with a gruff, 'Who do I look like? A toilet cleaner?'

The next day the waste disposal unit seizes up. Summoning all her courage, she says, 'Sorry to bother you, dear. The waste disposal's broken – would you try to fix it for me?'

'Who do I look like? Some sort of plumber? Get me a beer and sod off!' is the reply.

To cap it all, the next day the washing machine goes on the blink and, taking her life in her hands, the wife addresses the sofa-bound slob: 'Darling, I know you're busy, but the washing machine's packed up.'

'Oh, and I suppose I look like a bloody washing-machine man?' her old man says.

Finally fed up, she calls out three different repairmen to come and fix her appliances.

That evening, she informs her husband of this. He frowns angrily and asks, 'So how much will it cost?'

'Well, they said I could pay them either by baking a cake or having sex,' she says.

'What type of cakes did you bake?' he growls.

'Who do I look like? Delia Smith?'

Holy hotdog
What did the Buddhist say to the hotdog seller?
Make me one with everything.

Back to Priest School
Father Patrick was talking to his replacement in a small village church.

'Father Michael,' he says, 'you'll be looking after my flock from now on.'

'But where do I start?' the young priest replies. 'You've been hearing confessions for over 50 years, I'll be lost.'

'Don't worry,' says Father Patrick, 'I've written a list of sins and absolutions on the wall in the confessional box. Look up the sin and it will tell you next to it what to say. After a while you'll get to know the congregation and you'll be okay.'

One week later, Father Michael is sitting in the confessional box looking at his mentor's list when his first visitor arrives. 'Forgive me Father, for I have sinned,' says a female voice. 'I had to give my husband a gobble last night.'

The priest searches the wall but can't find the correct reply anywhere. In desperation he pulls open the curtain of the box and stops a choirboy.

'Oi! What did the old priest give for a gobble?'

'A Kit-Kat,' the lad replies.

The hygenic waiter
On being seated at a restaurant table, a gentleman becomes somewhat embarrassed when he knocks the spoon off with his elbow. A nearby waiter calmly picks it up and produces another shiny spoon from his pocket, which he places on the table.

Suitably impressed, the diner enquires, 'Do all waiters carry spare spoons on them?'

The waiter replies, 'Indeed, sir, it is in fact company policy, ever since our efficiency expert determined that 17.8 per cent of our clients knock the spoon off the table. By carrying a spare spoon on our person, we save on trips to the kitchen'

After the gentleman has finished his meal and paid the bill, he wanders over to the same waiter and says to him, 'You will, of course, forgive me, but do you know you have a piece of string hanging from your fly?'

'Indeed, sir,' the waiter begins, 'Our efficiency expert determined that we were spending too much time washing our hands after going to the toilet. Thus, by attaching this piece of string to my penis I avoid touching myself: I go, and then I return to work. It saves a lot of time.'

'But how do you put it back in your trousers?' asks the curious diner.

'Well sir, I can't speak on behalf of my colleagues, but I just use the spoon.'

The alligator dash

A very rich man who owns a huge house has a drop-dead gorgeous daughter. He's also interested in alligators and has a sumptuous swimming pool filled with different exotic specimens of the species. One day he decides to throw a party and invites hundreds of people. After everyone has had a few drinks, he announces that anyone who can jump into the pool and make it to the other side alive can have either £1 million or his daughter.

No one is willing to try this, until suddenly there's a splash, and he turns to see a bloke in the pool, swimming as fast as he can to the other side. Everyone cheers him on, as the alligators try to tear him apart. Amazingly, he makes it to the other side, somewhat ruffled, but completely unharmed. The rich man says, 'I say, that was amazing! So what's it to be: the million or my daughter's hand?'

The hero replies, 'Look mate I don't want your money or your daughter. I just want the bastard who pushed me in!'

Bear squared

How do you make a bear cross?
Just nail two bears together.

Clever lad

Little 10-year-old Freddie goes for a long weekend with his uncle, a wealthy Hampshire farm owner. One evening, as Uncle John and his wife are entertaining guests with cocktails, they are interrupted by an out-of-breath Freddie who shouts out, 'Uncle John! Come quick! The bull is fucking the cow!'

Uncle John, highly embarrassed, takes young Freddie aside, and explains that a certain amount of decorum is required. 'You should have said, "The bull is surprising the cow" – not some filth picked up in the playground,' he says.

A few days later, Freddie comes in again as his aunt and uncle are entertaining. 'Uncle John! The bull is surprising the cows!'

The adults share a knowing grin. Uncle John says, 'Thank you, Freddie, but surely you meant to say the cow, not cows. A bull cannot "surprise" more than one cow at a time, you know ...'

'Yes, he can!' replies his obstinate nephew. 'He's fucking the horse!'

Whole lotta shaking going on

Alf and Mabel have been married for 60 years, and they live in a home for the old and infirm. One day Alf comes into their room and announces, 'Mabel, I know we've been together for 60 years, and we've been through a lot of hard times together, but I'm afraid I've got some bad news. I'm leaving you.'

'Why?' gasps the shocked old lady.

'I'm going out with Vera next door,' he replies.

'Vera? What does she do for you that I don't?'

'She gives me oral sex,' admits Alf.

'But ... but Alfred, I give you oral sex too,' exclaims Mabel.

'Maybe,' says Alf, 'but you don't have Parkinson's Disease.'

The power of suggestion

A blonde walks in to her local clinic and asks to see the doctor. When she's admitted, the doctor is a little perturbed to see she's wearing headphones and asks her to remove them.

'I'm afraid I can't or I'll die,' she replies.

'Don't be so ridiculous,' the doctor says, reaching across to snatch them out of her ears. Immediately the woman turns red and falls on the floor.

In the name of science the doctor puts the headphones in his ears. 'Breath in, breath out ...' says a soothing voice.

Deathbed confession

Becky was on her deathbed with husband, Jake, maintaining a steady vigil by her side. His warm tears splashed upon her face and woke her from her near death slumber. 'My darling Jake, 'she whispered.

'Hush my love,' he said.

But she was insistent. 'I need to confess something to you.'

'There's nothing to confess, don't worry yourself.' Jake said tenderly.

'No, no – I must die in peace. I have been unfaithful to you with your father, your brother and your best friend,' she croaked pathetically.

'Hush now, Becky – don't torment yourself, I know all about it,' he said. 'Why do you think I poisoned you?'

The power of photography

While enjoying a drink with his mate one night, Trevor decides to try his luck with an attractive lady sitting by the bar. She lets him join her for a drink and to his surprise asks him to accompany him home. They spend the night hard at it. Finally they finish; Trevor rolls off, pulls out a cigarette and looks for his lighter. He asks his new love if she has a light.

'There might be some matches in the top drawer,' she replies.

Opening the drawer he finds some matches on top of a framed photo of another man. Naturally he begins to worry.

'Is this your husband?' he enquires nervously.

'No, silly,' she replies.

'Your boyfriend then?'

'No,' she replies, snuggling up to him.

'Who is he, then?'

'That's me, before the operation.'

Lucky dog!

A man and his dog walk into a pub, and turn to the assembled patrons. 'Ladies and gentlemen,' the man announces in a loud voice. 'I bet anyone here a pint of lager that my dog can talk.'

After much cynical muttering from the tables, the barman finally agrees to the bet – and is amazed as the hound perches himself on the barstool and delivers a fascinating diatribe about the situation in Ireland.

'That is truly wondrous,' says the barman, as he pours the man a pint. 'But I bet you another pint that your pooch can't go and get you a newspaper.'

After a moment's though, the man agrees and slips the dog a crisp fiver.

'And I want the change as well,' he says.

The dog nods and runs out of the pub. But an hour later he still hasn't returned. Worried, the man goes out to look for him and finds the pup in a nearby alleyway – shagging a local bitch.

'Oi!' the man yells. 'You've never done this before.'

The dog turns back to the man. 'Well,' he says, 'I've never had the money before.'

Bullets cost money, you know

A man goes in to a gun shop for a telescopic rifle sight. The assistant takes one out, points it at the window and says, 'This baby is good, you can see right into my house on the hill over there.'

The man looks through the sights and starts laughing.

'What's so funny?' asks the assistant.

'Well, I can see a naked man chasing a naked woman around your house,' replies the customer.

Snatching the scope back, the assistant looks through the sight – and sure enough, there is his wife being chased by an excited young man. Furious, the assistant says that he will give the man the telescopic sight for free if he can take the man's dick off with one bullet and kill his wife with another.

The man agrees and arranges himself behind the gun and looks through the sight. 'You know what?' he says. 'I think I can do this with one bullet.'

Sick joke

Two buckets of sick are out for a walk when one of them starts crying. 'What's the matter?' asks the other bucket.

'I was brought up down that alley,' replies the second bucket.

Domestic economics

A newly married couple get their first taste of financial hardship when, one day, the husband comes home, and announces he's redundant. Being a proud man and believing that he should always support his wife, his pride is somewhat hurt. His wife, however, assures him that he still loves him, and that things will get better.

Unfortunately they do not, and when the wife suggests that perhaps she should try to find a job, the husband humbly agrees. But things are not well in jobland, and soon the wife realizes that the only option left to her is to go on the game.

She assures her husband that it is merely a job, and will not affect their relationship. Soon after placing some ads in the local phone boxes, the wife receives her first prospective client. The husband agrees to wait upstairs whilst the client comes round and conducts his business with the wife in the couple's lounge.

The visitor is eager to know how much it costs for 'the full works', and in her nervousness the wife has completely forgotten to discuss prices with her husband. She dashes upstairs and asks him.

'Twenty quid,' he replies. The visitor appears disappointed at this news, claiming he has only got £7. So he asks what he could get for that.

The wife dashes upstairs again. 'He's only got £7, what should we do?' she asks.

'Tell him he can have a hand job for that, but no more,' replies the desperate husband.

The client seems delighted at what the wife has to tell him when she returns, and drops his pants to reveal a huge long cock that is the best-looking specimen the wife has ever seen. Instantly, she runs upstairs to her husband yet again.

'What's the matter now?' he asks.

The wife replies, 'Can you lend me £13?'

Declan the crab

Declan the humble crab and Katie the lobster princess were madly and passionately in love. For months they enjoyed an idyllic relationship, until one day Katie scuttled over to Declan in tears.

'We can't see each other anymore,' she sobbed.

'Why?' gasped Declan.

'Daddy says that crabs are too common,' she wailed. 'He says that no daughter of his will marry a creature that walks sideways.'

Declan was shattered, and walked away to drink himself in to oblivion.

That night, the great lobster ball was taking place. The lobster princess refused to join in the merriment. Suddenly the doors opened and Declan the crab strode in. The dancing stopped, and all eyes were on Declan as he made his way over to Katie's father. All could see that he was walking forwards. Step by step he made his way over to the throne and looked the King Lobster in the eye. There was a deadly hush.

Finally, the crab spoke. 'Fuck, I'm pissed.'

Q: What can you say to a man who's just had sex?

A: Anything you like – he's asleep.

Howzat!

A priest goes into a pub to avoid the rain and spies a member of his congregation in there looking miserably in to his pint.

'What's wrong, Brian?' asks the kindly man of God.

'It's my grandfather,' replies Brian. 'He's just died.'

'Well, did you not try to take him to Lourdes and get him cured?'

'We had a whip-round in the pub and I went with him, but we had only been there an hour when he died,' answered Brian.

'Well,' comforts the Priest. 'Sometimes the Lord moves in mysterious ways.'

'I think it was more likely to be the speed of the cricket ball that hit him in the head.'

Hog heaven

Hoping to start breeding pigs, a farmer goes out and buys some of the finest sows he can find. After several weeks, he notices that none of the pigs are getting pregnant. He calls a vet, who informs him that he should try artificial insemination. The farmer doesn't have the slightest idea what the vet means by this, but undeterred, he asks how he will know when his new purchases have become pregnant. He explains that his pigs will stop standing there and lay down and start rolling around in the mud.

Giving it some thought, the dumb farmer concludes that artificial insemination must require him impregnating his livestock himself – so he loads them into the truck and drives them out into the woods to have sex with them all.

The next morning, the farmer looks out of the window only to see his pigs standing around in the field. Desperately, he takes them out to the woods again and bangs them all twice for good measure before retiring to bed.

The next morning, he wakes up to find the pigs still standing around in the field. 'One more try,' he tells himself, and proceeds to load them up and drive them out to the woods. He spends all day shagging the pigs, and upon returning home, falls straight asleep.

The next morning, he cannot even raise himself to look at the pigs, so he asks his wife to look out and see if they're lying in the mud. 'No', she says. 'They're all in the back of the truck and one of them's honking the horn.'

Strength in numbers

Hacking his way through dense jungle, an explorer comes across a pygmy standing over a dead elephant.

'Did you kill this?' asked the explorer.

'Yes,' replied the tiny man.

'That's amazing! I've never seen such a thing. What did you use?'

'A club,' shrugged the pygmy.

'It must have been a bloody big club!'

'Indeed it was,' said the pygmy. 'There must have been about 300 of us.'

A disappointed father

Tommy ran home from school, as he couldn't wait to break his good news. 'Mum, Mum!' he yelled. 'I had sex with my geography teacher today!

Dad, Dad! Guess what, I had sex with my geography teacher.'

'I'm proud of you, son,' the father replied, to the mother's disbelief.

'I think now you're old enough to ride your brother's bike.'

Tommy's face dropped in disappointment.

'I can't. My arse hurts.'

Hard decision

A man goes to his doctor and admits that he has a sexual problem.

'I just can't get it up for my wife any more,' he says.

'Don't worry, Mr Williams,' says the doctor. 'Bring your wife in and I'll see what I can do.'

The couple come in the next day and the doctor asks the wife to remove her clothes. Then he asks her to turn around and jump up and down. He turns to the man.

'You're fine,' he says. 'She didn't give me an erection either.'

Genuine excuse

Pete rings his boss at work and says, 'Look, I'm really sorry, but I can't come to work today. I'm sick.'

'Sick!' screams his boss. 'Sick! This is the tenth time this month, Pete. Exactly how sick are you?'

'Well,' replies Pete. 'I'm in bed with my 12-year-old sister.'

A quiet drink spoiled

Three lads are enjoying a quiet night in a pub, when a fourth stumbles in and orders a beer. Spying the group, the drunk stumbles over, points at one of the boys and shouts: 'I've shagged your mum!'

The lads ignored him and returned to their pints. He shouts again: 'Up the arse!'

Although irritated, they ignore him again. The drunk stands up again points at the boy and yells: 'Your Mum's sucked my cock!'

The boy looks up wearily. 'You're drunk, Dad. Go home.'

How the press works

Two boys are playing football in the park when one of them is attacked by a rottweiler. Thinking quickly, his friend rips a plank of wood from a nearby fence, forces it into the dog's collar and twists it, breaking the dog's neck.

All the while, a newspaper reporter who was taking a stroll through the park is watching. He rushes over, introduces himself and takes out his pad and pencil to start his story for the next edition. He writes, 'Manchester City fan saves friend from vicious animal.'

The boy interrupts: 'But I'm not a City fan.'

The reporter starts again: 'Manchester United fan rescues friend from horrific attack.'

The boy interrupts again: 'I'm not a United fan either.'

'Who do you support, then?'

'Liverpool,' replies the boy.

So the reporter starts again: 'Scouse bastard kills family pet.'

Divine intervention

Father Morrissey wakes up one beautiful morning and decides to bunk off church and play golf instead. He convinces another vicar of his illness and gets him to deliver the sermon, then goes off to the course, praying he won't meet anyone from his congregation. On the first tee, he sees that he has the whole course to himself. Result!

Meanwhile, up in Heaven, Saint Peter turns to God and says: 'You're not going to let a man of the cloth get away with this?' God looks down at Father Morrissey just as he tees off. The ball flies 420 yards, bounces once, then rolls straight into the hole. 'And why on earth did you let him get a hole in one?'

The Lord smiles. 'Who is he ever going to tell?' he says.

Singer mishears crowd

Sir Cliff Richard is performing in Japan on the last leg of a successful world tour. The audience go wild as Cliff asks them if there is anything he can sing especially for them.

'Tits and fanny!' scream the audience.

'I can't sing that,' says Cliff. 'I'm a devout Christian.'

'Tits and fanny!' scream the crowd.

'Oh, come on,' says Cliff.

'Tits and fanny!' scream the crowd.

'Okay, okay,' says Cliff. 'But I don't know how it goes.'

'Tits and fanny ...' sing the crowd in unison. ' ... how we don't talk anymore.'

What's the difference...

...between a rebellious chicken and a randy solicitor?

One clucks defiance...

Playing through

Some friends were playing a round of golf when they heard shouts in the distance. Looking across, they watched amazed as a buxom lady ran onto the fairway, pulled off some of her clothes and sprinted off up the course. Not two minutes later, two men in white coats appeared and asked which way the woman had gone. They pointed up the course and the two men ran off in that direction.

Bemused, the golfers carried on with their game, but were again disturbed by another man. This time he was staggering over the hill, panting with the effort of carrying two buckets of sand. Between wheezes, the newcomer too asked which way the woman had gone, then tottered away. Increasingly baffled, the golf party ran after the figure. 'What the hell is going on?' they asked.

Gasping, the man explained: 'The lady has escaped from our treatment clinic. She has acute nymphomania, and as soon as she gets all her clothes off, the nearest man is ravished.'

'But why do you need two buckets of sand?' shouted the golfers after him.

'Well, I caught her the last time she escaped,' panted the man. 'This time, I needed a handicap.'

What do you call...

...a Scouser in a white shell suit?

The bride.

Three little words

An elderly gentleman shuffles into a newspaper office and asks if he can place a piece in the obituaries section.

'No problem sir,' says the young girl behind the desk. 'That'll be a pound per word.'

Nodding slowly, the old man writes 'Doris is dead' on a piece of paper, and forlornly passes it back to the girl.

'Is that all you want to put in it?' asks the girl.

The pensioner looks at her with sad eyes. 'I'm afraid I only have three pounds, my dear,' he says, and begins to shuffle out of the door.

The girl, feeling sorry for the old man, says she will go up and speak to the editor. 'Wait – I'll see if we can work something out.'

Moments later, she returns from the office, grinning broadly. 'Good news,' she says. 'The editor says you can have another three pounds worth of words.'

Smiling gratefully, the old man takes another piece of paper and thinks for moment. Shakily, he then writes: 'Doris Is Dead. Metro For Sale'.

Q: What's black and white and eats like a horse?

A: A zebra.

Patient takes advice too far

After suffering from severe headaches for years with no relief, Trevor is referred to a headache specialist by his family GP.

'The trouble is,' Trevor tells the specialist, 'I get this blinding pain, like a knife across my scalp and ...'

He is interrupted by the doctor, 'And a heavy throbbing right behind the left ear?'

'Yes! Exactly! How did you know?'

'Well, I myself suffered from that same type of headache for many years. It is caused by a tension in the scalp muscles. This is how I cured it: every day I would give my wife oral sex.'

'Is that all it takes?' says Trevor, intrigued.

'Oh no,' says the doctor. 'When she came she would squeeze her legs together with all her strength and the pressure would relieve the tension in my head. Try that every day for two weeks and come back and let me know how it goes.'

Two weeks go by and Trevor returns, grinning. 'Doc, I'm a new man! I haven't had a headache since I started this treatment! I can't thank you enough.'

'That's fine,' says the doctor. 'I was glad to pass on a personal cure.'

'By the way,' says Trevor, standing up to leave. 'You have a lovely home.'

The best ferret in the world

A man is having a quiet drink in a pub when a tramp comes up and asks, 'Wanna buy this for £50?' He pulls a ferret from his pocket.

'What the hell would I want to buy that for?' asks the man.

'This ferret will give you the best blow job of your life,' the tramp says.

The guy thinks his leg is being pulled, and tells the tramp to sling his hook. Undeterred, the tramps continues, 'Look, if you don't believe me, take it outside for a free trial.'

The guy takes the ferret out to the back of the pub. Straight away, the animal unzips his trousers and gives him the best blow job of his life. So the guy carries the ferret back into the pub, gives the tramp £50 and takes the animal home.

When his battleaxe of a wife opens the front door, the man proudly holds up the ferret.

'Look what I've bought for £50,' he proclaims.

'What on earth did you buy that for?' she asks angrily.

'This ferret gave me the best blow job of my life!' he exclaims.

'Well,' she says, annoyed. 'What the hell do you want me to do with it?'

The man replies, 'Teach it how to cook – and then fuck off!'

Bus stop

One day, a well-endowed, attractive young lady is sitting on the bus, when a good-looking fellow gets on and sits opposite her. Attracted to him, she starts smiling flirtatiously. Yet it is to no avail. The man ignores her. Surprised and frustrated, the young woman unbuttons her blouse further to reveal her bounteous cleavage and hitches her skirt up to show her stocking-tops. However, there is still no reaction.

Frustrated beyond belief, she tries a last-ditch attempt to capture his attention: she whips off her knickers, jumps onto his seat and straddles his face. Showing the first signs of emotion, the man smiles and shouts out,

'I may be blind, but I know that smell anywhere – it's Grimsby, my stop!'

First heard at the Hackney Empire, 1953

A drunk goes to the doctor complaining of tiredness and headaches.

'I feel tired all the time,' he slurs. 'My head hurts, I've got a sore arse and I'm not sleeping. What is it, Doc?'

Frowning, the doctor examines him thoroughly before standing back.

'I can't find anything wrong,' he says. 'It must be the drinking.'

'Fair enough,' replies the lush. 'I'll come back when you sober up.'

Making a boob

A doctor is examining a girl of admirable proportions. Holding his stethoscope up to her chest, he says, 'Okay, big breaths!'

'Yeth,' said the girl, 'and I'm only thixteen...'

Three hard rats

Three rats are relaxing in a bar. After a few jugs they start talking about how tough they are. The first rat says, 'When I woke up there was a matchbox of Rat-o-kill outside my hole. I ate the whole lot and didn't feel a thing.'

After a significant pause and a few more glasses, the second rat chips in, 'When I got up this morning, there was an enormous rat trap with a huge piece of prime cheese for bait. I stepped up, caught the bar on my back, ate the cheese and slipped out without even a bruise.'

At this, the third rat gets up and heads for the door.

'Where are you going?' ask the two other rats.

'Aw, I'm bored here. Think I'll go home and shag the cat again.'

Caught short

Two dwarfs have just won the Lottery, so they go out and hire two prostitutes and two hotel rooms. The first dwarf tries desperately all night to get an erection, but all he can hear from the next room is, 'One, two, three, huh!' This goes on all night.

The next morning, the second dwarf asks, 'So, how did it go?'

The first dwarf replies, 'Shit, I couldn't get an erection. How was your night?'

The second dwarf turns round and replies, 'Even worse, I couldn't even get on the bed.'

More camels ...

The recruit had just arrived at a Foreign Legion post in the desert, and asked his corporal what the men did for recreation. The corporal smiled wisely and said, 'You'll see.'

The young man was puzzled. 'Well, you've got more than a hundred men on this base and I don't see a single woman.'

'You'll see,' the corporal repeated.

That afternoon, 300 camels were herded in the corral. At a signal, the men went wild: sprinting into the enclosure and screwing the camels. The recruit saw the corporal hurrying past him and grabbed his arm.

'I see what you mean, but I don't understand,' he said. 'There must be over 300 camels and only a hundred of us. Why is everybody rushing? Can't a man take his time?'

'What?' exclaimed the corporal, startled. 'And get stuck with an ugly one?'

Tall order

A milkman is making his deliveries and finds a note attached to a customer's door saying, 'I need 45 gallons of milk.'

He knocks at the door and a beautiful, dumb blonde answers it.

'Is this a mistake?' the milkman asks.

'No,' she says. 'I was watching a talk-show and it said bathing in milk is a good aphrodisiac.'

'Really?' replies the milkman. 'Do you want that pasteurized?'

'No, up to my tits will be fine,' she says.

The ungrateful wife

A middle-aged woman reads a magazine article which claims that, as women get older, their fannies grow. Concerned about this (and her husband's reaction), she decides to carry out her own test. She places a mirror on the bathroom floor and stands over it, legs apart. While looking down, her husband happens to walk past.

'Watch out!' he cries and jumps at her, pushing her over.

'What are you doing?' the woman shouts. 'You could have broken my arm!'

'Don't be so ungrateful,' her husband replies. 'If you'd fallen down there, you could have broken your neck.'

Q: What did Donald Duck say to the prostitute?

A: Put it on my bill.

Crafty seadog

In search of adventure, an attractive young lady decides to head to the Far East and stows away on the first available ship. After a month, the ship's captain finds her – and is surprised that after a month at sea she's well fed and cared for. He realizes that she must have befriended someone on board, but is surprised when she confesses that it was his first officer. Apparently every morning he would give her a full English breakfast and a bath, and had said that he would continue to do so until they reached Japan.

'And what did he ask in return?' queried the captain.

'You might say he took advantage,' blushed the beauty.

'Too bloody right he did, ' chuckled the old sea dog. ' You're on the Liverpool to Birkenhead ferry.'

What do you get...

...if you cross an agnostic, an insomniac and a dyslexic?
A man who lies awake at night, wondering if there really is a dog.

Million-dollar question

A teenager comes home from school and asks his dad, 'What's the difference between potential and reality?'

His dad says, 'I'll show you. Ask your mum if she'd sleep with Robert Redford for a million dollars. Then ask your sister if she'd sleep with Brad Pitt for a million dollars.'

So the kid goes to ask his mum, 'Would you sleep with Robert Redford for a million dollars?' His mum says, 'Don't tell your father, but yes, I would.'

Then he asks his sister, 'For a million dollars, would you sleep with Brad Pitt?' She says, 'Yes!'

The kid goes back to his dad and says, 'I've got it. Potentially we're sitting on two million bucks – but in reality, we're living with a couple of slags.'

The bear truth

A baby polar bear is sitting on an iceberg with his mum. Suddenly he asks, 'Mummy, am I really a polar bear?' His mother replies,

'Why of course, dear.'

A minute later, he asks again, 'Mummy, am I really a polar bear?'

His mum says, 'I'm a polar bear, your daddy is a polar bear, you are a polar bear. Now carry on eating your seal!'

A minute later, the baby asks the question again. Annoyed, the mother shouts, 'Yes! Why do you keep asking?'

To which the baby shrieks, 'Because I'm fucking freezing!'

It always comes in higher ...

The police have just arrested Fred West. They take him down to the cells and start to interrogate him. They say, 'Right then, you bastard, how many have you killed?'

Fred says, '17.'

So the coppers spend weeks digging up his house – and find 25 bodies. They go back to Fred and say, 'You bastard, you told us you killed 17.'

And Fred says, 'Yeah, but I'm a builder. It was only an estimate.'

Leave the lights off

A guy on a date parks his car and gets his girlfriend in the back seat. They make love, and the girl wants to do it again almost instantly. They end up doing it a second, a third and a fourth time, until the bloke needs a rest and asks his girlfriend to excuse him as he needs to take a leak.

While out of the car, he notices a man a few yards away changing a flat tyre. He walks over and says, 'Listen, my girlfriend's over there in my car and I've already given it to her four times and she still wants more. If you give her one for me, I'll change your tyre.'

The lucky motorist readily agrees, climbs into the vehicle and begins shagging the insatiable girl. While he is banging away in the doggy position, a policeman shines a torch through the window.

'What do you think you're doing there?' he asks the man, who replies, 'I'm making love to my wife.' The policeman looks bemused and says, 'Why don't you do it at home?'

The man answers, 'Well, I didn't know it was my wife until you shone the torch on her.'

Cold comfort

A married couple receive a bank statement saying they have a huge overdraft. They also receive a final demand for the gas bill, so they agree to save money. That evening, while watching TV, the man gets up and tells his wife that he's off down the pub. Outraged, the wife informs him that he has no right to go off to the pub and leave her at home when they need to economize.

The husband nods and tells his wife to put her coat on.

Surprised, the wife asks, 'Why? Are we going out together?'

'No,' he says. 'I'm turning the heating off.'

Crocodile does tricks

A bloke walks into a bar with a crocodile. Predictably, most of the patrons scarper and the barman complains. But the owner of the croc says, 'No worries, mate, watch this.'

Picking up a bottle, he smashes it over the croc's head. No reaction, other than a wag of the head. The bloke then gets his cock out and puts it in the croc's mouth, but again the croc just wags its head. Then a fellow punter asks if he can try it.

'Help yourself, mate,' says the owner.

The punter proceeds to smash a bottle over the croc's head and then put his cock in its mouth. The croc just gives its usual response. Word spreads and several blokes try it. Then an old biddy walks up and asks for a go.

'Can I just make one request, though?' she says to the owner.

'Ask away,' he replies.

'Don't hit me so hard with the bottle.'

Revenge is a dish best eaten cold

One day a 12-year-old boy walks into a brothel, dragging a dead frog behind him and says, 'Hello, I'd like a girl for the night.'

The madam says, 'I'm afraid you're too young for one of my girls.'

So he gets out his wallet and gives her £200, to which she says, 'She'll be waiting for you upstairs.'

The boy says, 'She's got to have active herpes.'

'But all my girls are clean!'

So out comes another £200. The madam says, 'Okay.'

So the boy goes upstairs, dragging the dead frog. Half an hour later, he comes back down, still dragging the dead frog. By now the madam is curious, and asks, 'Why did you come in here dragging a dead frog and asking for a girl with active herpes?'

'Well,' he says, 'when I get home, I'll fuck the baby-sitter, and she'll get it. Then, when my parents get home, Dad will drive her home and have sex on the way, so he'll get it. Later, Mum and Dad will make love, and she'll get it. Then, when Dad has gone to work, the milkman will come round and fuck my mum, and he'll get it. And he's the bastard who killed my frog!'

A dream come true

For quite some time, a man has lived next door to a beautiful young girl. He curses his lack of confidence, as he's never said more than hello to the fantastic creature on his doorstep. Then one day, as he returns from work, the girl appears at her front door wearing a flimsy negligée and beckons him over. As she slides her arms around his neck, it's obvious she's coming on to him, and the man gets increasingly hot under the collar.

All of a sudden she looks up.

'Inside, quickly,' she whispers urgently, 'I can hear someone coming.'

Blind with lust, he follows her indoors where she strips off and stands in front of him, stark naked.

'So, honey,' she coos, 'what do you think my best attribute is?'

'Well,' the man stammers, 'It's ... er ... got to be your ears.'

The woman frowns at him incredulously.

'My ears?' she gasps. 'But why? Have you ever seen such flawless skin? Such pert breasts? Have you ever set eyes upon such a firm backside?'

'No – I agree,' says the man.

The woman shakes her head 'And yet you say my ears ...'

'Well it's like this,' he explains, 'When we were outside, you said you could hear someone coming.'

'So?' she demands.

The man gulps. 'Well, that was me.'

Beadle's about

Jeremy Beadle has gone on a secretarial course.
  He hopes it will improve his shorthand.

Like ships that pass in the night

After months of plucking up courage, Tony decides to take a
parachute jump. But after leaping out of the tiny Cessna aircraft, he
pulls the ripcord ... and nothing happens. Alarmed, he pulls his
reserve chute cord – and again, nothing happens. As he's
plummeting towards earth – and certain death – he spots another
man shooting upwards at rapid speed.
  'Do you know anything about parachutes?' cries Tony, as the
man passes him.
  'No,' comes the reply. 'Do you know anything about gas cookers?'

Drac attack

One day Dracula is walking down the street, when suddenly ten
tons of smoked salmon sandwiches, bread rolls, pitted olives,
chicken wings, chipolatas, tomato salad, pizza slices and crisps
descends on him from a great height, knocking him to the ground.
  'Oh no!' he gasps with his dying breath, 'It's Buffet the
Vampire Slayer!'

Rationing

Little Johnny is delivering newspapers one morning. He knocks at
the door of Mrs Smith, and tells her that her bill is due.
  'That'll be £5 please,' he says.
  'I'm a little short of cash,' Mrs Smith says. 'But if you want to
step in here I can pay you in sex.'
  Johnny steps in, and shuts the door. Mrs Smith unzips his pants,
pulls them down and is faced by the biggest cock she's ever seen.
She lies down on the hall carpet and is bemused to see Johnny
pulling something from his jacket pocket. He takes a handful of big
washers out, and slips them onto his massive cock.
  'You don't have to do that,' Mrs Smith says. 'I can take all of it.'
  Johnny looks down at Mrs Smith and says, 'Not for £5 you can't.'

Taking things literally

Three men are sitting in a pub, bored shitless. The first bloke says to the others, 'Right, let's play a game. When we get home tonight, we have to do the first thing our wives tell us to.'

The other two agree, and they all decide to meet up the next evening to discuss the results. When they are all back in the pub, the first man tells his tale. 'I got home and the wife was washing up, so I decided to help her. I started drying the dishes, and I dropped one. "That's right," she said, "smash the place up." So I got a sledgehammer and destroyed the entire house. Now she's divorcing me and I've been charged with wilful destruction.'

'You think that's bad,' the second man says. 'When I got home, I fell asleep on the sofa, dropped a fag and scorched the carpet. The wife came in and said, "Oh good, burn the whole house down." So I torched the place. I'm being divorced, and I'm also up for arson.'

'You lucky bastard,' the third man says. 'When I got home, my wife was in bed, so I climbed in next to her. I was feeling a bit amorous, and I started tickling her downstairs. She said to me, "You can cut that out for a start." Anybody want a toupée?'

Q: What do you call an Irish Lesbian?

A: Gaelic.

Does he work at Paddington?

Jimmy was applying for a job as a switch operator on the railroad. The chief engineer was conducting the interview.

'What would you do,' asked the engineer slowly, 'If the Northern Express was heading north on Track 1 and the Southern Central was heading south on Track 1?'

Jimmy frowned. 'Well,' he began, thoughtfully. 'I'd call my brother.'

The chief engineer looked at him for a second.

'Why would you call your brother?' he asked.

'He's never seen a train wreck before,' said Jimmy.

The nice gesture

Two men are sitting on a riverbank, fishing. Suddenly, they look up and see a funeral procession going over the bridge. One of the men takes off his cap and solemnly holds it over his heart.

'That was a nice gesture,' says the other man.

'Oh,' replies the first, 'it's the least I can do. We were married 25 years.'

Rest in puss

Little Tim was in the garden filling in a hole when his neighbour peered over the fence. Interested in what the cheeky-faced youngster was up to, he politely asked, 'What are you up to there, Tim?'

'My goldfish died,' replied Tim tearfully, without looking up, 'and I've just buried him.'

The neighbour frowned. 'That's an awfully big hole for a goldfish, isn't it?'

Tim patted down the last heap of earth. 'Well,' he replied, 'That's because he's inside your fucking cat.'

White as a sheet

As the congregation settled into the pews, the preacher rose to the lectern with a red face. 'Someone in this congregation,' he began gravely, 'has spread a rumour that I belong to the Ku Klux Klan.'

As whispering spread around the hall, the padre continued.

'This is a horrible lie – one I am embarrassed about and one which a Christian community cannot tolerate. I ask the party who did this to stand and ask forgiveness from God.'

No one moved, and the preacher continued. 'Do you not have the nerve to face me and admit this is a falsehood? Remember, you will be forgiven and in your heart you will feel glory.'

Again all was quiet. Then, slowly, a drop-dead gorgeous blonde rose from the third pew. Her head was bowed and voice quivered as she spoke.

'Reverend, there has been a terrible misunderstanding. I never said you were a member of the Klan.'

'Oh?' said the Father, 'So what did you say?'

The blonde chewed her lip sadly. 'I simply mentioned to a couple of friends that you were a wizard under the sheets.'

What's the difference...

...between Gary Lineker and an Essex girl?

Gary Lineker's never scored more than four times in 90 minutes.

The four parrots

Feeling very lonely because her husband had died the year before, a Jewish lady decides to buy a pet to keep her company. So, she goes to her local pet shop and explains her situation to the shop manager.

'I've got just the thing for you,' he says. 'This is Bella, a female parrot – she will chat sweetly to you all day.'

The Jewish lady is delighted and buys the bird. When she gets the parrot home she says, 'Come on, Bella – say something.'

Bella says 'My name is Bella. I like to fuck and I want some sex!'

The old lady is shocked and nearly passes out. She leaves it for an hour or so and approaches the parrot once more. But no luck: 'My name is Bella and I want to fuck!'

The lady decides enough is enough and plans to return the parrot immediately.

However, just as she's about to leave, the local rabbi comes round. She explains her bad luck with the parrot.

'Don't worry,' says the rabbi, 'I've got three parrots at home and I've taught them so well that all they do is pray all day! Let me take Bella to them and they'll make her a good parrot.'

The widow agrees and so the rabbi leaves with Bella. He gets home and tells his parrots, 'This is Bella, she is bad, you must teach her to be good.'

Bella shouts, 'My name is Bella, I like to fuck and I want sex now.'

The rabbi's parrots look at each other and one shouts, 'I told you if we prayed long enough ...'

Beer call

Returning from an exhausting day at work, a man plops down on the couch in front of the TV.

'Hey, darling,' he shouts to his wife, 'Get me a beer before it starts.'

His wife sighs and fetches him a beer. 'Actually,' says the man as she's walking away, 'I'll probably need another beer before it starts.'

She looks cross, but fetches another tinny and slams it down next to him. But after gulping down both beers, the husband is still not satisfied. 'Quick, get me another beer,' he says. 'It's going to start any minute!'

'No, I won't!' screams the furious wife back. 'Is that all you're going to do tonight? Drink beer and sit in front of that TV? You're nothing but a lazy, drunken, fat slob – and furthermore...'

'Damn,' sighs the man. 'It's started.'

Sporting chance

Finishing his ploughing run early one evening, a farmer heads home – hoping to spend time with his gorgeous young wife. But, upon entering the farmhouse, he hears panting and moaning coming from the bedroom. Furious, he grabs his 12-bore shotgun, edges his way upstairs and inches the bedroom door open. There, sure enough, is his young farmhand, pumping away on top of his wife. Enraged, the farmer bursts in waving his shotgun. His wife screams and runs away in panic – leaving the terrified farmhand, shaking on his knees, in the middle of the floor.

The farmer presses his gun at the lad's testicles.

'Boy!' he barks, 'I'm going to blow these off. Anything to say?'

'Please!' stutters the young buck. 'Give me a chance!'

The farmer narrows his eyes. 'Okay,' he snarls. 'Swing 'em.'

The spoilt child

A man takes his spoilt son to the fair on his birthday, and promises he can have whatever he wants for the duration of the day.

'Dad, Dad, can I go on the big wheel?' the boy whines, and the father duly takes him on the big wheel. This is followed by the bumper-cars, the waltzer, three hot dogs and a toffee apple.

'Dad, Dad, let me have a go on the shooting range,' the child then asks. The boy wins a teddy, and demands to name it whatever he wants. Dad agrees, and the boy shouts, 'I'll call him Wanker!' For the rest of the day, he talks to Wanker in a loud voice, much to the shame of his father.

As they're getting into the car to go home, the father accidentally leaves the teddy on the roof of the car. As they set off, the bear falls onto the road.

'Daddy, Daddy, Wanker's off!' the little boy cries, to which the old man says, 'God, son, I know it's your birthday – but I think you've had quite enough for one day.'

He had a hunch ...

Quasimodo, the Hunchback of Notre Dame, returns home from a hard day ringing the cathedral bells – and finds his wife standing in the kitchen with a wok.

'Fantastic,' he says, 'Is it Chinese tonight, Esmerelda?'

'Oh, no,' she says, 'I'm ironing your shirt.'

Taking the piss

A man is sitting in the pub having a quiet pint when a gremlin comes in and asks for a half. He downs his drink quickly, then runs along the bar, sticks his head in the man's pint and shakes it around. The man is bemused, but continues to drink as the gremlin returns to his seat. The little beastie orders a second and third half and after each one does exactly the same thing. The man finally loses his patience and grabs the gremlin by the scruff of the neck.

'If you stick your head in my pint one more time, I'll rip your dick off!' shouts the angry drinker.

'Ain't got one,' says the gremlin.

The man looks confused. 'If you haven't got a cock, how do you piss?' he asks the gremlin.

'Like this,' says the gremlin, and sticks his head in the man's pint, shaking it around.

The secret of a long life

Sat on a park bench, a small boy is munching one chocolate bar after another. After seeing him starting on his sixth, a man on the bench across from him shakes his head.

'Son,' tuts the gentleman, 'Eating all that chocolate isn't good for you. It will give you acne, rot your teeth and make you fat.'

The small boy looks back at him. 'My grandfather lived to be 107,' he replies.

The man nods sagely. 'But did your grandfather eat six candy bars at a time?'

The boy looked at him. 'No,' he said, 'He just minded his own fucking business.'

Fountains of Wayne

An Essex girl goes to the local social benefits office to claim her family allowance, and tells the officers that she has ten children.

'Wow!' says the clerk. 'What are their names?'

'Wayne, Wayne, Wayne, Wayne, Wayne, Wayne, Wayne, Wayne, Wayne and Wayne,' the woman answers, smiling proudly.

The man looks at her dubiously. 'Really?' he says. 'So what if you want them to come in from playing outside?'

'That's easy – I just shout Wayne and they all come running,' answers the woman.

The clerk is not convinced. 'And what if you want them to come to the table for dinner?' he asks.

'Again,' says the claimant, 'I just shout 'Wayne – dinner's ready!'

'But wait a minute,' says the man, his brow furrowed. 'What if you just want one of them to do something?'

'That is slightly more difficult,' says the woman, nodding. 'Then I have to use their last names.'

Snow joke

Why are women such poor skiers?

There's not much snow between the bedroom and kitchen.

The thoughtful wife

George the postman was on the final day of his job after 35 years of serving the same neighbourhood, come rain or shine. At his first house, he was greeted by the entire family applauding him, and sent on his way with a healthy gift envelope. At the second house, he was presented with a case of fine wine, at the third he left with a box of Havana cigars.

At the fourth house, George was greeted by a beautiful blonde in a baby-doll nightie, who took him by the hand upstairs to the bedroom and treated him to the best sex of his life. Afterwards she led him to the kitchen and cooked him breakfast.

As the stunning woman poured the coffee, the postie noticed a £1 coin next to his cup. 'What's the money for?' he asked.

'Oh,' the woman replied. 'Last night I told my husband that today was your last day, and I asked him what we should give you as a special treat. He said, "Fuck him. Give him a pound." The breakfast was my idea.'

Beetlemania

A man is sitting at home watching TV late one night when there's a knock at the front door. The man angrily answers the door to find a 6-ft stag beetle standing on the step. After he asks the beetle what the hell he thinks he is playing at calling at such a late hour, the creature lays into him with a series of vicious kicks and punches. It then walks away, while the man crawls back inside his house and calls an ambulance.

At the hospital the man is reluctant to tell the doctor how he came about his injuries, but eventually relates the incredible tale of the stag beetle, expecting to be laughed at.

To his surprise the doctor is sympathetic, explaining to the man that there is a nasty bug going about.

Q: Why are men like public toilets?

A: They're either vacant, engaged or full of shit.

Spelling test

A young woman visits the doctor for a breast examination. When he sees her he is surprised to see an 'O'-shaped mark on her chest.

'Oh', she explains. 'That's from my boyfriend's Oxford University jumper. He likes to wear it when we have sex and the crest rubs against my skin.'

A couple of weeks later, another girl is in for a breast examination. She whips her top off, and there is a 'C' in the middle of her chest. The doctor raises an eyebrow while the girl explains that her lover likes to wear his Cambridge University jumper during sex.

Weeks later, a third girl comes in for an examination and she has a 'W' on her chest. 'Ah!' cries the doctor. 'Let me guess, you have a boyfriend at Warwick?'

'No,' smiles the girl. 'I've got a girlfriend at Manchester.'

Dangerous discharge

A woman who's pregnant with triplets is walking down the street, when out of the bank runs a robber. In the ensuing gunfight, he shoots the woman three times in the stomach.

At the hospital the woman is told that her babies are unhurt, and she gives birth a month later to two girls and a boy. All goes swimmingly for 16 years, until one day the mother finds one daughter crying. 'What's wrong, dear?' she asks concerned.

'Well I was doing a wee and a bullet came out!'

'Oh ...' says the woman, relieved, and proceeds to tell her daughter of that fateful day 16 years ago.

A month passes and the second daughter comes to her mum crying, with the same problem. 'Not to worry', says the mum. 'I'll explain it to you ...'

Another month passes and the boy comes in very concerned and close to tears. The kindly mother takes the boy in her arms and asks him, 'Were you doing a wee and a bullet came out, my love? Because if you did, it's okay.'

'Nah,' replies the lad. 'I was having a wank and I shot the dog!'

Upper-class twit of the year

Tarquin the upper-class git comes across a beautiful naked woman lying in the forest with her legs spread wide open. Not believing his luck, he approaches her and asks her if she's game.

The woman replies 'Yes', so he shoots her.

Too-late tailor

Joe is being plagued by terrible headaches. One day, after years of suffering, he decides to see a migraine specialist. The doctor tells Joe to strip, inspects him all over, and announces that he's found the cause of his problem.

'Your testicles are pressing against the base of your spine,' says the medic. 'The pressure builds up, and you get an excruciating headache.'

Joe is appalled. 'Tell me, doctor, is there anything I can do about it?' he asks.

'I'm afraid I have bad news. The only answer is to get rid of the testicles,' says the doctor.

Joe considers the pros and cons of a life without balls and sex – but then he thinks about the agony of his daily headaches, and without too much difficulty decides to go for the snip.

He comes round from the operation and leaves the hospital. Walking along the street, he smiles as he realizes that the pain has completely disappeared. To celebrate, he decides to treat himself to some new clothes, so he makes his way to a top tailor to get fitted.

Inside the tailor's, he asks to see a pair of trousers. The tailor looks at Joe and says, 'You'll need a 36-inch waist, 33-inch inside leg.'

Joe is amazed at the accuracy of the tailor's eye, and asks for a shirt. 'That'll be a 42-inch chest, 16-inch neck,' the tailor says, and Joe is once again stunned by his accuracy.

Finally, all that is left is a pair of underpants. '36?' guesses the tailor incorrectly.

'No, sorry, I'm a 34,' Joe says. 'I've worn a 34 since I was 18.'

'This is not possible,' frowns the tailor. 'If a man of your size wore a size 34, the pants would press his testicles into the base of his spine, causing the most horrific headaches.'

Two men in a boat

After weeks of floating adrift in a tiny boat, two men are forlornly watching the sea for signs of a ship. All of a sudden a huge hand emerges from the water near the boat. It leans all the way over to the left, and then all the way over to the right. Then it happens again – moving all the way over to the left then back to the right, before slipping silently beneath the surface.

The men look at each other.

'Christ,' says one. 'Did you see the size of that wave?'

The talking tortoise

A lonely man goes to the pet shop to buy an animal for some company.

'I have the perfect pet for you,' says the owner. 'It's an amazing tortoise: it will do almost everything – and it even talks.'

'I'll take it,' says the man.

Later on that evening, the man decides to put his pet's skills to the test. 'Tortoise, go down to the shop and buy me a paper!' he cries, placing the tortoise on the floor outside the living room.

A year later, the man is still watching TV when he remembers his tortoise. 'Bloody hell! That tortoise is so slow I'd best go and look for him.' He steps out of his front door and, to his surprise, nearly steps on his missing pet.

'You're so bloody slow, you've been gone for nearly a year. Where's my paper?'

To which the disgruntled tortoise replies, 'Well if you're going to be like that, I won't go!'

We love you really, Peter

Bill died and went to heaven, where he was met at the gates by an angel who led him to a large warehouse. Each wall was lined with thousands of clocks.

'Each clock represents a person's lifetime,' said the angel. The hands on one of the clocks suddenly spun around furiously, taking an hour off the time.

'What was that?' asked Bill curiously.

The angel explained that each time someone acted like a wanker, an hour was knocked off their life.

The pair carried on walking, then Bill asked the angel if he could possibly see the famous pop star Peter Andre's clock.

'Oh, yes,' said the angel. 'But you'll have to come into the office. We've been using it as fan during this hot spell.'

Calling all cars

Scotland Yard are having a crackdown on Viagra smugglers. Police are reported to be looking for 20 hardened criminals.

He's been stung before

One day Jane met Tarzan in the jungle. She was very attracted to him and during her questions about his life she asked him what he did for sex.

'What's that?' he asked. She explained to him what sex was and he said 'Oh, I use a hole in the trunk of a tree.'

'Tarzan, you have it all wrong,' she says horrified, 'but I will show you how to do it properly.'

She took off her clothes, laid down on the ground and spread her legs wide. 'Here,' she said, 'You must put it in here.'

Tarzan removed his loincloth, stepped closer and then gave her an almighty kick in the crotch. Jane rolled around in agony. Eventually she managed to gasp, 'What the hell did you do that for?'

'Just checking for bees,' said Tarzan.

Bad exchange

A Japanese man walks into a currency exchange in Trafalgar Square and hands 10,000 yen over the counter. The woman smiles and hands him back £70. The following week, he again walks in and puts down 10,000 yen – but this time the teller only gives him £60.

'Why less this week?' he asks the teller.

The lady smiles and says, 'Fluctuations.'

The Japanese man storms out, and just before slamming the door, turns around and says, 'Well, fluc you Blittish, too.'

Eskimo humour

An Eskimo is out for a drive one day when his car breaks down and he is forced to call out the Alaskan AA. The Eskimo stands in the howling wind and waits for the mechanic to arrive. When the mechanic reaches the broken car, he sets to work, looking under the bonnet until he locates the problem.

He looks up at the Eskimo and says, 'You've blown a seal, mate.'

To which the Eskimo hastily replies, 'No I haven't! That's just frost on my moustache.'

Q: What does a man with a ten-inch dick have for breakfast?

A: Well, this morning I had bacon, eggs and orange juice.

The well-hung fly

While out shopping one day, a woman spots her husband cheating with another woman in a restaurant. Waiting until he returns home, the wife pretends everything is normal – cooking his dinner, ironing his shirts and waiting for him to go up to bed. As soon as he is asleep, she stalks into the bedroom, pulls off the covers and cuts off his penis with a bread knife. As the husband wakes up, screaming, the wife panics and runs downstairs, still clutching the severed member in her bloody hand. Suddenly realizing the consequences of her actions, she leaps into the family saloon and speeds off into the night.

It's not long before she skids over the roundabout and onto the nearby motorway. Accelerating up to 90 mph, she soon attracts the attention of a police car and decides she has to get rid of the evidence. Opening the sunroof, she throws the flaccid organ out – only to see it bounce of the cop car windscreen.

'I think this woman must be a nutter,' says the police sergeant, hot in pursuit.

'I don't know about that,' says second officer, 'But did you see the size of the cock on that fly?'

While the cat's away ...

Early one morning, a milkman is doing his rounds. He goes up to one of the houses and knocks on the door to collect the milk money. A small boy answers the door smoking a huge Havana cigar, swigging from a bottle of lager, his arm around what appears to be a call girl.

The milkman looks at the small boy and asks, 'Is your mum or dad in?'

The little lad replies, 'Does it look like it?'

Man finds topless woman

Unemployed for a number of years, Barry finally lands a job working for the local railway company. One night he meets up with some friends in the pub. 'So how's the new job, Barry?' asks one of his mates.

'Brilliant,' he replies. 'The other day I was out working when I found a woman tied to the tracks. I untied her, took her back to my place for a cup of tea and ended up shagging her all night. It was fantastic! Missionary, doggy-style, wheelbarrow – you name it, we did it.'

'Yeah?' enquires one of his friends. 'But was she good-looking?'

'I dunno,' sighs Barry. 'I couldn't find the head.'

The truth dawns

This woman's husband had been slipping in and out of a coma for several months, yet she had stayed by his bedside every single day. One day, when he came to, he motioned for her to come nearer. As she sat by him, he whispered to her, his eyes full of tears. 'My dearest, you have always been with me. All through the bad times: when I got fired, you were there to support me. When my business failed, you were there. When we lost the house, you stayed right here. When my health started failing, you were still by my side. You know what?'

'What dear?' she gently asked, smiling, as her heart began to fill with warmth.

'I think you're bad luck.'

He can hold his drink

In their local pub, a man and a woman are having a pint. When the man goes to the toilet, another man sits in his seat and starts chatting to the woman. 'I'm going to shag you here and now,' proclaims the man.

'No you won't – I'll get my husband,' she replies.

'And then,' continues the man, 'I'm going to strip you naked and lick your body.'

'When my husband gets back, he'll kill you!' she warns.

'And once that's over with, I'm going to fill your pussy up with beer and then drink it through a straw!'

'Right, that does it!' she yells, running off to get her husband. A few minutes later, she returns with him and explains what the pest had said.

'He said he was going to shag me,' cries the lady while her husband takes off his coat. 'And then he said he wanted to lick my naked body,' she sobs as her husband rolls up his sleeves. 'And worst of all, he said he was going to fill my pussy with beer and drink it all up through a straw!'

At this, the man rolls his sleeves down, puts his coat back on and heads for the door. 'What are you doing?' protests the woman.

To which the man replies, 'I'm not fighting anyone who can drink that much beer!'

What's the difference...

...between an oral thermometer and a rectal thermometer?
    The taste.

The Pope's four conditions

The day arrived in the Vatican for the Pope's annual physical – and the Holy See were dismayed to hear he'd been diagnosed with a rare form of testicular cancer. A genito-urinary specialist was called and, after examination, told him the only cure is to have sex. After some thought, the Pope licked his dry lips and spoke. 'I agree,' he says. 'But under four conditions.'

As uproar broke out, a single voice cried out from the hubbub: 'And what are these conditions?'

The room stilled. There was a long pause, before the Pope croaked, almost inaudibly: 'First, the girl must be blind, so she cannot see who I am.'

The cardinals nodded.

'Second, she must be deaf, so that she cannot hear who I am. And third she must be dumb so that if somehow identifies me, she can tell no one.'

The was another pregnant pause.

'And the fourth condition?' a Cardinal piped up.

The Pope grinned. 'Big tits.'

What do you call...

...a fanny on top of a fanny on top of a fanny on top of a fanny? A block of flaps.

Pet lovers

Harry was hired to play his trumpet on the score of a movie, and was especially thrilled because he got to take two long solos. After the sessions, which went wonderfully, Harry couldn't wait to see the finished product and asked the producer when he could catch the film. A little embarrassed, the producer explained that the music was for a porno flick that would be out in a month, and he told Harry where he could go to see it.

A month later Harry, with his collar up and wearing glasses, went to the theatre where the picture was playing. He walked in and sat way in the back, next to an elderly couple. The movie started, and it was the filthiest, most perverse porno flick ever. Jerry couldn't believe it as group sex, S&M and golden showers shot across the screen – and then, just when it couldn't get any worse, a dog got in on the action. Quick as a flash, the dog has had sex with all the women, in every orifice; and with most of the men.

Embarrassed, Harry turned to the old couple and whispered, 'I'm only here for the music.'

The woman turned to Harry and whispered back, 'That's okay, we're just here to see our dog.'

The Devil's decision

A womanizer dies and goes to hell for his sins. He's greeted by the Devil, who tells him he has the choice of three rooms for his eternal stay. Asking if he can view them before he decides, the man is led to the first room.

He opens the door to discover a million people standing on their heads on a concrete floor.

'I don't like the look of that,' says the man. 'I want to see the next room.'

So Satan leads him further. When they reach the second room, the man opens the door to reveal a million people standing on their heads on a wooden floor.

'No, that's not for me either,' says the philanderer, shaking his head.

Eventually, they reach the final room, and the man peeks round the door to find a million people standing knee-deep in shit, smoking fags and drinking coffee. Despite the atrocious smell, he decides this is the best option and tells the Devil of his decision.

But five minutes later, the devil returns, claps his hands and orders:

'Okay, you lot. Coffee break's over. Back on your heads!'

Go, sister!

Two nuns are sitting in the traffic waiting for the lights to change when suddenly a vampire appears in front of them.

'Oh sister, what shall we do?' stammers the younger nun.

'Do not worry,' came the reply. 'Show him your cross.'

The younger nun winds down the windscreen and yells, 'Fuck off, you little twat!'

Free ride

This nun's standing at a bus stop when a double-decker pulls up. As she gets on, the nun notices she's the only passenger on the bus, so she turns to the driver and asks, 'Could you do me a very special favour, Mr Driver?'

'If I can,' he replies.

'Well, the thing is, I have a serious heart problem and I want to have sex for the first time before I die.'

'Erm, okay,' answers the driver.

'There are two conditions, though,' continues the nun. 'Firstly, we can't do it if you're married, because I don't want to commit adultery. Secondly, it has to be anal sex, because I have to die a virgin.'

The bus driver gives a nod, so they clamber upstairs and get down to it. When it's all over, though, the driver's racked with guilt.

'I'm so sorry, Sister, but I have a terrible confession – I'm married with three kids.'

'Don't fret, Mr Driver,' replies the nun, sympathetically. 'I have a confession, too. I'm on my way to a fancy-dress party and my name's Kevin.'

A man who loves his job

The mayor of a town hears that a local sewage worker has been working without a single day off in 25 years. Impressed, the Mayor decides such an excellent worker deserves a personal visit.

After being kitted out in the necessary waders, the Mayor meets the man down in the sewers, and asks him how he could do such an unpleasant job for so long.

'It's actually quite interesting,' says the man. 'For instance, you see that turd over there?'

The mayor squints into the murky waters. 'Yes?'

'Well, that's from the butcher's shop on the High Street,' says worker. 'You can tell from the bits of sawdust stuck to it.'

'That's amazing,' says the Mayor, genuinely impressed.

'And that brown trout over there,' says the man. 'You can tell from the smell of petrol that it's from the carsey in the local mechanics.'

'Unbelievable!' says the Mayor. 'You truly are a poo maestro. But what about the bum cigar over there?'

'Oh, that's easy' says the worker, following his gaze. 'It's from my house.'

'How do you know?' replies the leader of the city.

'Well,' says the man. 'It's got my sandwiches tied to it.'

Q: Have you heard of the new shampoo for gypsies?

A: It's called Go And Wash.

Unlucky Arthur

A travelling salesman is touring an area in deepest rural Wales, and stays the night at a farmhouse. After a fine meal with the farmer, the salesman turns to his kind host and asks if there's any possibility of renting some 'companionship' for the evening.

'Well,' mulls the farmer. 'I'm afraid there's not many women around here like that. But there's always Arthur ...'

'Oh?' says the salesman, intrigued. 'How much does he charge?'

'It'll cost you £10,' comes the reply.

The salesman thinks about this. 'Seems a bit expensive,' he says.

'Well,' says the farmer, 'The local magistrate takes out £4 because he doesn't approve of that sort of thing.'

'So that's £4 for him and £6 for Arthur,' says the salesman.

The farmer shakes his head. 'No, the local constable also takes £4 because he doesn't approve of that sort of thing.'

'Christ,' says the salesman. 'So the magistrate gets £4, the bobby £4 – that only leaves £2 for Arthur.'

'No – we have to pay Gareth and Dai to hold him down,' says the farmer. 'You see, Arthur doesn't approve of that sort of thing either.'

What's the difference...

...between an egg and a wank?

You can beat an egg.

The bells! The bells!

On hearing that her elderly grandfather had just passed away Jennie went straight round to visit her grandmother. When she asked how her grandpa had died, her gran explained 'He had a heart attack during sex on Sunday morning'

Horrified Jennie suggested that shagging at the age of 94 was surely asking for trouble.

'Oh no' her gran replied, 'We had sex every Sunday morning, in time with the church bells, in with the dings and out with the dongs.'

She paused, and wiped away a tear. 'If it wasn't for that damn ice cream van going past, he'd still be alive'.

The memory man

Dave the scouser is touring the US on holiday and stops in a remote bar in the hills of Nevada. He's chatting to the bartender when he spies an old Indian sitting in the corner – complete with full tribal gear, long white plaits and wrinkled face.

'Who's he?' asks Dave.

'That's the Memory Man,' says the bartender. 'He knows everything. He can remember any fact. Go and try him out.'

So Dave wanders over, and thinking he won't know about English football, asks: 'Who won the 1965 FA Cup Final?'

'Liverpool,' replies the Memory Man, instantly.

The tourist is amazed. 'Who did they beat?'

'Leeds,' comes the reply – again, quick as a flash.

'And the score?'

The wise brave does not hesitate: 'Two-one.'

Thinking that details may fox him, Dave tries something more specific.

'Who scored the winning goal?' he asks.

The Red Indian doesn't even blink: 'Ian St John.'

The Liverpudlian is flabbergasted and, returning home, he regales his relatives and friends with his tale. But it's not enough – and soon he's determined to return and pay his respects to this amazing man. Ten years later he's saved enough money, and returns to the US. After weeks of searching through the towns of Nevada, Dave finds the Memory Man in a cave in the mountains – older, more wrinkled, resplendent in his warpaint and headdress.

Humbled by this vision, the scouser steps forward, bows and greets the brave in the traditional native tongue: 'How.'

The Memory Man squints at him.

'Diving header in the six-yard box,' he says.

Ask a stupid question ...

The phone at the local hospital rang, and the duty medic picked it up to hear a man speaking frantically on the other end.' My wife is pregnant and her contractions are only two minutes apart!' he babbled.

'Is this her first child?' the doctor asked.

'No, you idiot!' the man shouted. 'This is her husband!'

One-way street

An elderly man is driving down the MI when his mobile rings. Answering it, he hears his wife on the other end.

'Albert,' she says, 'Please be careful when you're driving back. I just heard on the radio that there's a maniac on the MI. He's driving the wrong way!'

'It's not just one,' Albert replies, 'There's fucking hundreds of them!'

Getting the jump on a bouncer

A man drives from Aberdeen to London for a night out. He is stopped at the door of a very posh restaurant by an enormous bouncer, who tells him he can't come in without a tie.

'But I've just driven all the way from Aberdeen!' the man moans. It's no use, however – strictly no tie, no entry. So the man returns to his car and looks for something that will make do. He finally finds some jump leads and fashions himself a bootlace-style affair, then returns to the club.

'Can I come in now?' he asks. The bouncer looks him up and down and replies, 'I suppose so, but make sure you don't start anything.'

What's the difference...

...between Twiggy and a fake American dollar?

One's a phoney buck...

You'd have put the same word in

A young cleric is preparing to board a plane when he hears the Pope is on the same flight.

'This is exciting,' he thinks, 'I've wanted to see the Pope in person.' He's therefore even more surprised when the Pope sits down next to him, and starts work on a crossword puzzle.

'This is fantastic,' thinks the young priest. 'I'm really good at crosswords. Perhaps if the Pope gets stuck, he'll ask me for assistance.'

Almost immediately, the Pope turns to him. 'Excuse me,' he croaks, 'but do you know a four letter word referring to a woman? It ends in '-unt'?'

Only one word leapt to the priest's mind. 'My goodness,' he thinks, beginning to sweat. 'I can't tell the Pope that. There must be another word.'

Racking his brains, it finally hits him, and he turns to the Pontiff. 'I think the word you're looking for is 'aunt'.' he says, relieved.

'Of course,' says the Pope. 'Hmm. You don't have any Tippex, do you?'

The lousy hunter

Cletus the slack-jawed redneck goes up to the mountains for a spot of bear hunting. On his first day, he spots a mighty grizzly, takes aim with his rifle, fires – and misses. A few seconds later, the bear comes up behind him and taps him on the shoulder.

'You're trying to kill me, aren't you?' he says to Cletus, and Cletus nods, terrified. 'Well,' says the bear, 'it's your choice – either I bugger you or I kill you.'

That night, with a very sore arse, Cletus heads into town and buys a bigger rifle. The next day, he returns to the woods and spots his grizzly. He aims, fires and misses again. The bear offers him the same choice, and the hunter is once again shafted by the beast.

Back in town, Cletus buys an even bigger rifle and returns once more to kill his quarry. Suddenly, he spots the bear and shoots. But a few seconds later, he feels a heavy claw tapping him on the shoulder.

'You're not really here for the hunting, are you?' says the bear.

Six items or less

A newly wed couple had just moved into a new neighbourhood and were anxious to meet other people, so they decided to join their local church. They met up with the reverend, who told them, 'We're not interested in having any part-time undedicated members in our congregation. Belonging is a big commitment. So in order to test your resolve, I'm going to ask you two to give up sex for 30 days. After all, Jesus used to head out into the desert for 40 days at a time, so I don't think this is too much to ask. If you can pass this test, we'll let you in.'

So the couple agree and go home, They come back 30 days later and the reverend asks them, 'Well, how did it go?'

The husband replies, 'For the first few weeks we were okay. But I started getting pretty pent-up in the last half of the month. The final straw came on the 29th day. My wife dropped a head of lettuce on the floor and bent over to pick it up, and there I was, staring at her nice, firm ass sticking up at me. I mean, I couldn't help it – I threw up her skirt, got her down on the floor and we had wild, passionate sex right then and there.'

The reverend says, 'I'm sorry, but that means you will no longer be welcome in our church.'

'To hell with that!' said the husband. 'We'll no longer be welcome in Tesco's!'

Q: What did Cinderella do when she got to the ball?

A: She choked.

Too many questions

After 50 years of happy marriage to Lena, Ole becomes very ill and realizes that he will soon die. In bed one night, Ole turns to his wife.

'Lena,' he asks. 'When I am gone, do you think you will marry another man?'

Lena gave it some thought. 'Well, yes,' she said. 'Marriage has been good to me and I think that I surely will marry again.'

Ole was taken aback. 'Why Lena,' he cried, 'Will you bring your new husband into our house?'

'This is a fine house,' said Lena, 'Yes, I think we will live here.'

'But Lena,' Ole gasped, 'Will you bring your new husband into our bed?'

Lena said 'Ole, you made this bed, a good strong bed. Yes! Sure I will bring my new husband into this bed.'

Ole gulped. 'But Lena,' he said in a quite voice, '...You won't ... ah ... let your new husband use my golf clubs, will you?'

Lena smiled at her husband. 'Oh, Ole!' she grinned, misty-eyed. 'Of course he won't use your golf clubs! He is left-handed.'

Q: What do you say to an out-of-work actor?

A: 'Large BURGER AND FRIES, please.'

Slow food

A man and his wife are driving through the Welsh countryside when they came across a roadsign:

'Llanfairpwllgwyngyllgogerychwyrndrobwllllantysiliogogogoch.'

After the husband attempts to say it, his wife starts laughing – and quickly, the pronunciation soon becomes an argument. So much so, in fact, that they're still debating as they pull into a restaurant in town. As they're settling their bill, the wife can't help questioning the cashier.

'Excuse me, but would you mind settling an argument between my husband and me?' she asks. 'Could you pronounce the name of where we are? Only please do it very slowly.'

The cashier rolls her eyes, and leans forward.

'Liiiiiiittttlllllleeeee Chhhheeefffff,' she says.

What's the best way...

...to remember your wife's birthday?

Forget it once.

What do you call...

...an Australian with a sheep under one arm and a goat under the other?

Bisexual.

Superior firepower

A patrol of Iraqi soldiers are driving through the desert when the commander hears a voice from behind a sand dune shout, 'One British Special Forces soldier is worth a thousand Iraqi soldiers!'

The commander tells his officers to send ten men over the hill to sort him out. After sounds of a firefight, a voice shouts from behind the sand dune, 'One British Special Forces soldier is worth a thousand Iraqi soldiers!'

The commander then orders 100 men over the sand dune. After noises of a firefight, one wounded Iraqi soldier crawls back down the sand dune then says to his commander, 'It's a trap. There are two of them!'

Armless

A man wakes up in a hospital bed after a terrible accident and cries, 'Doctor! Doctor! I can't feel my legs.'

The doctor comes over to the poor chap's bedside and says, 'Of course you can't. I've amputated both your arms.'

Bring her in at two-thirty

One day, a man walks into a dentist's surgery and asks how much it costs to extract wisdom teeth.

'£80,' the dentist says.

'That's a ridiculous amount,' the man says. 'Isn't there a cheaper way?'

'Well,' the dentist says, 'if I don't use an anaesthetic, I can knock it down to £60.'

'That's still too expensive,' the man says.

'Okay,' says the dentist. 'If I save on electricity and wear and tear on the tools, and simply rip the teeth out with a pair of pliers I could get away with charging £20.'

'Nope,' moans the man. 'It's still too much.'

'Hmm,' says the dentist, scratching his head. 'If I let one of my students on work experience have a crack, I suppose I could charge a fiver.'

'Marvellous,' says the man. 'Book the wife in for next Tuesday.'

Why do men name their dicks?

Because they don't want a total stranger making 90 per cent of their decisions.

Therapy?

A man walks into a pub and orders a drink. He necks it, takes out his cock, and pisses all over the bar. The landlord is furious and tells the man to get out. He apologises profusely, saying he doesn't know what came over him, and that he will see a psychiatrist and get help.

A week later, the man goes back into the pub, orders a drink, takes out his cock and pisses all over the bar. Again, the furious landlord tells him to get out, and again the man apologises, and says he will definitely get some help from a psychiatrist for his unusual condition. He then leaves.

The following week, the man comes in and the landlord stops him before he can order a drink.

'It's okay,' says the man, 'I've been in treatment with my psychiatrist. Everything's fine.'

The landlord decides to give the man one more chance, and pulls him a pint. The man drinks it, then gets his cock out and pisses all over the bar.

The landlord is stunned.

'I thought you'd been to see a psychiatrist,' he says.

'I have,' the man replies.

'But you've just pissed all over my bar again,' the landlord says.

'I know,' says the man. 'But I don't feel guilty about it any more.'

Q: Why are girls like pianos?

A: When they're not upright, they're grand.

The black hole

While out walking in the country, a man comes across a hole. Curious, he finds a small pebble and tosses it into the hole. He hears no sound, so picks up a slightly bigger one and throws that into the blackness. Again, he hears no sound. He picks up an even bigger rock, throws it into the hole, and again listens at the opening for some sound. Again, there is only silence. Looking around for something really big to chuck into the apparently bottomless pit, he finds a huge boulder and hurls it into the hole.

As he is kneeling at the side of the hole waiting for some sound, a goat comes charging down the road towards him. He manages to scramble out of the way in the nick of time, and the goat falls down into the black hole.

A few moments later, a farmer comes across the hill and approaches the man. 'Have you seen a goat around here?' the farmer asks, and the man, somewhat embarrassed that the goat has fallen down the hole while he was right next to it, answers that he hasn't.

'That's odd,' says the farmer, 'It must be around here somewhere because I left it tied to an enormous boulder.'

If your name's not down ...

A Man United fan dies on match day and goes to heaven in his Man United shirt. Arriving at the top of the ethereal staircase, he knocks on the pearly gates – and out walks St Peter in a City scarf.

'I'm sorry, mate,' says St Peter, 'No Man United fans in Heaven.'

'What?' exclaims the man, astonished.

'You heard, no Man United fans.'

'But, but ... I've been a good man,' replies the Man United supporter.

'Oh, really,' says St Peter. 'What have you done, then?'

'Well,' said the guy, 'A month before I died, I gave £10 to the starving children in Africa.'

'Oh,' says St Peter, 'Anything else?'

'Well, two weeks before I died I also gave £10 to the homeless.'

'Hmmm. Anything else?'

'Yeah. On the way home yesterday, I gave £10 to the Albanian orphans.'

'Okay,' said St. Peter, 'You wait here a minute while I have a word with the Boss.'

Ten minutes pass before St. Peter returns, and looks the fan straight in the eye.

'I've had a word with God and he agrees with me,' he says. 'Here's your £30 back – now fuck off.'

Heard it before

An Englishman, Irishman and a Scotsman walk into a bar. 'What the hell is this?' the barman shouts. 'Some kind of a joke?'

Walk like a man

The ambitious coach of an all-girls athletics team decides to start using steroids in an attempt to improve his girls' dismal performance. After a few weeks, the team begins to whip all the others in their area, so the coach decides to increase the drug dosage, tasting glory for the first time in his short, undistinguished career.

The team continues to perform well and even looks like making the national finals. The coach thinks long and hard, and – seeing the shining gold medals in his mind's eye – he adds more steroids to the girls' diet.

The team goes mental, winning every event and qualifying for the finals. Then, the night before the big day, disaster strikes. Penelope, a 16-year-old hurdler comes to the coach's office.

'Coach,' she sobs, 'I have a problem. Dark, wiry hair's growing on my chest.'

'Oh my God!' the coach screams. 'How far down does it go?'

'To my balls,' Penelope says, 'which is another point I wanted to raise.'

What do you call...

...an aardvark that's just been beaten up?

A vark.

Discommunication

A very, very drunk man flops onto a bus seat next to a priest. His tie is stained, his face plastered with lipstick and a half-empty bottle of gin is sticking out of his trouser pocket. He opens his newspaper and starts reading, but after a few minutes turns to the priest and asks, 'Hey, Father, do you have any idea what causes arthritis?'

'Yes,' the priest replies sternly. 'It's caused by loose living, being with cheap, wicked women, drinking too much alcohol and having complete contempt for your fellow man.'

'Well, I'll be damned,' the drunk mutters, and returns to his paper. The bus carries on its way, and a few minutes later the priest, feeling guilty about what he has just said, nudges the man and apologizes to him.

'I'm very sorry,' says the holy man. 'I didn't mean to come on so strong. It was mean-spirited and inconsiderate of me. How long have you been suffering from arthritis?'

'I haven't,' says the drunk. 'I was just reading here that the Pope has.'

The frog chorus

A tramp walks into a bar and orders a drink.

'I don't think you're going to be able to pay for that, are you?' says the barman.

'Okay,' says the tramp. 'If I promise to show you something you've never seen before, will you give me a drink?'

Reluctantly, the barman agrees, and the tramp pulls a hamster out of his pocket and puts it on the bar. The furry creature runs over to the piano and bangs out a brilliant version of Imagine.

'That was amazing,' admits the barman as he pulls the tramp's pint.

Once he's downed it, the tramp asks for another.

'I'll need another miracle in return,' says the barman. So this time the tramp pulls out a frog and puts it on the bar. The frog clears his throat and sings Bohemian Rhapsody.

At this point, a man sitting in the corner of the bar comes up and gives him £100 for the frog.

When he's gone, the barman says to the tramp, 'Blimey, that's cheap. You could have got much more.'

'It's okay,' replies the tramp. 'The hamster's a ventriloquist.'

What are the odds on that?

Two men are trying to play a round of golf when they catch up with two women. They watch with mounting frustration as the women manage to hit every water hazard, bunker and piece of rough – without waving them through, as golf etiquette requires. After two tedious hours of waiting, one of the men decides enough is enough and walks over to ask them if he can play through. He strides up the fairway, but halfway up stops suddenly and quickly returns.

'I can't do it,' he says to his playing partner. 'One of those women is my wife, and the other is my mistress! Maybe it'd be better if you went to talk to them.'

The second man agrees, but halfway there he stops and returns, just like his colleague had done.

'What's up?' asks the first man.

'I tell you what,' says the second man, smiling sheepishly. 'It's a small world, isn't it?'

Forget-me-not

Two elderly couples are enjoying a friendly conversation when one of the men turns to the other.

'Arthur, I've been meaning to ask you,' says the pensioner. 'How's your course at the memory clinic going?'

'Outstanding,' replies Arthur. 'They teach us all the latest psychological techniques: visualisation, association and so on. It's made a huge difference for me.'

'That's great,' says his mate. 'What was the name of the clinic again?'

Arthur goes blank, then wrinkles his brow. 'Wait there, I can do this.' He closes his eyes, and his lips move as he thinks to himself.

'What do you call that flower with the red petals and thorns?' he says, finally.

'You mean a rose,' says his friend.

'Yes, that's it!' say Arthur, and turns to his wife. 'Rose, what was the name of that clinic?'

Miracle cure

After a nasty car accident, a man's wife slips into a coma. After spending weeks at her bedside, the husband is summoned to the hospital by the excited staff.

'It's amazing,' says the doctor, breathlessly. 'While bathing your wife, one of the nurses noticed she responded to touching her breasts.'

The husband is very excited, and asks what he can do.

'Well,' says the doc. 'If one erogenous zone provokes a response, perhaps the others will too.'

So the husband goes alone into the room, where he slips his hand under the covers and began to massage her clit. Amazingly, the woman begins to move and even moan a little. The man tells the doctor, waiting outside.

'Excellent!' he said. 'If she responds like that, I think you should try oral sex.'

Nodding, the husband returns to the room – but within minutes the heart monitor alarms go off, and the medics pile into the room.

'What happened?' shouts the doctor, as he checks the prone woman's pulse.

'I'm not sure,' replies the man. 'I think she choked.'

Q: What do you call a smart blonde?

A: A golden retriever.

Those aren't pillows!

Three guys check into a hotel, but the clerk tells them that, because the lodge is fully booked, they'll all have to share a bed. However, being completely exhausted, they decide to take it.

Next morning, the guy who slept on the left says, 'Wow, I had the weirdest, most vivid dream. I dreamt I was having a wank!'

The bloke on the right says, 'You too?'

The guy in the middle says, 'You're both disgusting. I had an ordinary dream. I dreamt I went skiing.'

Tree hugger

Driving his car through the countryside, a middle-aged man spots a naked youth with his arms tied around the trunk of a tree. The driver slows and winds his window down and he hears the naked lad wailing for help. After looking around to check he's not getting into some sort of trap, he gets out of his car to investigate.

'Oh, thank God!' the young man cries. 'I've had a terrible day!'

'I can see that,' says the driver, noticing the bruises and whip-marks on the young man's back. 'What on earth happened to you?'

'Well,' moans the young man, 'I was driving along when I saw this young woman in a pair of cut-offs and a bra hitch-hiking. I stopped to give her a lift, and as soon as I jumped out to put her rucksack in the boot two enormous blokes jumped out of the undergrowth, stripped me, tied me up and beat me, stole all my belongings and drove off in my car.'

'Oh dear, gorgeous,' says the driver, unbuckling his belt. 'It's just not your day, is it?'

Divine intervention

A rabbi and a priest are involved in a bad car crash. Their vehicles are totally demolished but both clergymen are uninjured. After they crawl out of their wrecked cars, the rabbi sees the priest's collar.

'So,' says the rabbi, 'you're a priest. I am a rabbi. Just look at our cars. Both are completely demolished and you and I stand here unscathed. God must have intended for us to meet and become great friends and live together in peace for the rest of our days.'

'I agree with you totally,' says the priest. 'This must be a sign from God. You will be my closest friend for as long as we both may live.'

'Look at this,' the rabbi continues. 'Here is another miracle already. Look here in the back. A bottle of Mogen David wine, unbroken. Surely God wants us to seal our friendship with a drink.' With this, he pops the cork, and hands the bottle to the priest, who takes several swigs and passes it back to the rabbi. But he just hands it back to the priest.

'Aren't you having any?' the priest asks.

'No,' the rabbi replies. 'I think I'll just wait for the police.'

Tool time

Having heard from the jury, the judge asked the accused serial killer to stand. 'You have been found guilty of murdering your postman with a chainsaw,' he said, sternly.

'You lying bastard!' screamed a man in the gallery, leaping to his feet.

The judge stared in astonishment, before turning back to the killer to continue with his verdict: 'You are also guilty of killing a housewife with a hammer.'

'You miserable shit!' yelled the man, again leaping to his feet.

'Sir,' the judge said, 'I am seconds away from charging you with bringing the court into disrepute. Kindly explain your outrageous interruptions.'

'I lived next door to that bastard for 20 years,' the man snarled, 'and did he ever have a garden tool when I needed one?'

Lucky eighteen

An Englishman, American, and Arabian were in a bar talking about their families. The Englishman said, 'I have ten kids at home and if I had another one I would have a soccer team!'

'Well,' said the American guy, 'I have 15 kids at home and if I had another one I would have a football team!'

'Well,' said the Arabic guy, 'I have 17 wives at home.' He paused, sipping at his drink. 'If I had another one I would have a golf course.'

Hard reading

Did you hear – Stevie Wonder got a cheese grater for his birthday. He said it was the most violent book he'd ever read.

The three corpses

Three smiling corpses are lying in a morgue in Alabama, and a detective goes into the coroner's to find out the cause of death. The coroner points to the first dead man.

'This is Cletus,' he says. 'He died after winning $23 million on the state lottery.'

He then moves onto the second smiling corpse. 'This is Bo,' the coroner says with a grin. 'He died having oral sex with Trudy-May.'

Finally he moves onto the last smiling corpse. 'This is Roscoe,' says the coroner. 'He died after being struck by lightning.'

'Well,' asks the detective. 'Why in the hell was he smiling?'

'Oh,' says the coroner. 'He thought he was having his picture taken.'

What a blow!

After stumbling upon an lamp in his cellar, a old man tries to clean it and is astonished when a genie appears and grants him one wish. The pensioner thinks hard, then unselfishly decides that peace in the Middle East would help humanity more than any petty personal gain.

'Hmm,' says the genie. 'I think that's beyond even my powers. It's a conflict as old as time itself, with intractable religious, social and economical issues involved. Could you please choose again?'

The old man thinks for a moment then asks if just once, possibly, he could receive a blow job from his wife.

The genie looks at him coldly. 'Okay,' he says. 'When you say the word peace, do you mean ...'

Thanks fur the memories

One Saturday, a man and a woman walk into a very posh shop.

'Show the lady your finest mink!' the man demands. So the owner of the shop goes in the back and comes out with a full-length coat.

As the lady tries it on, the owner sidles up to the man and whispers, 'Ah, sir, that particular fur goes for £50,000.'

'No problem!' says the man. 'I'll write a cheque!'

'Very good, sir,' says the owner. 'You may come by on Monday to pick the coat up, after the cheque clears.' So the man and the woman leave.

On Monday, the man returns on his own. The owner's outraged. 'How dare you show your face in here? There wasn't a penny in your account.'

'Sorry,' grins the man, 'but I wanted to thank you for the most wonderful weekend of my life!'

Twisting in the wind

After hearing that one of the patients in a mental hospital had saved another from a suicide attempt by pulling him out of a bathtub, the director reviews the rescuer's file and called him into his office.

'Mr James,' says the official, 'Your records and your heroic behaviour indicate that you're ready to go home. I'm only sorry that the man you saved later killed himself with a rope around the neck.'

'Oh, he didn't kill himself,' Mr James replied. 'I hung him up to dry.'

Home remedy

Young Timmy pricks his finger on a drawing pin at school, and calls out to his teacher that he need to soak it in some cider.

'Cider!' the teacher exclaims. 'What for?'

'Because,' Timmy says, 'my sister says whenever she gets a prick in her hand, she always puts it in cider.'

Sweet nothings

Settling down at the bar to enjoy his drink, a man suddenly hears a voice say, 'You've got lovely ears, you have. Really lovely.'

He looks around, but doesn't see anybody, so he carries on with his drink.

A few seconds later, he hears the same voice saying, 'I really like your haircut, it really suits you.' Again, he looks round, and again he sees nothing.

He goes back to his pint, but as soon as it reaches his lips he hears the same voice. 'What a beautiful smile, it makes you look stunning.'

This time the man beckons the barman over. 'Did you hear that voice telling me how nice I looked?' he asks.

'Oh, think nothing of it,' says the barman. 'That's the peanuts on the bar – they're complimentary.'

If you want to know the time ...

The police are ordered to clean up the high street for a big parade, and are patrolling the pavements when a drunk staggers towards them.

'Excuse me, offisher,' he says to one constable. 'Could you pleash tell me the time?'

The constable frowns at him. 'One o'clock,' he replies – before whacking the drunk over the head with his baton.

'Christ,' said the drunk, reeling. 'I'm glad I didn't ask you an hour ago.'

Her indoors

Frank is enjoying a pint in the pub one afternoon with a friend.

'My wife will be on the plane now,' he says with a wistful smile.

'Really,' his friend says. 'Where's she off to, then?'

'Oh, nowhere,' says Frank. 'I've left her at home taking a couple of inches off the kitchen door.'

Odds against

After her business goes bust, a blonde woman named Sharon finds herself in dire financial trouble – so desperate, in fact, that she resorts to praying.

'God, please help me,' she wails. 'I've lost my business, and if I don't get some money, I'm going to lose my car as well. Please let me win the lottery.'

Saturday night comes, and Sharon watches aghast as someone else wins it. Again, she begins to pray: 'God, please let me win the lottery! I've lost my business, my car, and I'm going to lose my house as well.'

Next Saturday night comes, and Sharon still has no luck. Once again, she prays.

'God, why haven't you helped me?' she cries, angrily. 'I've lost my business, my house, my car and now my children are starving. I've always been a good servant to you – PLEASE let me win the lottery just this once, so I can get my life back in order.'

Suddenly, there is a blinding flash of light as the heavens open above, and Sharon is confronted with the glowing, ethereal vision of God Himself.

'Sharon,' he booms. 'Meet me halfway on this. Buy a ticket.'

What's the difference...

...between a jumbo jet and a Brummie?

A jumbo jet stops whining when it gets to Majorca.

Never lie to kids

Little Johnny's mother is taking a bath, having recently been discharged from hospital where she had all of her pubic hair removed. Johnny comes into the bathroom as she's drying off, and asks her what happened to the hair.

'I've lost my sponge,' she says, and sends Johnny out to play.

A few moments later, Johnny reappears and tells his mother he thinks he's found her sponge.

'Oh, really,' his mum asks. 'Where is it?'

Johnny answers, 'The lady next door is washing daddy's face with it.'

What a prick

An extremely drunk man looking for a whorehouse stumbles into a chiropodist's office instead. Laboriously, he weaves over to the receptionist. Without looking up, she waves him over to the examination bed.

'Stick it through that curtain,' she says.

Looking forward to something kinky, the drunk pulls out his penis and sticks it through the crack in the curtains.

'That's not a foot!' screams the receptionist.

'Christ!' replies the drunk. 'I didn't know you had a minimum.'

Two for the price of one

'I'm telling you, I've never been happier,' Carol tells her friend, 'I've got two boyfriends. One is just fabulous – handsome, sensitive, caring, considerate and he's got a fantastic sense of humour.'

'Well what on earth do you need the second one for?' asks her envious friend.

'Oh,' Carol replies, 'the second one is straight.'

Past her prime

A self-obsessed bodybuilder is admiring his physique in the mirror one morning, and complimenting himself on his Herculean frame. Even his suntan is almost perfect, he notes – except, he realizes to his horror, for his groin, which is a pale, alabaster white. Annoyed, he decides to go to the beach and correct the situation. Arriving on an apparently deserted part of the shore, he undresses completely and buries himself in the sand – leaving only his knob above ground to catch the sun's rays.

However, before long, two old women come strolling along and notice his member waving in the sea breeze. After prodding it with her cane, one of the pensioners tuts. 'There is just no justice in the world,' she says.

The other old lady looks at her. 'What do you mean by that?' she says.

The first woman frowns. 'I'm 80 years old, and I've been chasing these things all my life,' she says. 'Now the damn things are growing wild and I'm too old to squat.'

Q: What do you call a sheep tied to a lamppost in Wales?

A: A leisure centre.

Flies never lie

While driving a truckload of manure, an old farmer is stopped by a policeman. 'You were speeding,' says the cop. 'I'm going to have to give you a ticket.'

'If you must,' the farmer says, watching the cop shoo away several flies.

'These flies sure are terrible,' the cop complains, swatting irritably.

'Yep,' the farmer says. 'Them are circle flies. They call them that because they circle a horse's tail.'

The cop looks at him angrily. 'You wouldn't be calling me a horse's ass now, would you?' he barks.

'Nope, I'm not,' replies the farmer. 'But you just can't fool them flies.'

Smooth operator

The local paper in Leeds carries an advert for the job of 'fanny shaver'. A young hopeful rings up the number shown, and the man answers the phone asks him some questions. 'First things first,' he says. 'Are you single?'

'Oh yes,' says the applicant.

'That's good,' says the man, 'we've had a lot of trouble in the past with people who are married. Their wives get annoyed. Now, secondly, do you have a current ten-year passport?'

'Yes,' says the young applicant.

'Brilliant,' says the man. 'Often we find that people have a problem with travelling all over the globe. They seem to find the strain of jetting from LA to Milan to New York staying at top-class hotels a little bit too much to take.'

'Oh no, not me,' says the young hopeful. 'I love to travel.'

'Great,' says the man. 'And what about supermodels? Do you think you'd have a problem getting close to some of the most beautiful women in the world? You might even have to party with them and keep them company. How would you deal with that?'

'I'd be fine,' says the applicant. 'I love talking to women and I don't think I'd be intimidated.'

'Excellent,' says the man. 'Now, what about the shaving of the fanny? Would you get flustered peeling bikini bottoms off beautiful women, foaming them up and shaving their pubic regions? This sort of intimacy can often make a man all fingers and thumbs, you know.'

'No way,' says the young man. 'I have no problem with nudity or intimacy with gorgeous women. I'd be both discreet and charming.'

'Well,' says the man, 'you sound as if you could be just right for the job. I'll post you a coach ticket to Croydon.'

'Is that where my first job is?' asks the applicant.

'Oh no,' says the man. 'That's where the queue for the interviews starts.'

Sorted!

One fine day in the forest, Mr Rabbit is on his daily run, when he sees a giraffe rolling a joint.

'Giraffe, oh Giraffe!' he calls. 'Why do you do drugs? Come run with me instead!' So the giraffe stops rolling his joint and runs with the rabbit.

Then they come across an elephant doing lines. 'Elephant, oh Mr Elephant, Why do you do drugs? Come run with us instead.' So the elephant stops snorting, and goes running with the other two animals.

Then they spy a lion preparing a syringe. 'Lion, oh Mr Lion' cries the rabbit, 'Why do you do drugs? Come run with us instead.'

But no – with a mighty roar, the lion smashes the rabbit to smithereens.

'No!' cry the giraffe and the elephant. 'Why did you do that? All he was trying to do was to help you out!'

The lion growls at them. 'That fucking rabbit always makes me run around the forest when he's whizzing his tits off.'

Anal intruder

One day a man has a terrible stomach complaint and goes along to his doctor to see what can be done about it. The doctor tells him that he is very ill, but that he can cure his condition with a course of suppositories, inserted deep into his arse every six hours.

'Right,' says the doctor, 'bend over and I'll do the first one for you.' The man bends down and the doctor sticks the suppository deep into his hole. He then gives the man his course and sends him home.

At home six hours later the man realizes that he can't stick the suppository far enough up his arse on his own, and he asks his wife to help him insert the slippery bullet. After explaining to her what to do the man bends over. His wife puts one hand on her husband's shoulder to brace herself and thrusts the suppository really hard into his arse. To her horror, the man lets out a desperate, blood-curdling scream.

'My God!' she cries. 'What's the matter? Have I hurt you?'

'No,' replies the man. 'But I've just realized that when the doctor did it he had both hands on my shoulders.'

What's got three pairs of balls...
...and screws you twice a week?
The National Lottery.

Brawn, not brains
After hours of drinking heavily, Bob is sitting in a bar when, through his bloodshot eyes, he notices a figure sitting next to him. Feeling very jovial, the bloke turns to the blurry figure and says: 'Do you want to hear a blonde joke?'

The figure next to him snorts. 'Listen, mate,' comes a female voice, 'I weigh 175 lbs and am the British Women's kick-boxing champion. I am also blonde. My blonde friend next to me weighs 190 lb and is the Women's European arm-wrestling champion. Finally, my other friend at the end of the bar weighs 235 lb and is the Women's World power-lifting champion. She, too, is a natural blonde. Now, do you still want to tell that blonde joke?'

The guy pondered this for a while.

'Hmmm,' he replied finally. 'Not if I have to explain it three times.'

What's the difference...
...between a dead dog in the road and a dead lawyer in the road?
There are skid marks in front of the dog.

Don't get lost in the woods
After graduating from the University of Arkansas, a young journalist gets a job at a tiny provincial newspaper in the middle of the prairies. His first assignment is to write a human-interest story, so he goes out to the country to do his research. Driving through the cornfields, he spies an old farmhand and introduces himself.

'I was just wondering, sir' the young hack asked. 'Out here in the middle of nowhere – has anything ever happened that made you happy?'

The old-timer furrowed his weathered brow for a moment.

'Yep!' he exclaimed, suddenly. 'One time my neighbour's daughter, a good-looking girl, got lost. So we formed a posse, and went out and found her. After we all screwed her, we took her back home.'

The young journo blanched. 'I can't print that!' he cried. 'Can't you think of anything else that happened that made you happy?'

The farmer thought again. 'Yeah!' he said, finally. 'One time one of my neighbour's sheep got lost. After forming a posse, we found it and all screwed it before we took it back home.'

'Christ!' says the young man. 'I can't print that either!' He thinks for a while. 'Okay – has anything ever happened around here that made you sad?'

The old man looked at the ground. 'Well,' he said sheepishly. 'I got lost once.'

Q: What's got 75 balls and screws old ladies?

A: Bingo.

Memory lapse

A young man walks out of a newsagent's and spies an old man on a park bench crying his eyes out. So the youth goes over to the howling pensioner to see if he's all right. 'Are you okay?' he asks.

'No, it's my birthday today, I'm 82,' blubs the old man.

'Eighty-two! But you look great for your age, you should be happy,' continues the young man.

'Yeah, and I got married yesterday too – to a 25-year-old blonde bombshell,' explains the old man.

The sympathetic young man thinks he's sussed the old man's misery and continues his line of enquiry, 'And you're too old to fulfil your conjugal responsibilities, I suppose?'

'No, not all, we enjoy a full and loving sexual relationship and get down to it five times a day. That's not the problem at all,' says the old man, who is still crying.

'Look, mate, I'm 25 and even I don't enjoy that much sex, you lucky sod,' says the dumbfounded lad. 'So why are you crying?'

The old man looks up and says wistfully, 'I've forgotten where I live.'

Lap of luxury

What has eight legs and eats pussy?

Me, you and Tatu.

What a dump!

A drunk staggers down the main street of a town and up the church steps. He manages to open the church door and falls into the silent building. On his hands and knees he weeps as he struggles to pull himself to his feet, half crawling and half walking towards the front of the church. He crashes from pew to pew softly crying, 'Oh God help me, God help me,' until he finally makes it into the confessional box.

Having observed the man's sorry progress the priest sits silently in the booth, waiting to hear the drunk's tale. He waits for several minutes, hearing the drunk moan and groan, until finally there is a lengthy silence from the drunk's side of the confessional. At last the priest speaks.

'May I help you my son?' he says.

'I don't know father,' the drunk replies. 'It depends on whether or not you have any paper on your side.'

Take matters into your own hands

Plucking up the courage, a young man goes to a massage parlour for the first time. As he's not sure when to ask for the dirty deed, he lies on the leather bed, frustratedly getting more and more aroused. After a few minutes, the masseuse notices his growing erection. 'Perhaps sir would like a wank?' she breathes.

The man gulps. 'Yes please,' he stutters.

With that, the lady leaves the room, and returns a full 20 minutes later. 'Well,' she says, popping her head round the door. 'Finished?'

Load of balls

A man enters a barbershop for a shave. While the barber is foaming him up, he mentions the problems he has getting a close shave around the cheeks. 'I have just the thing,' says the barber – and takes two small wooden balls from a nearby drawer. 'Just place these between your cheek and gum.'

The client places the ball in his mouth and the barber proceeds with the closest shave the man has ever experienced. After a few strokes the client is very impressed.

'Just one thing,' he asks in a garbled voice. 'What if I swallow them?'

'No problem,' says the barber. 'Just bring them back tomorrow like everyone else does.'

The generous judge

'Mr Quinn, I have reviewed your case very carefully,' the divorce court judge said, 'And I have decided to award your wife a sum of £500 a month.'

'That seems more than fair, your Honour,' said Mr Quinn. 'And I shall do my best to send her and the kid a few quid each month myself.'

Thinking ahead

A man walks into a bar and sees a beautiful woman sitting on her own. Thinking quickly he buys a drink and goes over to sit next to her.

'Hello,' he says, 'Can I show you something?'

The woman looks him up and down. 'Okay,' she says, 'What is it you want to show me?'

The man rolls up his sleeve and points to his watch.

'You see this watch?' he says. 'It enables me to tell anything about the person I am talking to without asking them a single question.'

'Rubbish,' the woman replies, 'Your watch can't tell you anything about me.'

'Right,' the man says, and he stares intently at the watch for a few seconds, 'I can tell you haven't got any knickers on.'

'Sorry,' the woman replies, 'But your watch must be broken. I've got knickers on.'

The man looks at his watch in confusion, then gradually a smile of recognition spreads across his face.

'Oh, that's right,' he says, 'I set it ten minutes fast this morning.'

A fishy story

A beautiful young lady wearing a lovely summer dress is sitting peacefully in a railway carriage on her own when a crusty traveller enters the compartment, eating a tray of king prawns. The filthy youth sits down opposite the woman, shelling his prawns and flicking the debris onto the floor, occasionally tossing one onto the young lady's lap with a sneer. When he's finished his meal he casually screws up the carton he's been eating out of and throws it at the girl's face.

The young lady then calmly stands up, picks up the shells from the floor, put them in the carton and throws the whole sorry mess out of the window. She then walks over to the communication cord and pulls it.

'You silly bitch,' the crusty says with a sneer, 'That'll cost you a £50 fine.'

'Yes,' the young lady replies, 'And when the police smell your fingers it'll cost you ten years.'

Last requests

Three criminals are in hell waiting to be punished for their sins, and the Devil says, 'Before I plunge you into the fiery abyss, you can have one cool beer as a last privilege.'

The first criminal in the line-up is Jeffrey Dahmer.

'What drink do you want?' asks Satan.

'I would love a Budweiser,' replies Dahmer, and sure enough he's given a can of it before being tossed into agony.

The Devil repeats his question to the second criminal.

'I would like some Foster's,' says Ronnie Kray, and he gets some of the amber nectar before his punishment.

Finally, the Devil asks the third man, Fred West, what beer he'd like before being burnt for eternity.

'Oh, that's easy,' says Fred. 'I could murder some Tennent's.'

Not reading the signs

There once was a mobster who employed a deaf and dumb accountant. For years all went well between the two, until one day the mobster decided to doublecheck his books and found that he was short by $10 million. Enraged, he sent for the accountant, who returned accompanied by his brother, who could speak sign language.

'Tell your bastard brother I want to know where my $10 million's gone,' the furious gangster swore at the brother.

After a quick exchange the translating brother reported that the accountant knew nothing about the missing millions.

The angry Mafioso then pulled out a gun and held it to his accountant's head. 'You tell this lying son of a whore that if he don't tell me where my money is in the next 20 seconds, I'll blow his fucking brains out.'

The brother duly translated this message, and the accountant furiously signalled back that the money was hidden under a bed in his house.

'Well,' growled the thug, 'What did the little rat say?'

'He said,' replied the brother, 'that you haven't got the balls to do it.'

In hot water

Nervously pacing up and down a hospital corridor, a man waits as his wife gives birth to their first child. After a long labour the doctor comes out and tells the man that he is the father of a baby boy. The man is overjoyed, and rushes in to his wife who smiles weakly and gives him the child.

Overcome, the tearful father asks the midwife if there is anything he can do to help. Sensing that the dad wants to share in the occasion, the midwife tells him to take the baby and bathe it next door.

After a few minutes the midwife pops in to see how the man is getting on – then jumps back in dismay when she sees what the new dad is doing. He has two fingers firmly lodged up the infant's nose and is dragging the child through the water in figure of eights.

'Good God!' she shouts. 'That's not how to bathe a newborn!'

'It bloody well is,' the man replies, 'when the water's this hot.'

Calm down! Calm down!

At the end of a tiny deserted bar is a huge Scouse bloke – 6 feet 5 inches tall and 350 lbs. He's having a few beers when a short, well-dressed and obviously gay man walks in and sits beside him. After three or four beers, the queer finally plucks up the courage to say something to the big Liverpudlian. Leaning over, he cups his huge ear: 'Do you want a blow job?' he whispers.

At this, the massive Merseysider leaps up with fire in his eyes and smacks the man in the face. Knocking him off the stool, he proceeds to beat him all the way out of the bar. Finally, he leaves him, badly bruised, in the car park and returns to his seat as if nothing has happened.

Amazed, the bartender quickly brings over another beer. 'I've never seen you react like that,' he says. 'Just what did he say to you?'

'I'm not sure,' the big Scouser replies. 'Something about a job.'

Courting controversy

Following a hard day in court, a judge decides to go to the pub. Nine pints and seven whiskies later, he staggers out of the boozer and starts to walk home. Unfortunately, on his way he feels sick and he throws up all over his suit.

Arriving home, he uses his fine legal mind to explain the mess to his wife.

'Some filthy tramp vomited all over me,' he moans, and his sympathetic wife makes him a nice cup of tea.

The next day the judge comes home and decides to make his story more convincing. 'You'll never guess what?' he says to his wife, 'The tramp that threw up on me was in court today. I gave him six months!'

'Well,' she replies, 'You should have given him a year, because he shat in your pants as well.'

What's the difference...

...between a blonde and a bowling ball?

You can only get three fingers in a bowling ball.

Fit for duty?

During a shortage of eligible men, a bear, a pig and a rabbit are called up for national service. While waiting for the medical examinations, they all admit they're terrified of being killed.

'I'm ungainly and pink,' says the pig, truthfully. 'The enemy will see me a mile off – so I decided to chop my tail off.'

The rabbit nods sagely – and the bear realizes the bunny's ears have been removed. 'I just hope it works,' says the rabbit.

Mystified, the bear watches as both animals enter the examination room – then return, smiling.

'We're free to go,' says the rabbit. 'They said a rabbit without ears is not a proper rabbit, and a pig without a curly tail is not a proper pig!'

He's about to leave with the pig when the bear pipes up.

'Hang on a minute!' he cries. 'I'm massive and slow – I'd not last a day.'

The other two look at the bear. 'Well,' says the rabbit, 'Your sharp teeth could be useful in combat. You might want them removed ...'

Nodding miserably, the bear lies down – and the other animals start kicking his fangs out. Eventually the dazed bear, blood pouring from his mouth, stumbles through the door. A moment later he returns.

'Did you get let off?' says the pig.

'Yesh,' splutters the bear. 'Apparently I'm too fat.'

Hard to believe

A elderly gentleman shuffles into a drug store and asks for Viagra.

'That's no problem,' says the pharmacist. 'How many do you want?'

'Just a few, maybe four,' says the pensioner. 'But could you cut them into four pieces?'

'That won't do you much good,' replies the pharmacist.

The customer looks at him and sighs.

'I'm 83 years old – I'm not interested in sex anymore,' he says. 'I just want it to stick out far enough so I don't piss on my shoes.'

Beer goggles

What is the difference between a dog and a fox?
About eight pints.

Can't see the woods for the tree

A traffic policeman pulls a car over on a lonely back road and approaches the lady driver. 'Ma'am, why were you weaving all over the road?' he asks.

'Oh, officer!' the woman replies. 'Thank goodness you're here! I almost had a terrible accident. Swerving to avoid a tree, I looked up to find another tree right in front of me. So I pulled the car over to the right and there, yet again, was another tree in front of me!'

The copper nods, then points to the rear-view mirror.

'Ma'am,' he says, patiently. 'That's your air freshener.'

Is it malignant?

A man walks into a bar with a big green bullfrog on his head.

'Where did you get that?' the barman asks.

'Would you believe,' the bullfrog replies, 'it started out as a tiny little wart on my arse?'

The missing pen

A doctor is sitting in his surgery preparing to write out a prescription for a patient. He reaches into the top pocket of his white coat and pulls out a rectal thermometer.

'Damn!' he swears. 'That means some arsehole must have my pen.'

Never satisfied

A Jewish grandmother is watching her grandchild playing on the beach – when a huge wave washes over him, pulling him out to sea. Falling down on her knees in the sand, the grandma begins to pray:

'Please God, save my only grandson! He is my life and the future of our family! With all my years of faith, please return him to us safely!'

Just then a huge wave rolls back onto the beach, bringing the bewildered lad back onto the sand, good as new.

The grandma looks up to the sky. 'He had a hat,' she bellows.

Always read the instructions

Three new inmates are sitting in their cell, contemplating their futures. The first one takes out a mouth organ. 'At least I can keep myself amused by playing a little music. It'll help to pass the time.'

The second takes out a pack of cards. 'We can while away the time playing poker,' he says.

The third man takes out a box of tampons. 'What the hell are you going to do with those?' the other two ask.

He grins and says, 'It says on the box I can ride, swim, ski and play tennis with these.'

Hidden love

An elderly Frenchman went to his parish priest, and asked to confess.

'Of course, my son', said the priest.

'Well, Father, at the beginning of World War Two, a beautiful woman knocked on my door and asked to hide from the Germans. I concealed her in my attic, and they never found her.'

'That's a wonderful thing, my son, and nothing that you need to confess,' said the priest.

'It's worse, Father. I was weak, and told her that she had to pay for rent of the attic with her sexual favours,' continued the old man.

'Well, it was a very difficult time, and you took a large risk – you would have suffered terribly at their hands if the Germans had found you hiding her.'

The man nodded solemnly, as the padre went on. 'I know that God will balance the good and the evil. He will judge you kindly,' the priest concluded.

'Thanks, Father', said the old man. 'That's a load off of my mind. Can I ask another question?'

'Of course, my son', said the priest.

'Do I need to tell her that the war is over?'

Role reversal

A female journalist goes out to Kuwait to do a story on gender roles, just before the outbreak of the Gulf War in 1991. She notes with some dismay that the women of the country customarily walk about 10 feet behind their men. Several years later the same journalist returns to the country to see if there has been any change in these gender roles. She is surprised to find, on her return, that the men now walk ten feet behind their women. Amazed at this, she approaches a young lady.

'This is marvellous,' she says. 'What enabled the women here to effect such a reversal of roles?'

'Simple,' the young woman replies. 'Land mines.'

Q: What is the definition of a tampon?

A: Dracula's teabag.

Lateral thinking

Three men reach the final round of tests to join the SAS, and are called together to speak with the interviewer.

'Do you love your wife?' says the officer.

'Sir, yes I do, sir,' say the recruits in unison.

'And do you love your country?'

'Sir, yes sir,' say the men.

'But what do you love more, your wife or your country?'

The recruits do not hesitate: 'Sir, my country, sir.'

The interviewer stares at them: 'We want you to prove this. Your wives are sitting in separate rooms nearby – take this gun and go and kill your loved one.'

The first man gulps and stares at the gun for a few minutes.

'I can't do it,' he says, and leaves.

Turning white, the second man goes into the room, and all is silent for about five minutes. Soon the door opens and the man, sweaty with his tie loosened, puts down the unfired gun and leaves.

The final interviewee looks long and hard and the revolver, then slowly paces into the adjoining room. After a brief silence, the interviewer hears the sound of a gunshot. There's a brief pause, then an almighty crashing sound and a woman's scream.

Grinning and breathless, the final recruit emerges from the room and puts the gun on the table. The interviewer looks up at him and says 'What the hell happened?'

'The gun you gave me was filled with blanks,' says the man, breathing heavily. 'So I had to beat her to death with the chair.'

A man's best friend

Leaving a cafe with his morning cup of coffee, a man notices a most unusual funeral procession approaching the nearby cemetery. Moving up the street slowly is a black hearse, followed closely behind by a second black hearse. Behind this, with head bowed, walks a solitary man walking a pit bull on a leash. Behind him are about 200 men walking single file.

Curiosity getting the better of him, the man respectfully approaches the man walking the dog.

'I know now is a bad time to disturb you,' he says to the mourner. 'But I've never seen a funeral like this. Who has passed away?'

The bereaved looks up. 'Well, that first hearse is for my wife.'

'What happened to her?' the first man asks.

The funeral-goer looks down at his pit bull. 'My dog attacked and killed her.'

The man nods solemnly 'Well, who is in the second hearse?'

'My mother-in-law,' the man answers. 'She was trying to help my wife when the dog turned on her.'

A poignant and thoughtful moment of silence passes between the two men.

'Could I borrow that dog?' says the first man, finally.

The mourner looks at him wearily. 'Get in line.'

That's the spirit

A landlord is shining glasses behind the bar when in walks a businessman. 'What'll you have?' asks the publican.

'A scotch, please,' replies the businessman.

The bartender hands him the drink, and says 'That'll be two quid.'

'What are you talking about?' says the man, angry. 'I don't owe you anything for this.'

The ugly bug ball

After a heavy night, a man rolls over to find possibly the ugliest woman in the world sleeping peacefully beside him. Aghast, he very gently slides his arm out from under her, gets up, and dresses as fast as he can. Stopping only to leave a £20 note on the bureau, he tip-toes out – only to feel a tug on his trouser leg. Looking down, he sees a girl just as ugly as the one in the bed.

'What?' she smiles, toothlessly. 'Nothing for the bridesmaid?'

What do you call...

...a woman with one leg shorter than the other?

Eileen.

The lazy sons

Ron and Reg are sitting in the café moaning about the younger generation. 'My son must be the laziest little bastard in Britain,' Ron says, sipping his tea.

'You've got no chance, mate,' Reg answers. 'My boy Gary is the laziest little shit I've ever seen.'

The two men continue to argue and decide to visit each other's houses to witness the lazy lads first hand. First they go to Ron's house, where his son is lying on the sofa watching *This Morning*.

'Nip up the road and get me 20 Marlboro will you?' Ron asks his lad.

'Get them yourself,' the boy says. 'I'm watching television.'

'Go on, son,' Ron says. 'I'll give you a tenner if you just go and get me some fags.'

'Bollocks,' the boy says. 'I'm not shifting.'

Ron and Reg then head over to Reg's house. They walk into the living room where the curtains are shut and the telly is blaring out *Oprah*. Jimmy, Reg's son, is sitting in front of the fire, the room is unbearably hot and the boy is weeping softly. The two men stare at the boy in disbelief: an 18-year-old lad sitting at home openly crying over a television show. Jimmy doesn't even look up as the two men come into the room, he just sits in his chair, staring at the television screen, crying like a baby.

Annoyed at his son's apathy, Reg finally walks over and turns off the television. But it doesn't do any good and Jimmy just carries on weeping, staring into space.

'What's the matter, son?' Reg asks.

'I'm burning,' Jimmy replies.

Watching your figure

A nought and a figure of eight are walking through the desert, when the nought turns the eight and says, 'Why have you got that belt pulled so tight?'

Skilled worker

A dog walks into the Job Centre and asks the man at the counter if they have any vacancies. The man is stunned. 'You're a talking dog!' he cries. 'What a wonderful talent you have. I'm sure we can find work for you no problem.'

At this the dog becomes agitated. 'Look,' he says. 'Don't mess me about. Have you got any jobs or not?'

'Okay,' says the man. 'Just sit tight. I'll make a call and I'll have you working in no time.'

With that the man phones Billy Smart's Circus. 'I've got a talking dog here,' the man says to Billy. 'Can I send him down to you?'

Billy is ecstatic. 'All my life I've been looking for a talking dog,' he says. 'You get him down here tomorrow morning and he can name his wage.'

The dog's still wary. 'What will I be doing for Mr Smart?' he asks.

The man is puzzled. 'I imagine you'll be the Talking Dog in the circus,' he says.

'Oh, that's no good to me, mate,' the dog says. 'I'm a plumber.'

Q: What's the definition of trust?

A: Two cannibals going down on each other.

The cowpoke

Three cowboys were sitting around a campfire, out on the lonesome trail, each with a tale of bravado for which cowboys are famous.

'I must be the meanest, toughest cowboy there is,' the first cowboy said with a drawl. 'Why, just the other day, a bull got loose in the corral and gored six grown men before I wrestled it to the ground, by the horns, with my bare hands.'

The second cowboy couldn't stand to be bested. 'Why, that's nothing,' he said. 'I was walking down the trail yesterday when a 15 feet rattler made a move for me. I grabbed it with my bare hands, bit its head off and sucked down all of its poison. And I'm still here to tell the tale.'

All this time, the third cowboy remained silent, and the first two turned to look at him as he slowly stoked the red-hot coals with his penis.

What's the difference...

...between a woman in a church and a woman in the bath?
One's got hope in her soul...

It's a small world

A Czechoslovakian man feels his eyesight is getting worse, and visits an optician. He sits down in the chair, and the optician points at the bottom line of the eye-test: CZYFHRGRV.

'Can you read this?' asks the doctor.

'Read it?' says the Czech. 'Doc, I know the guy!'

Roadkill

A young brickie starts work on a farm, and the boss sends him out to the local supplier for more cement. As dusk falls, though, he's still not returned – so the boss calls him on the CB radio.

'I've got a problem, Boss,' comes the reply. 'I've hit a pig!'

The foreman sighs. 'Ah well, these things happen sometimes,' he says, sympathetically. 'Just drag the carcass off the road so nobody else hits it.'

'But he's not dead, boss,' says the young man. 'He's tangled up on the bull bar. I've tried to untangle him, but he's kicking and squealing in a horrible way. He's a real big mutha, boss – I'm afraid he's going to hurt me!'

'Never mind,' says the boss. 'There's a shotgun in the back of the truck. Get that and shoot him. Then drag the carcass off the road and come home.'

Another half an hour goes by, but there's still no word from the youngster. The boss gets back on the CB. 'What's the problem, son? Did you drag the pig off the road like I said?'

Through the radio crackle comes the reply: 'Yeah boss – but his motorbike is still jammed under the truck.'

Have you heard?
Robert De Niro is making a film about the Harold Shipman murders. It's called The Old Dear Hunter.

Eighteen hours to live
A woman comes home from the doctor and tells her husband she has only 18 hours to live.

'That's terrible!' cries her husband, 'What would you like to do during your last hours? I'll try to make it as memorable as possible for you.'

'Well,' she said, 'First, I want to take a long romantic walk, then have a quiet dinner at my favourite restaurant. But ultimately, I want to go to bed with you and make passionate love all night long.'

'Gee, honey,' says her husband, shaking his head 'I don't know about that "all night long" stuff. After all, I've got to get up in the morning.'

Drunk driving (iv)

A man is driving home after drinking one too many following a round of golf. After pulling him over to the side of the road, a policeman informs him that he is too drunk to drive.

'Too drunk to drive?' the man says. 'Officer, I can barely putt!'

What's the difference...

...between an Airfix model without adhesive and David Beckham? One's a glueless kit...

It's a question of timing

Three old men are sitting around chatting about their respective toilet habits. 'The best thing that could happen to me,' says the 80 year-old, 'would just to be able to have a good pee. I stand there for 20 minutes, and it dribbles and hurts. I have to go over and over again.'

The 85-year-old nods in agreement. 'The best thing that could happen to me,' he laments, 'Is if I could have one good bowel movement. I take every kind of laxative I can get my hands on and it's still a problem.'

But the 90 year-old is shaking his head.

'That's not my problem,' he says. 'Every morning at 6:00am sharp, I have a good long slash. And then at 6:30am sharp I usually crimp off a length too.'

'So what's the problem?' chorus the others.

'Well,' says the pensioner, 'The best thing that could happen to me would be if I could wake up before 7:00am.'

Q: How do you make a blonde's eyes twinkle?

A: Shine a torch in her ear.

The spelling contest

A boy comes home from school looking sheepish. 'Dad,' he moans, 'We had a class spelling contest today, and I failed on the very first word.'

'Ah, that's okay, son,' says his father, looking over his glasses at him. 'What was the word?'

The son looks even more miserable. 'Posse,' he replies.

His father bursts out laughing.

'Well, no wonder you couldn't spell it,' he roars. 'You can't even pronounce it!'

Under arrest

Did you hear Vanessa Feltz was held at by customs at Heathrow – for smuggling drugs?

Allegedly, she had 40 lbs of crack in her knickers.

What's the difference...

...between a snow-woman and a snowman?

Snowballs.

Building site blunder

An Italian, an Irishman and a Chinese fellow are hired at a construction site. The foreman points out a huge pile of sand and says to the Italian guy, 'You're in charge of sweeping.'

He then turns to the Irishman. 'You're in charge of digging.'

Finally, he turns to the Chinaman. 'And you're in charge of supplies. Now, I have to leave for a little while. I expect you guys to make a dent in that pile.'

Two hours later, the foreman returns to find the pile of sand untouched, and the Italian and Irishman standing nearby looking sheepish.

'Why didn't you sweep any off it?' he asks the pair.

The Italian looks at him. 'We didn't have a broom or shovel. You said the Chinese guy was in charge of supplies, but he disappeared and I couldn't find him.'

Annoyed, the foreman storms off to find the errant Oriental. Just then, the Chinaman leaps out from behind the pile of sand.

'Supplies!' he yells.

The future's Rosy

While on a day out in Blackpool a man decides to go and visit a fortune teller. He goes into the hut of Gypsy Rose Lee and sees a middle-aged lady sitting at a table staring into a crystal ball. He sits down and she begins to tell his fortune. A smile breaks out and she begins to laugh.

'You're going to come into great wealth,' she says. 'You'll marry a beautiful woman and have a long and happy life, full of laughter and great sex.'

At this the man stands up, draws back his arm and delivers an almighty haymaker at the fortune teller, catching her right in the middle of her face and breaking her nose. She falls to the floor, stunned by the punch. Bleeding from her nose, she asks the man why he lamped her.

'Oh,' he says, 'I always like to strike a happy medium.'

Wishful thinking

An old woman goes into a sex shop and asks the assistant if she can have a look at an assortment of vibrators. Despite a wide range of colours, shapes and sizes, none of them appeal to the old lady. She looks up and says to the assistant, 'Can I have a look at that tartan one up there on the shelf?'

'No,' replies the shop assistant. 'That's my thermos flask.'

Taking things too far

Taking his seat on a flight, a businessman is bemused to see a parrot in the next seat. The plane takes off and the man asks the stewardess for a coffee. As he does, the parrot screeches, 'Yeah, and get me a double whisky too, you ugly cow!'

The stewardess walks off to get the drinks, but on her return has forgotten the man's coffee. She apologizes, and as she turns to get the coffee the parrot again squawks, 'Yeah, and get me another whisky you slack-arsed tart!'

By now the stewardess is rattled, and she returns with the whisky, but again no coffee. The man, having observed the parrot's success, decides to try the rude approach. 'I've asked you for coffee twice!' he bellows, 'Now get your lazy butt back there and get me a cup of coffee.'

Moments later he and the parrot are dragged from their seats and thrown out of the emergency exit by two stewards. They plunge downwards for a few seconds, then the parrot looks at the man and squawks, 'For someone who can't fly, you sure are a ballsy prat!'

Q: Did you hear about the girl who went fishing with five men?

A: She went home with a red snapper.

The slowest takeaway in the world

One evening a husband and wife are sitting at home, waiting for dinner guests to arrive. After putting the casserole in the oven the wife turns and screams, 'I've forgotten the nibbles! We can't have a party without nibbles! Go down into the garden and fetch some snails. I'll boil them up and serve them with a little garlic butter and lemon.'

The husband sets off to the end of the garden with a bucket and starts hunting for the snails. No sooner has he started when a beautiful woman leans over the fence and casually asks him if he wants to pop over to her place for a quick drink. The husband thinks that a quick snifter before dinner can't hurt, so he climbs over the fence and goes in.

After downing a martini, the woman grabs the man and begins kissing him. One thing leads to another and soon the pair are hard at it in bed. So hard, in fact, that the husband falls asleep for a couple of hours. Waking up in a panic, he grabs all his clothes and his bucket of snails, jumps back over the fence and hurtles into his own kitchen where his wife has nodded off. He trips up as he enters through the door and spills his bucket of snails over the lino and wakes her.

'Where the hell have you been?' she screams. The husband looks up at his livid wife, looks down at the scattered snails on the floor and shouts,

'Come on lads, we're nearly there!'

Bang! Hish! Bang! Hish!

Joe was visiting a friend's rubber factory one day. They entered the first room, to the loud sound of 'Bang! Hish! Bang! Hish!'

'What are you making here?' asked Joe.

'Teats for a baby's bottle,' replied the owner. 'The bang makes the teat and the hish puts the hole in the end.'

The next room, however, was filled with different sounds: 'Bang! Bang! Bang! Bang! Hish! Bang! Bang!'

'This is where we make condoms,' explained the owner.

'So why,' asked Joe, 'Do the machines go hish every now and then?'

'Well,' says the owner, 'We have to make sure there are enough babies for our teats.'

Q: How do Greeks separate the men from the boys?

A: With a crowbar.

Radical surgery

When Ralph first noticed that his penis was growing larger and staying erect longer, he was delighted – as was his wife. But after several weeks – when his spam javelin had grown to nearly 20 inches – Ralph became quite concerned, so he and his wife went to see a prominent urologist. After an initial examination, the physician explained to the couple that, though rare, Ralph's condition could be helped through corrective surgery.

'How long will Ralph be on crutches?' the wife asked anxiously.

'Crutches? Why would he need crutches?' responded the surprised doctor.

'Well,' said the wife coldly, 'You are planning to lengthen his legs, aren't you?'

Drive in comfort

Prior to competing in the 2001 Open Championships, Tiger Woods is touring the links courses in Ireland and pulls into a petrol station in his huge Mercedes.

'Howdy,' he says to the attendant. 'Can you fill her up?'

But as he pulls out the keys, two wooden tees fall out of his pocket.

'Sweet Mary!' says the attendant. 'And what are they?'

Tiger looks down, and smiles.

'They're for putting my balls on while I'm driving.'

'Bejasus!' cries the attendant. 'Those fellas at Mercedes think of everything.'

Home from home

A guy walks into a bar down in Alabama and orders a gin and tonic. Surprised, the bartender looks at him.

'Ain't you from around here, boy?' he sneers.

'I'm from Pennsylvania,' the guy replies.

The bartender frowns. 'What do you do there?'

'I'm a taxidermist,' comes the reply.

The bartender laughs incredulously. 'A taxidermist!' he cries. 'What the hell is a taxidermist?'

The guy looks at him. 'I mount dead animals.'

The bartender smiles and turns to the rest of the bar. 'It's okay, boys,' he shouts. 'He's one of us!'

Eating disorder

Two men are sitting in the waiting room at a doctor's surgery. The first man is gingerly holding his shoulder with a look of severe pain on his face, while the second has baked beans in his hair, fried egg down the front of his shirt and two sausages sticking out of his front pockets. The two men weigh each other up for a few minutes, then the second man asks the first what happened to him.

'My cat got stuck up a tree,' the man says, gripping his arm. 'I went up after him and fell out. I think I've broken my shoulder.'

The second man nods in sympathy.

'What about you, then?' the first man asks. 'What's wrong with you?'

'Oh, it's nothing serious,' the second man replies. 'I'm just not eating properly.'

Groin strain

George's girlfriend decided she wanted to please her man, so one day she went out and bought a pair of crotchless panties. That night she lay on the bed and waited for George to come home. When he got in he was greeted by the sight of his woman lying on the bed with her legs spread, wearing nothing but her new underwear.

'Hi Georgie,' she said in a throaty voice. 'You want some of this?'

'Jesus Christ, no!' George screams. 'Look what it's done to your knickers!'

What's Meg short for?

Because she's got really little legs.

It fell down the stairs ...

In a bid to encourage teamwork, representatives of the Navy, Army and Metropolitan Police are invited to a cross-forces outward-bound competition. With the scores even at the end of the weekend, the three groups are set one final task: to troop into the woods and bring back a rabbit.

The Navy go in first: there's 15 minutes of quiet rustling, before a single shot rings out. Before long, one naval officer emerges grinning from the undergrowth – clutching a bunny shot neatly between the eyes.

Next up were the Army– who, it became obvious from the smoke and crackling, were adopting a slash 'n' burn technique. After an afternoon, one of the infantrymen emerged beaming – holding another rabbit, albeit slightly charred.

Finally, it was the turn of the Met – highly confident they could secure victory. They descend into the foliage, and quickly there are the echoes of gunfire. This continues for hours until – a full day later – the policeman walk out, triumphantly holding up ... a slightly bloodied squirrel

'What the hell are you doing?' shouts the coordinator. 'You're supposed to get a rabbit.'

In reply, one of the Met officers wordlessly holds up the battered rodent. 'Listen to me,' it squeaks, wild-eyed. 'I'm a rabbit! For the love of God, I'm a rabbit!'

Drunk driving (v)

A man and a woman leave a party in their car late one night. After a couple of miles a police car signals the man to pull over. The policeman walks up to the couple.

'Good evening, sir,' he says. 'Do you realize you were doing 60 mph in a 55 mph zone?'

'I'm afraid I didn't,' the man says. 'I must have put my foot down to keep up with the traffic. I'm terribly sorry.'

'He's lying, officer,' the man's wife suddenly shouts. 'He clearly told me he was going to thrash the car's arse off to get back in time for the football.'

The policeman nods his head. 'I also noticed you were weaving in and out of the traffic in a reckless manner,' he says.

'Yes, I was,' the man replies. 'An insect flew into my eye and I lost control for a moment. I'm very sorry. Next time I'll pull over.'

'He's such a liar,' the man's wife interrupts again. 'He was laughing like a madman and pretending to be James Hunt.'

At this point the man finally snaps. 'For fuck's sake woman,' he bellows. 'Shut your blabbering mouth before I fill it!'

'Does he always speak to you like this?' the cop asks the wife.

'Oh no, officer,' the wife says. 'Only when he's had eight pints and a couple of bottles of wine.'

The quick-thinking sentry

A private is alone on sentry duty when the phone rings in his box.

'Hello? Hello?' a voice shouts down the phone. 'Are there many vehicles in the officer's car park?'

The sentry steps out of his box and looks across the road, where a solitary Bentley is parked. He goes back to the box and answers the caller.

'Only that fat bastard General Jackson's car,' he says.

'Do you know who you're talking to?' booms the voice down the line. 'This is General Jackson!'

'Do you know who you're talking to?' the private replies, completely unflustered.

'No,' General Jackson answers.

'Well, fuck off then, fat arse,' the private replies.

Did you hear about...

...the two lesbian twins?

They even lick alike.

Slide rule

A woman is drying herself after a shower when she suddenly slips and lands spread-legged on the bathroom floor. After trying to stand, she's realizes she's landed so hard her crotch created a vacuum, sucking her to the floor.

She calls out to her husband for help. He tries with all his strength to lift her but she won't budge. So he goes next door and gets his neighbour. Both pull like oxen but she just won't move. She's well and truly stuck to the floor. Suddenly the neighbour says, 'Why don't we just get a hammer and break the floor tiles around her and lift her up that way?'

'Great idea,' says the husband, 'but just let me rub her boobs a little to arouse her.'

'Why?' asks the confused neighbour.

'So we can slide her into the kitchen. The tiles are cheaper in there.'

Royal fertility

Which king has had the most children?

Jonathan.

Now wash your hands ...

A very attractive young lady walks up to the bar and calls over the barman, a tall fellow with a thick, full beard. The woman leans over the bar in her low-cut dress and reaches out to touch the man.

'Are you the landlord?' she asks, gently stroking his lustrous beard and running her fingers through his hair.

'No,' gulps the barman, only just managing to pull his eyes away from her ample cleavage. 'I just work here.'

'Well,' says the forward young lady, caressing the barman's beard with both hands. 'Can I talk to him?'

'Er, no,' says the by now highly excited barman. 'He's not actually in tonight.'

'Well, when you see him,' the blond purrs, gently caressing the barman's face, 'tell him there's no toilet roll in the ladies.'

Q: What do you get when you cross an apple with a nun?

A: A computer that never goes down on you.

The eager employee

A young executive was working late one night, trying to impress his new boss. He stepped out of the office for a minute to get some coffee, and saw his boss standing at the shredder with a piece of paper in his hand.

'Do you know how to work this damn thing?' his boss bellowed.

The young man ran over and took the paper out of his hand. 'Oh yes, sir,' he said. 'It's quite simple.' He then fed the piece of paper into the shredder.

'Thank you, son,' the boss said. 'A couple of copies will be fine.'

Drop 'em!

With his elderly wife, Bill the pensioner goes to the doctor for his annual physical. After testing him with the stethoscope, the physician turns to him. 'Well, Bill,' he says. 'You seem fine but I'm going to need a urine sample, a stool sample and a sperm sample.'

Hard of hearing, Bill turns look at his wife. 'What did he say?' he yells.

His wife bellows back: 'He said he needs your underwear.'

Does it come with a candle?

A man runs into a fishmongers with a giant carp under his arm. 'Do you sell fishcakes?' he says to the shop owner.

'Of course we do,' comes the reply.

The customer breathes a sigh of relief. 'Thank God,' he says, gesturing to the fish. 'It's his birthday.'

Second choice

One morning Martha walks down to the post office to cash in her pension. Standing in the queue she spies her good friend Wynn, whom she hasn't seen in a couple of months. After an initial chat, the pair meet outside for a good old chin-wag.

'Hello Martha,' Wynn says. 'How have you been?'

'I've been fine,' Martha answers. 'A bit of trouble with the hips but nothing major.'

'Oh good,' Wynn says. 'And how's George?'

'He's okay,' Martha says. 'The gout plays up now and then, but he gets by.

How have you been?'

'Well,' says Wynn, 'I've not been too good actually.'

'Oh dear,' says Martha. 'What's happened?'

'Two months ago Albert was out in the garden picking his cabbages when I heard a terrible scream,' Wynn says. 'It was a massive heart attack. He was dead before the ambulance got there.'

'Dear Lord!' Martha says. 'What on earth did you do?'

'What could I do?' Wynn says. 'I opened a tin of peas.'

Spreading the news

An old man stumbles into the confessional.

'Father!' he shouts. 'I'm an 81-year-old man and last night I made love to two 19-year-old twins!'

'Well,' the priest replies, 'are you married? Have you committed adultery?'

'No, Father,' the old man says. 'My wife passed away several years ago.'

'Have you remarried, my son?' asks the priest.

'No, Father,' the old guy replies.

'You're Catholic?' the priest asks.

'No,' the aged Lothario replies. 'I don't believe in religion.'

'Well,' says the priest, 'why on earth did you feel the need to come and tell me?'

'If you'd slept with two 19-year-old twins,' the old git answers, 'wouldn't you be telling everyone?'

Car trouble

A boy is walking down the road one day when a car pulls over. 'If you get in the car,' the driver says, 'I'll give you £10 and a packet of sweets.' The boy refuses and keeps on walking.

A little further up the road the man again pulls over. 'Okay,' he says. 'How about £20 and two packets of sweets?'

The boy tells the man to piss off and carries on walking.

Still further up the road the man again pulls to the curb.

'Right,' he says. 'This is my final offer – £50 and all the sweets you can eat.'

The little boy stops walking, goes towards the car and leans in. 'Look,' he hisses. 'You bought the fucking Skoda, Dad, and you have to live with it.'

Puss in Boots

A midget goes to the doctor's, complaining that her lady's area hurts like hell every time it rains. The doctor helps her onto the examination couch, and begins to examine her. After a while, he has to admit that he can't find anything wrong with her bearded clam at all.

'I tell you what,' says the physician. 'Next time it rains, come into the surgery so I can give your lamb hangings the once over while you're in pain.'

The dwarf agrees, and two days later returns to the doctor's waiting room during a torrential downfall. As she's in absolute agony, the doctor agrees to see her right away, and lifts her onto the examination table for a closer look.

'Yes, I can see the problem now,' he says, and reaches for the scalpel.

The pygmy woman is alarmed, but feels she's in the hands of a professional. Thirty seconds later, it's all over and she is lifted down from the table.

'How does that feel?' asks the doctor.

The gnomic girl wanders around the room for a while.

'There's no pain at all,' she replies, smiling. 'Amazing – what did you do?'

'It was easy,' says the physician. 'I just took an inch off the top of each wellie.'

Miss Piggy

One day, a lonesome cowboy wanders into a saloon in a dusty hell-hole of a town and heads straight to the bar for an ice-cold beer. He swigs back his beer, then he asks the barman where he might find a little lady to take the taste of the trail out of his mouth.

'Ain't no women for a hundred miles,' the barman says. 'But there's a barnyard out back chock full of prime livestock. Feel free to go out and help yourself to any of the animals.' Disgusted, the cowboy swears he would never stoop so low as to have sex with another species.

However, the next night he is overcome with longing and loneliness, and he creeps into the barnyard to take a little look-see. He spies a fine-looking piglet and takes her back to his hotel room, where he gives the little porker a bubble bath, grooms her real nice and ties a tiny pink ribbon behind her ears. Then he tucks his new friend under his arm and takes her down to the bar for a drink.

But as he walks through the swinging doors of the saloon, a deathly hush falls over the crowd. Dozens of the townfolk are sitting around with their animals, and the new cowboy can't work out why all the men are staring at him with such obvious shock.

'What's the matter with you people?' he yells. 'You're all doing the same thing.'

At this a man at the back of the saloon stands up and says, in a solemn voice, 'We sure are, mister, but you can bet your life we'd never do it with the sheriff's gal.'

What's six inches long...

...and gets women excited?

A £50 note.

He's had his chip

Elderly and cancer-ridden, a man lay dying in his bed. In death's agony, he suddenly smelled the aroma of his favourite chocolate chip cookies wafting up the stairs. Gathering his remaining strength, he lifted himself out of bed and slowly made his way out of the bedroom. Bracing himself by leaning on the banister, he stumbled downstairs, his muscles screaming with the pain of the effort.

He finally reached he kitchen and breathing heavily, he leaned against the door-frame. Was he already in heaven? There, spread out upon newspapers on the table, were literally hundreds of his favourite chocolate chip cookies. Was it a divine gift? Or one final act of love from his devoted wife, making sure he left this world a happy man?

Mustering his strength, he threw himself toward the table, landing on his knees. His parched lips parted, imagining the wondrous taste of biscuit that would make his last hours tolerable. Shakingly, his withered hand snaked over to the plate at the edge of the table. But, suddenly, it was smacked with a spatula.

'Stay out of those,' said his wife. 'They're for the funeral.'

I want to break free

A man is involved in a terrible cycling accident, in which he breaks all of his limbs. Waking up in hospital several days later, his legs hoisted in the air and his arms encased in plaster, he finds the doctor looking at him from a chair next to his bed.

'Oh,' the doctor says, 'you're awake. How do you feel, my man?'

'Considering I've had such a terrible accident, I really don't feel too bad,' the injured man replies. 'In fact, I feel pretty darn good.'

But as he finishes saying this, he suddenly leans to his left. The doctor, realizing the man has no means of support, grabs him and props him upright.

Later on a nurse comes by to check on him and asks him how he's getting on.

'As I said earlier,' the injured man says, 'when you consider what I've been through I actually feel super.' And again, he begins to fall to one side. The nurse jumps forward and sits him upright, then goes on her way.

The next day the man's wife comes in and asks her husband how he's feeling. 'As I've told everyone,' the man says, 'I feel fine. I just wish these buggers would let me fart in comfort.'

Like a virgin

A young woman goes to see the doctor to ask his advice on a very sensitive matter. 'I'm getting married on Saturday,' the distraught young lady cries, 'and my husband is convinced I'm a virgin. What he doesn't know is that I lost my virginity years ago. Is there any way I can convince him I am still chaste?'

'Medically, no,' the doctor replies. 'But I do have a suggestion which may help. On your wedding night, when you're getting ready for bed, slide an elastic band around your thigh. When your husband enters you, simply twang the band with your fingers and tell your husband the sound is your hymen snapping.'

On the big day, the newlyweds go up to their honeymoon suite. The bride goes into the bathroom and slips the elastic band around her thigh. The couple then get down to some serious married sex. Just as her husband enters her, the bride snaps the band and moans with what she thinks is a mixture of ecstasy and pain.

'What the hell was that?' her husband cries.

'Oooh,' the woman moans. 'That must have been my virginity snapping, honey.'

'Well,' shouts her husband, 'snap it back again. It's caught round my bollocks.'

Q: What's black, triangular and sings?

A: Kate's bush.

Big mamas

Newly married, George and Tina retire to their honeymoon bedroom – and breathlessly start undressing each other for the first time. As Tina's panties slide off, George eyes nearly pop out.

'Ooh!' he cries, 'You've got a lovely big arse!'

Furious, Tina whacks across the face and pushes him out onto the balcony in just his socks. He's standing there, freezing, when the bloke in the room next to him is similarly pushed out.

'Shit – it's my wedding night,' says the man. 'And I've been thrown out for saying my wife had really big tits.'

Just then a third naked man is also forcefully ejected onto the next balcony.

'I suppose you put your foot in it as well' said George.

'No,' says the new bloke, shaking his head. 'But I bloody well could have.'

Tough decision

An old woman is complaining to her equally ancient friend that she no longer has sex with her husband.

'He looks at me, with my tits like rooftiler's mailbags, and my saggy arse and old minge,' she moans, 'and he's completely turned off.'

Her 88-year-old friend looks at her with scorn and says, 'What you want to do is get down to Anne Summers and get yourself some sexy underwear. No red-blooded man can resist the sight of a woman in pingers and red satin bra.'

The following day the old lady goes down to the sex shop and buys herself a peephole bra and a pair of crotchless panties. That night she hides on top of her bedroom wardrobe, waits until her husband gets into bed, then, clad only in her new shagging gear, leaps from the wardrobe with a mighty banshee scream of 'Superfanny!'

She lands on top of her shocked husband who, after several seconds, says,

'I think I'll have the soup, if that's all right.'

Strict discipline

One day, while cleaning her young son's room, a mother finds a sado-masochist magazine on top of his wardrobe. Unsure of how to confront him, she keeps the magazine and shows it to her husband when he comes home from work. Slowly, he flicks through the pictures of leather-clad dominatrix and whips, before handing it back to his wife without a word. 'Come on,' she says, exasperated. 'What should we do about this?'

He looks back at her solemnly.

'Well,' he says. 'I don't think you should spank him.'

Big girl

Arnold is in bed shagging his big, fat wife when the phone rings. He answers it and says, 'Could you call back later. I'm in the tub.'

No need to rush

Just after taking off, the captain of a jumbo makes his customary announcement to the passengers about the length of the journey, expected arrival time and so on. But after he's finished he forgets to turn off the microphone, turns to his co-pilot and says:

'Right, I'll finish off this sandwich, then I think I'll nip back and fuck that new red-headed stewardess.'

In horror, the stewie, who is at the rear of the plane, rushes down the aisle to prevent the captain's indiscretion going any further. An old lady grabs her arm as she goes past.

'Why be in such a rush, dear,' she says, 'He said he had to finish his sandwich first.'

Cheap round

A man walks into a bar and orders ten pints of lager, with a further 12 vodka chasers. The barman then watches, amazed, as the bloke downs them one after the other. Recovering, the customer says, 'I shouldn't have done that with what I've got.'

'What have you got?' says the barman.

The bloke looks at him guiltily. 'Oh, about a quid.'

Almost cured

After years in a psychiatric institute, a patient seems finally well enough to be released – so undergoes a final examination by the chief psychiatrist.

'Tell me,' says the doctor, 'if we release you, what do you intend to do with your life?'

The inmate thinks for a moment. 'While I look forward to returning to my proper life, I would certainly avoid making the same mistakes. I was a nuclear physicist, and the stress of my work in weapons research lead to my breakdown. Consequently, in the future I shall confine myself to less stressful work in pure theory.'

'Marvellous,' says the shrink.

'Or else,' ruminated the inmate, 'I might teach, or write books – I could help educate the next generation of scientists.'

'Absolutely,' said the head. 'So many possibilities. But what if it doesn't work out?'

The patient grins. 'Oh, that's fine,' he says confidently. 'I can always fall back on the fact I'm a teapot.'

Q: What do Christmas trees and priests have in common?

A: Their balls are just for decoration.

Clever dick

A rich, lonely widow decides she needs a man in her life – so she places an advert in the local paper. It reads:

Rich widow looking for kind man to share life and fortune with. Must never beat me up or run away – and has to be great in bed.

For several months, her phone rings off the hook and applications pour through her letterbox – but none seem to match her qualifications. Then one day the doorbell rings. She opens the door to find a man, with no arms and no legs, lying on the welcome mat.

'Who are you?' she asked, perplexed. 'And what do you want?'

'Hi,' he replies, 'your search is over, for I'm the man of your dreams. I've got no arms – so I can't beat you up – and no legs, so I can't run away.'

'Hmm,' she says, unconvinced. 'What makes you think that you're so great in bed?'

He looks at her smugly. 'Well,' he grins. 'I rang the doorbell, didn't I?'

What's the difference...

...between a randy Swiss admiral and an efficient hoover?

One sucks and sucks and never fails...

And not a drop to drink ...

Following a dramatic escape from a burning freight vessel, two men are adrift in a lifeboat. While rummaging through the boat's provisions, one of the men finds an old lamp. Remembering old wives' tales of luck, he rubs the lamp vigorously – and to the amazement of the castaways, a genie emerges from the spout and offers them one wish.

Without giving much thought to the matter, the first man has an idea.

'I know,' he blurts out, 'Make the entire ocean into beer!'

The genie nods sagely, claps his hand – and, with a deafening crash, the entire sea turns into the finest brew ever sampled by mortals. Simultaneously, the genie vanished to his freedom. Only the gentle lapping of beer on the hull disturbs the stillness as the two men considered their circumstances.

Beaming, the man turns around to find the other man looking at him in disgust.

'Nice going!' he said after a long, tension-filled moment. 'Now we're going to have to piss in the boat.'

Flat out

After suffering years of torment from her friends, an extremely flat-chested woman finally decides to buy a bra, and goes to a high-class lingerie store. 'Excuse me,' she says to the assistant. 'Do you have a size 28AAAA bra?'

'Certainly not!' replies the saleswoman, haughtily – so the customer leaves and tries her luck in the next shop. Unfortunately, the response is the same: everywhere she goes she is rudely rebuffed. After trying eight lingerie stores, she angrily storms into a nearby bargain department store. Marching up to the sales clerk, she unbuttons her blouse.

'Do you have anything for these?' she yells.

The lady looks at her closely.

'I'm not sure,' she says. 'Have you tried Clearasil?'

Hide and seek

It's been a particularly good day for a travelling salesman and he needs just one more sale to get his commission. He knocks at the door of the Smith family home. A small boy comes to the door, steps out onto the doorstep and whispers: 'What do you want?'

The salesman looks at the boy. 'Hello,' he says. 'Is your mummy home?'

'Yes,' the boy says, 'but she's very busy.'

'Okay,' says the salesman. 'What about your daddy. Can I have a quick word with him?'

'Nope,' whispers the boy. 'He's busy, too.'

The salesman pauses, but is desperate for his commission.

'What about your brothers and sisters? Do you have any?'

'Yes,' the little boy whispers, 'but they're all very busy as well.'

'Grandparents?' the salesman asks.

'Nope,' the boy says. 'They're tied up as well.'

'Are there any other adults in the house?' the salesman asks, exasperated.

'Yes,' the boy says. 'There's two firemen and a policeman here at the moment.'

'You mean your entire family, two firemen and a policeman are all in the house, but they're too busy to see me. What are they doing?'

'Looking for me,' the little boy whispers.

You make me sick

Walking past an alleyway late one night, a policeman sees a tramp with two fingers shoved firmly up the arse of another tramp, who is kneeling on the floor.

'What the bloody hell do you two think you're playing at?' he asks.

The tramp doing the fingering stops, then looks up at the inquisitive copper to offer his explanation.

'It's quite simple really, officer,' he says. 'My good friend and companion here has drunk far too much today, and I am simply trying to make him sick it up.'

'Well,' the policeman says, 'sticking your fingers up his bumhole won't make him sick.'

'No, I know that,' says the fingering tramp. 'But sticking them in his mouth afterwards should do the trick.'

What did the plumber say...

...when he left his wife?

'It's over, Flo.'

Time's up

Concerned about his recent sexual performance, a man goes to see a doctor. After a couple of tests, the specialist sits him down for a quiet talk.

'I'm sorry,' the quack says, 'but it would appear that you have simply worn out your penis. By my reckoning you have 30 shags left, then that's it. Your sex life is over.'

The man walks home in a deep dark depression. His wife is waiting for him in their front room.

'Oh my God!' she cries when the man tells her of his misfortune. 'Thirty shags! We can't waste a single one of them. Every one must be special. Let's draw up a schedule right now.'

'I've already made a schedule on the way home,' the man says. 'And your name isn't on it.'

Q: Why do blondes take the Pill?

A: So they know what day of the week it is.

Mum's the word

Kevin is driving over the Severn Bridge one day when he sees his girlfriend, Sharon, just about to throw herself into the water far below. Kevin slams on his brakes and shouts, 'Sharon! What do you think you're doing?'

Sharon turns around with a tear in her eye and says, 'Hello, Kevin. You got me pregnant, so now I'm going to kill myself.'

At this Kevin gets a lump in his throat.

'Sharon,' he says. 'Not only are you a great shag, but you're a real sport, too.'

Free advice

After a chance meeting at St Andrews, Dave and Linda fall in love.

There's a whirlwind romance, and over a candlelit dinner they discuss getting married. Dave, wanting to do the right thing, decides to come clean.

'Look, Linda,' he says, with a furrowed brow. 'I have to tell you – I'm a complete golf nut. I live, eat sleep and breathe golf. It's my life.'

'Well,' says Linda, 'Since you're being honest, so will I. I've been keeping a secret – I'm a hooker.'

Dave stares at her for a moment.

'I see,' he says, pensively. 'It's probably because you're not keeping your wrists straight when you make contact with the ball.'

Q: Why do Australians whistle when they have a shit?
A: So they know which end to wipe.

You pays your money ...
The Queen visits a local hospital for the opening of a new wing, and is making a tour of the wards when she comes across a red-faced patient who's masturbating frantically.

'Good grief,' HRH says. 'What on earth is this patient's problem?'

'Well, your Majesty,' the ward sister says, 'he has a rare condition. He has to pull himself off at least eight times a day or his scrotum will swell like a balloon and eventually explode.'

'I see,' the Queen says, and moves along to a small room, where the curtains are drawn around the bed. HRH royally draws back the drapes and is shocked to discover a nurse kneeling on the bed performing oral sex on a male patient.

'And what, may I ask,' Elizabeth II says, 'is this man suffering from?'

'Oh,' says the ward sister, 'he's got the same disease as the last man, only he's on BUPA.'

What's the difference...
...between a British and an Iraqi soldier?

Don't know? Welcome to the United States Air Force!

A bit of a mouthful

It's a boring summer evening at Buckingham Palace, and after mindlessly teasing the corgis for an hour, the royals sit down for a quick game of 20 questions. Soon, the Queen's turn arrives, and after a quick discussion the rest of the family returns – sniggering, for the object she has to guess is horse's cock.

'Off you go then, Lizzie,' says Prince Phillip, trying not to laugh out loud.

'Er, is it bigger than a bread box?' says the monarch.

Snorting quietly, Princess Anne assures her that, yes, the item in question is bigger than a bread box.

'Umm... can I fit it in my mouth?' says the Queen.

Hiding his guffaws, Prince Charles replies no, she could not fit it in her mouth.

'Oh,' says the Queen, 'Is it a horse's cock?'

The frustrated grandmother

Patrick is walking down the street when he notices his grandfather sitting on his porch, in a rocking chair – with nothing on from the waist down. 'Grandpa,' he asks, 'why are you sitting out here half-nude?'

The old man looked at him sheepishly.

'Well,' he said. 'Last week I sat out here with no shirt on, and I got a stiff neck. This was your Grandma's idea.'

An offer he can't refuse

A young man enters the chemists and nervously approaches the counter.

'Excuse me, miss, but could I talk to the owner?' he asks the girl behind the counter.

'I am the owner,' says the young lady. 'Any business you wish to conduct in here, you can talk to me about.'

'Well,' the young man replies, 'it's just that it's rather embarrassing.'

'Don't be so silly,' the chemist says. 'I've heard everything in my years behind this counter, from genital warts to infected haemorrhoids.'

'Okay,' says the young fella with a blush. 'I've had this massive erection for three days. It's like a steel rod and it doesn't hurt, but I'm afraid it'll never go down. What do you think you can give me for it?'

'Wait here a moment,' the chemist says, and she turns away and walks into a back room. A few minutes later she re-emerges and steps back up to the counter.

'My sister and I,' she says, 'have discussed the situation, and we'll give you 15 per cent of the business and an immediate cash pay-out of £20,000.'

How many mice...

...does it take to screw in a lightbulb?

Two, but how do they get in?

Economic realities

Ted begrudgingly agrees to go into town shopping with his wife. But after a while he gets a bit bored and decides to nip off to the pub for a swift couple of pints. Walking up the road towards the public house, he passes a prostitute standing on the corner of the pavement. Bored by the prospect of another dull night in front of the box with his old lady, he asks her how much she'd want for penetrative sex.

'£20 for full sex,' the lady of the night replies.

'And what about a blow job?' the man asks.

'£15,' the whore answers.

'A quick hand-yank?' the man asks hopefully.

'Even that's a tenner,' the prozzie says.

'I've only got £3,' the man says. 'What can I have for that?'

'Oh Christ, I can't help you,' the tart says. 'You won't get an awful lot for £3.'

Dejected, the sad man leaves and goes back to meet up with his missus. They finish off their shopping and walk arm-in-arm to the bus stop.

Who should be on the other side of the road but the streetwalker. And on seeing the man, the whore bellows:

'I said you wouldn't get much for £3!'

Quid pro quo

A man is relaxing in his back garden, sitting in the shade, sipping a beer and listening to the cricket on the radio. As he chills out, his wife struggles with a manual mower, pushing up and down the large lawn, sweating and red-faced.

The man's next-door-neighbour sees the woman battling with the mower and shouts across the fence.

'You pathetic excuse for a man,' he yells, 'sitting there sipping your beer while your poor wife cuts the grass. You should be bloody well hung.'

'I am,' the man shouts back. 'That's why she's doing the grass.'

Emergency medicine

A guy walks into a pharmacy and asks for a bottle of Viagra.

The pharmacist eyes him suspiciously.

'Do you have a prescription for that?' he asks.

'No,' says the guy, 'but will this picture of my wife do?'

Getting your priorities right.

It's FA Cup Final day at Wembley Stadium and a young man is very disappointed when he finds his cheap seat is at the very rear of the stand, with a poor view of the pitch. A few seconds after kick-off he notices there is an empty seat near the front, so wanders up and casually sits down. After ten minutes he turns to the old man next to him.

'What kind of an idiot would book seats this good,' he says, 'and not bother to turn up?'

'Actually,' the old man says, 'the seat is mine. I reserved it for my wife, but she's now deceased. We've been coming to Cup Finals since 1960 – in fact, this is the first time I've ever been without her.'

'Oh my goodness,' the young man says, 'I'm very sorry. But tell me, isn't there anyone else you could have given the seat to – a son or daughter, perhaps?'

'Oh, I couldn't do that, ' the old man says. 'They're all at the funeral.'

The amputee pool

Some amputees are at the swimming baths. One amputee, who has only one arm, bets the others that he can swim the length of the pool in under one minute. To prove it, he jumps in and begins to frantically churn through the water. Fifty-eight seconds later, to the amazement of the able-bodied swimmers, he is back at poolside.

Then a second amputee steps up. Although he has no arms and only one leg, he says he'll better the time, and jumps in. Fifty seconds later he is back to rapturous applause.

Next a man with no arms or legs jumps in, and with an incredible effort hauls himself through the water in 47 seconds. This gets a huge round of applause, until a head silences the crowd by announcing that he'll do the pool in 45 seconds. The head moves himself with his lips along to the pool's edge and dives in. Ten seconds later a spectator, realizing that the head is still underwater, jumps in to pull him out.

'What happened?' the spectator asks.

'Jesus,' the head splutters, 'what a time to get cramp.'

Ask a stupid question ...

While walking down the street a man notices that a fellow pedestrian has a small orange instead of a head. Somewhat perturbed by this strange sight, he asks the man with the orange for a head how he came to have a fruit in place of his bonce.

'Well,' orange-head says, 'I found a lamp when I was out for a walk yesterday, and when I rubbed it a genie appeared. He granted me three wishes. First, I wished for £20 million.'

'And did you get it?' the man with the normal head asked.

'Yes,' the orange-headed man replied. 'So for my second wish I asked for a group of gorgeous willing women to appear and fulfil all my sexual fantasies. And that happened too.'

'My God, man,' the normal bloke said. 'What on earth did you ask for on your last wish?'

'Isn't it obvious?' said the man. 'I wished I had an orange for a head.'

The ice-cream challenge

A guy walks into an ice-cream parlour and, bored with the taste of vanilla and strawberry, asks for a fish-and-chip-flavour cone. The owner rubs his chin and says, 'That's tricky. Give me ten minutes.'

Ten minutes later, the guy comes back and asks for his ice-cream. He licks it and says, 'Mmmm, that tastes great, just like a bag of chips. But what about the fish?'

The owner looks pleased and replies, 'Turn it around.' The guy does this, licks it and, lo and behold, it tastes like fish.

'Amazing,' he says. 'Now can I have one that tastes like faggots and peas?'

'That's tough,' says the ice cream man. 'Give me ten minutes.'

Ten minutes later, the guy comes back and picks up his ice cream.

'Mmmm, just like mushy peas,' he says. 'But what about the faggots?'

'Just turn it around,' says the gelati salesman.

'Oh yeah,' says the man. 'It's just like faggots. Now give me one that tastes like a woman's fanny.'

'That's difficult,' says the owner. 'Give me half an hour.'

So the man wanders off, returning 30 minutes later for his ice cream. He licks it and goes: 'Urghhhhh! Horrible! That tastes like shit!'

But the owner simply winks at him and says, 'Turn it around.'

What do you call...

...a camel with four humps?
   A Saudi Quattro.

A blonde goes ice fishing

A blonde wanted to go ice fishing. She'd seen many books on the subject, and finally, after getting all the necessary items together, she made for the nearest frozen lake. After positioning her footstool, she started to make a circular cut in the ice. Suddenly, from the sky, a voice boomed:
   'THERE ARE NO FISH UNDER THE ICE!'

Startled, the blonde moved further down the ice and began to cut yet another hole. Again, from the heavens, the voice bellowed:'THERE ARE NO FISH UNDER THE ICE!'

The blonde, now quite worried, moved way down to the opposite end of the ice, set up her stool, and tried again to cut her hole. The voice came once more:

'THERE ARE NO FISH UNDER THE ICE!'

She stopped and looked skyward.

'Is that you, Lord?' she asked to the heavens.

'No,' the voice replied, 'This is the Ice-Rink Manager'

Q: Did you hear about the constipated accountant?

A: He couldn't budget.

Ballet lover

Various drinkers are enjoying an afternoon pint in the White Horse when a large, sweaty woman walks in, wearing a sleeveless sundress. She raises her right arm – revealing a big, hairy armpit – and points to rest of the customers. 'What man out there,' she booms, 'will buy a lady a drink?'

A deathly hush descends on the bar as the patrons try to ignore her – before a skinny little drunk pipes up. 'Bartender!' he says, slamming his hand on the bar, 'I want to buy that ballerina a drink!'

Baffled, the bartender pours a double whisky and the woman chugs it down. She wipes her mouth and, again, turns to the patrons. 'What man out there,' she roars, again revealing her hairy armpit, 'will buy a lady a drink?'

Once again the little drunk slaps his hand down on the bar and says, 'Bartender! I'd like to buy the ballerina another drink!'

After serving the lady her second drink, the bartender approaches the inebriated man. 'It's your business if you want to buy the lady a drink,' he says. 'But why do you call her a ballerina?'

The drunk squints at him. 'Sir,' he replies. 'In my eyes, any woman who can lift her leg up that high has to be a ballerina.'

One on the house

A man walks into a bar and, in a strange strangulated high-pitched voice, orders a pint of beer. The barman gives him his glass of beer and asks him what is wrong with his throat. At this the man raises his head, tilts backhis chin, and reveals a horrific scar.

The scar runs right across his throat, from ear to ear.

'Jesus!' the barman cries, 'That's nasty. How did you get that mate?'

The man takes a swig of his pint and then struggles to get out an answer: 'In the Falklands.'

'The Falklands?' the barman shouts. 'Then this drink is on the house. I have the utmost respect for you boys who put their lives on the line in that conflict.' At this, he slides over a glass of brandy to the scarred man.

'Muchas gracias,' the man says.

Amazing Grace

In ancient Rome, a Christian was being pursued by a lion. But as he ran through the city streets dodging back and forth, it became obvious that things were hopeless and the lion would catch him.

Clutching at straws, the hapless man turned suddenly, faced the beast and dropped to his knees.

'Lord,' he prayed, desperately. 'Turn this lion into a Christian!'

Instantly, the lion fell to its knees and prayed, 'For what we are about to receive ...'

Hedging your bets

Three men are sitting outside a maternity ward, waiting for their children to be born. One is from Liverpool, one is from Manchester and the third is a dreadlocked Rastafarian. After a few hours a doctor sees them.

'I've got some good news and some bad news,' he tells them. 'The good news is that you're each the father of a healthy baby boy.'

The three men sigh thankfully.

'The bad news,' he continues, 'is that we seem to have mixed the babies up and we don't know which child belongs to whom.'

The three new parents huddle together and come to the conclusion that each will recognize his own son. The Scouser steps forward and offers to claim his child first, and accompanies the doctor out of the waiting room.

He returns quickly with a black baby cradled in his arm.

The Rastafarian obviously claims the baby as his own, to which the Liverpudlian retorts: 'I don't care what you say, mate – one of the other two is a Manc.'

A brain went into a pub...

...and said, 'Can I have a pint of lager please, mate?'

'No way,' said the barman. 'You're already out of your head.'

Doggone

This man takes his sick dog to be seen by the vet. When it's his turn to be seen, the vet leads the poorly hound into the treatment room. He returns ten minutes later and says to the owner:

'Excuse me, sir, but could you say 'Ahhhh ...'.'

The dog's owner replies: 'Why do I have to say 'Ahhh ...'?'

The vet replies: 'Because your dog's dead.'

The human statue

A woman is in bed with her lover when she hears her husband opening the front door. 'Hurry!' she says, 'Stand in the corner!' She quickly rubs baby oil all over him, before dusting him with talcum powder.

'Don't move until I tell you to,' she whispers. 'Just pretend you're a statue.'

Her husband enters the room. 'What's this, honey?' he enquires.

'Oh, it's just a statue,' she replies nonchalantly. 'The Smiths bought one for their bedroom. I liked it so much, I got one for us too.'

No more was said about the statue, not even later that night when they went to sleep. Around 2am, the husband got out of bed, went to the kitchen and returned with a sandwich and a glass of milk.

'Here,' he said to the 'statue'. 'Eat something. I stood like an idiot at the Smiths' for three days, and nobody offered me as much as a glass of water.'

The hopeful shopper

A woman wanders into a chemist and glances at the display counter. 'Excuse me,' she asks the pharmacist after a few moments. 'Do you sell extra-large condoms?'

'Yes we do,' comes the reply. 'Would you like to buy some?'

'No,' says the woman, looking around. 'But do you mind if I wait around until someone does?'

A point of principle

A man walks up to a woman seated in a bar.

'Excuse me,' he says, 'I'm doing a survey. Would you have sex with a man you didn't know for one million dollars?'

The woman mulls over the proposition for a minute.

'Yes,' she replies. 'I would sleep with a man I don't know for a million dollars.'

The man nods. 'OK then – would you sleep with me for fifty cents?'

Insulted, the woman snorts.

'Of course not!' she cries. 'How could you ask me such a thing?'

The man looks at her slyly.

'Well, we've already established that you're a whore,' he replies. 'Now I'm just haggling over the price.'

What do you call...

...two lesbians in a closet?

A liquor cabinet.

Pieman Prat

A bloke walks into a pub with a meat and potato pie balanced on his head. He walks up to the barman and says, 'Can I have a pint of bitter, please.'

'Certainly,' says the barman, and starts pulling a pint. But he can't resist asking: 'You do realize, sir, you have a meat and potato pie on your head?'

The bloke says: 'Yes, I always have a meat and potato pie on my head on a Wednesday.'

'Ah!' says the barman. 'But today is Tuesday!'

'Oh no,' says the bloke. 'I must look like a right twat.'

Q: What do you call a Welshman with a sheep under each arm?

A: A pimp.

The randy rooster

A poultry farmer wakes up to find that his elderly rooster has died in the night. With 200 hens and no chicks, he decides he needs a new rooster.

He goes to the local market and spies Randy, a prize specimen of a rooster: tall, lean with a wild look in his eye.

'He'll service every hen you've got, no problem,' says the owner. 'He's a sex machine.'

The farmer decides Randy is worth the extra money, and takes him back to the barn. The effect is amazing – Randy bursts out of his carrying box, and immediately starts on the startled chickens in the coop.

Shocked, the farmer grabs the crazed rooster and holds him back.

'Whoah there, Randy,' he says. 'You'll wear yourself out, and there are a lot of chickens left.'

But as soon as the farmer releases him, he's away again – the feathers flying as his little chicken behind pumps away. Worse, he then sprints out of the barn and sees a flock of geese. As he finishes, the farmer watches in disbelief as he then starts on the pigs, then is off into the field after the cows.

Within hours Randy has had half the animals on the farm, and the farmer goes to bed – concerned his expensive rooster won't even last the day. Sure enough, the farmer wakes the next day to find Randy dead as a doornail, lying in the middle of the farmyard. As buzzards circle ominously overhead, the farmer says: 'Oh Randy, I told you to pace yourself, but you just wouldn't listen.'

The rooster opens one eye, and looks towards the buzzards.

'Shhh,' he says, 'they're getting closer ...'

Fame!

After days of abdominal pain, a man goes to the doctor for some tests. Returning a few weeks later, he asks for the results.

'Hmm,' says the doc, looking up from his paperwork. 'I have some good news and some bad news.'

The patient is visibly concerned. 'I suppose I'd better have the good news first.'

'Well,' sighs the doctor. 'We're going to name a disease after you.'

Never trust a man in a white coat

About to undergo a minor operation, a beautiful young girl is laid on a gurney by a nurse and left alone in the corridor. While she's away, a young man in a white coat approaches, takes the sheet away and starts examining her naked body. He walks away and talks to another man in a white coat. The second man comes over and does the same examinations. When a third man starts examining her body, the girl starts growing impatient.

'All these examinations are great,' she says. 'But are you starting the operation?'

The first man shrugs his shoulders.

'I have no idea. We're just painting the corridor.'

What does an elephant...

...use as a tampon?

A sheep.

The pushy stranger

Brian is asleep in bed with his wife when there's a loud knocking at the front door. He rolls over, looks at the clock and sees that it's 3am.

'Sod that for a game of soldiers,' he says and goes back to sleep.

Five minutes later the knocking starts again, this time louder.

'Aren't you going to answer that,' mumbles his wife.

Sighing, Brian drags himself out of bed, goes downstairs and opens the door.

A man is standing there, getting soaked in the pouring rain.

'Excuse me, mate,' he says, 'But you couldn't give us a push, could you?'

'A push?' says Brian, 'It's three in the morning, and I was asleep – piss off.'

He slams the door, goes back to bed and tells his wife what happened.

'Brian, you are a dick. Remember that night we broke down in the rain on the way to pick up the kids, and you had to knock at that man's door to get us started again? What would have happened if he'd told us to piss off?'

Sheepishly, Brian gets dressed and goes downstairs. Opening the door, he can't see the stranger so he shouts: 'Mate – do you still want a push?'

'Yes please, mate,' comes the reply.

Brian peers into the darkness.

'So where are you then?'

'I'm over here on the swings.'

Why do blondes...

...have big belly buttons?

From dating blond men.

What a winker

George had gained an interview for a job at a top City company, but unfortunately, he had a problem with one of his eyes – it winked constantly.

'We'd love to take you on,' said the managing director, 'But that winking is too distracting.'

'Wait! I can make it stop by taking two aspirin,' said George. Reaching into his pocket, he then pulled out a dozen condom packets and placed them on the deck before finding two aspirin. He took the tablets and winking instantly stopped.

'That's all well and good,' said the MD said, 'But we don't condone womanizing here.'

'No, no. You've got it all wrong,' said George. 'Have you ever asked for aspirin at the chemists while you're winking?'

Woman's work

While flying from London to New York at 36,000 feet, a Boeing 747 suddenly develops engine trouble and starts plummeting towards the Atlantic. As she realizes what's going on, the head stewardess crashes into the pilots' cabin, stands in front of the captain and rips off her blouse, saying:

'Captain, make me feel like a woman one more time before I die!'

The pilot rips his shirt off and says: 'Here you go then, love – iron this.'

Payback time

Two lawyers are standing in the queue at the bank one busy lunchtime, when a man walks in brandishing a handgun. The thief makes his way along the queue of customers and tells them all to empty their pockets, take off their jewellery and put it in the sack he is holding.

As he gets closer and closer to the pair of lawyers, one of them takes his wallet out of his back pocket, opens it, and hands his companion a crisp £50 note.

'What's this?' the friend asks.

'Oh,' says the first lawyer, 'it's the £50 I owe you.'

Swing low, sweet chariot

What does a 75-year-old woman have between her knees that a 25-year-old doesn't?

Her nipples.

Miracle worker

Jesus and Saint Paul are sitting in Heaven, talking about all the pollution on Earth and wondering what can be done about mankind's filthy ways. Jesus says he's going to pop down to Skegness to see the situation for himself, and Paul agrees to join him.

When they get there, Jesus asks what the huge metal pipe is for.

Paul tells him it's used to take human waste out to sea where the muck kills dolphins, so Jesus decides to take action and strides out across the waves. Walking alongside, Paul is soon knee-deep in filthy water, while Jesus scoots along on top of the sea. Ever hopeful of some help he slogs on, and Jesus keeps walking on water ... but soon the water is up to Paul's chin.

'Master,' he calls, 'I will follow you anywhere, but I'm up to my neck in shitty water and I think I'm going to drown.'

At this Jesus stops walking and looks at Paul.

'Well,' he says, 'why don't you just walk on the pipe like me, you silly prick?'

Q: How do you know when you're at a Norfolk wedding?

A: Everyone is sitting on the same side of the church.

Mother knows best

Young Mary has just got married but is quite a traditionalist, and is still a virgin on her wedding night. As a result, her husband Tony agrees to let Mary's mother stay over to quell any fears the girl might have. On the big night the young couple go upstairs and Tony takes off his shirt to reveal a hairy chest. Young Mary runs down to her mother.

'Mother!' she cries. 'Tony has a hairy chest!'

'It's all right,' her mother says. 'All good men have hairy chests.'

Mary goes back upstairs and Tony takes his trousers off to reveal hairy legs. Again Mary runs down to her mother.

'Mother!' she wails. 'Tony has hairy legs!'

'Don't worry, my child,' her mother says. 'All good men have hairy legs.'

Mary goes back upstairs, and Tony takes off his shoes and socks to reveal a left foot with no toes. Again the naive young girl runs to her mother.

'Oh, mother,' she moans, 'Tony only has a foot and a half.'

At this, her mother sits her down on the sofa.

'You stay down here, little one,' she says. 'This is a job for your mother.'

Shouldn't they be in water?

Jean goes round to visit her next-door neighbour Sally, where she notices some freshly cut flowers lying on the sideboard.

'Are these from your husband?' she asks.

Sally nods, and puts the kettle on.

'I suppose you'll be lying flat on your back with your legs spread later tonight' Jean says.

'Oh no,' says Sally. 'I'll just put them in a vase.'

Hot dog

A well-to-do lady is at the vets one day with her two dachshunds – one male, the other female. Whilst examining them both, the vet enquires as to whether the bitch has 'been dressed', or the dog given the snip.

In a casual tone the lady replies, 'Oh, that's not necessary. The bitch stays up the stairs and the dog stays downstairs'.

'And how does that prevent them from mating,' asks the vet?

'Have you ever seen a dachshund trying to climb stairs with a hard-on?' replies the lady.

The 20th anniversary

A wife wakes up in the middle of the night to find her husband missing. Hearing sobbing from the living room, she goes down to find her husband crying his eyes out. 'What's the matter?' the woman asks.

'You remember 20 years ago,' the man sobs, 'when I got you pregnant and your father said I had to marry you or go to jail?'

'Sure, honey,' the kindly wife replies. 'So what?'

'Well,' the man gasps through desperate sobs, 'I would have been released tonight.'

Ultimate sacrifice

While serving a life imprisonment, a murderer breaks free and goes on the run. He breaks into a house near the prison and ties up the young couple he finds in the bedroom. Bound to a chair, the young husband is helpless as the psychopath gets onto the bed where his wife is tied and starts to nuzzle her neck. After a while he gets up and leaves the room – and the husband takes his chance to bounce the chair across the room to his young wife.

'Darling,' he hisses. 'I saw him kissing you. He can't have seen a woman in years. Please cooperate: if he wants to have sex, just go along with it and even pretend you like it. Whatever you do, don't fight him or make him mad. Our lives may depend on it!'

'Darling', says the wife, spitting out her gag, 'I'm so relieved you feel that way. He wasn't kissing me ... he was whispering to me that he thinks you're really cute and asked if we kept the Vaseline in the bathroom.'

Memory lapse

An elderly man walks into a brothel and tells the madam he would like a really young girl for the night. The old steamer gives him a puzzled look and asks the fellow how old he is.

'Why,' the man says, 'I'm 98 years old.'

'Ninety-eight!' the madam exclaims. 'Don't you realize you've had it?'

'Oh,' he says, 'how much do I owe you, then?'

A job well done

On their 30th wedding anniversary, a couple decided to go back to the same hotel where they spent their blissful first night together. Just as she had 30 years before, the wife emerges from the bathroom totally nude and stands seductively in front of him.

'Tell me, darling,' she purrs. 'What were you thinking 30 years ago when I came out of the bathroom like this?'

'I took one look at you,' says her husband, eyeing her thoughtfully. 'And thought I'd like to screw your brains out and suck your boobs dry.'

'And what are you thinking now, baby?' she asked huskily.

'Hmmm,' he mulls. 'I'm thinking I did a pretty good job of it.'

Mental arithmetic

Timmy comes home with his report card, and his mother is angry to read he's received another D in maths.

'I warned you,' she chastises him, 'If you didn't get better grades this term, I was going to have to send you to the Catholic school.'

So the Timmy was packed off the local convent – from where, a term later, his mother is overjoyed to see him come home with an A in maths.

'I can't believe it!' she exclaims. 'What happened at Catholic school to cause such an improvement?'

'Well, I knew those people weren't kidding around,' he says, pulling off his satchel, 'when I walked into class the first day and saw that guy nailed to the plus sign.'

Hot shit

With a screech of brakes, an ambulance pulls up at the local casualty ward and a hippie is wheeled out on a gurney. The doctor questions his long-haired colleagues. 'So what was he doing then?' says the physician. 'Acid? Cannabis?'

'Sort of,' replies one of the hippies, nervously thumbing his caftan. 'But we ran out of gear, so I made a home-made spliff.'

'And what was in that?' replies the doctor.

'Um, I kind of raided my girlfriend's spice rack,' says the hippie. 'There was a bit of cumin, some turmeric and a little paprika.'

'Well that explains it,' the doctor replies, looking at them gravely. 'He's in a korma.'

Look right, look left

A middle-aged woman has a heart attack and is rushed to hospital on the very cusp of death. After being given a quick jolt of the defibrillator the woman is revived, and she tells the doctors that she had a near-death experience.

'I saw God, ' the beaming woman explains. 'He told me that it was not my time and that I had a good 30 to 40 years of life left on this earth.'

The woman makes a good recovery from her trauma, and as a result of her meeting with God she decides to really enjoy her life. She decides she wants to completely revamp her image and checks into a clinic for the works: face job, liposuction, boob job and hair colouring. After a few weeks to recover the makeover is complete, and the woman checks out and walks along the street feeling bright and breezy and full of hope for the future. She steps out at a zebra crossing and a lorry ploughs into her, killing her instantly.

The woman goes up to Heaven and stands in front of God in a fury. 'I thought you said I had a good 30 or 40 years left!' she cries indignantly.

'What can I say?' God says, obviously embarrassed. 'I didn't recognize you.'

Blockbuster riddle

What do the films *The Sixth Sense* and *Titanic* have in common?
Icy dead people.

Undercover operator

A man and his wife are driving home in their expensive new car one night when they both get horny, and decide to christen the sparkling motor with a shag. Pulling into a lay-by they get down to business, but soon realize their nice new motor's actually too small for the amount of erotic manoeuvring they want to do. The guy suggests they climb out and have a go under the car, which he promises his wife will provide ample clearance for his heaving buttocks, so the couple slip under the pristine vehicle and go at it like the clappers. In fact, they're enjoying themselves so much that they don't notice when a policeman comes over and taps the man on the back of his exposed legs.

'What do you think you're doing?' the copper asks the man.

'I'm just fixing my car,' the chap calmly replies.

'No you're not!' the policeman says through hysterical laughter. 'You're having sex in public, and I'm going to nick you for indecent exposure.'

'How do you know I'm lying?' the indignant man asks.

'Well,' the copper replies, 'for a start you're facing downwards on top of a naked woman. Secondly, I don't see any tools anywhere. And thirdly, your car was stolen five minutes ago.'

What do you call...

...five Barbies in a row?

A barbecue.

The baffled parrot

A magician gets a job on the Titanic. During his first performance, the captain's loud-mouthed parrot shouts out, 'It's up his sleeve! It's up his sleeve!' and ruins his act. The next night, the parrot again jumps in, yelling, 'It's in his pocket!' and, 'He's swapped them over!'

Throughout the whole voyage, no matter how good a trick the magician does, the parrot always spoils it.

Then the boat hits the fateful iceberg and sinks into the freezing depths. The magician manages to get into a lifeboat, and is joined by the parrot. At first, the bird refuses to talk, but after two weeks adrift, it finally cracks.

'Okay,' it says, 'you win. What have you done with the ship?'

Q: How do you know when your wife has died?

A: Sex is still the same, but the dishes start piling up.

The boogieman

A barrister walks into a bar and sits down next to a drunk. Soon the lawyer realizes the drunk is carefully studying something in his hand and holding it up to the light.

'What do you have there?' asks the curious barrister.

The drunk shakes his head.

'Damned if I know. It looks like plastic and it feels like rubber.'

'Let me take a look,' says the lawyer, and rolls it between his fingers.

'Yeah, you're right,' he says. 'It does look like plastic and feel like rubber, but I don't know what it is. Where did you get it?'

The drunk looks at him. 'Out of my nose.'

What goes...

...down a washing line at 100mph?

Honda pants.

Hungry bum

A man goes to the doctor's and says, 'Doctor, I really need some help. I can't seem to get an erection.'

The doctor examines him carefully and suggests a number of remedies – all to no avail.

'Herbal remedies, Viagra, hydraulic pumps – nothing seems to work,' says the man.

'Well,' the doctor says, 'There is a last-ditch option. Scientists at the local hospital are doing some experimental work with elephant muscle tissue transplants. But I have to warn you, they are not sure of the side-effects.'

The guy thinks for minute: 'Look, doctor, I'm desperate. I'll do anything.'

So he's booked in for the operation, it all goes perfectly – and six weeks later the man has recovered enough to try his luck with a gorgeous secretary in his office. So they're sitting at dinner, enjoying their starters when the man starts to get horny. Sure enough, he's getting hard – and thinks his troubles are finally over.

Suddenly, the zip on his trousers splits open, his knob bursts out onto the table, grabs a bread roll out of the secretary's hand and disappears under the table again.

The woman is amazed. 'Wow,' she says, 'Can you do that again ... later?'

The man looks thoughtful.

'Well,' he says, 'I don't know if I can fit another bread roll up my arse.'

Why is working in an office... just like Christmas?

You do all the work, but the fat guy in the suit gets all the credit.

Why do elephants...

...have trunks?

Because sheep don't have strings.

Sweet smell of success

Sitting at home one night with his wife, a man is casually tossing peanuts into the air and catching them in his mouth. As the couple take in the latest episode of *Watchdog* the man loses concentration for a split second, and a peanut goes into his ear. He tries to get the nut out, but succeeds only in forcing the thing in awfully deep.

After a few hours of fruitless rooting the couple decide to go to the hospital, but on their way out of the front door they meet their daughter coming in with her boyfriend. The boyfriend takes control of the situation: he tells them he's studying medicine and that they're not to worry about a thing. He then sticks two fingers up the man's nose and asks him to blow – and lo, the nut shoots from the ear and out across the room.

As the daughter and her boyfriend go through to the kitchen to make a pot of tea, the man and his wife sit down to discuss their luck. 'So,' the wife says, 'what do you think he'll become after he qualifies? A GP or a surgeon?'

'Well, ' says the man, rubbing his nose, 'by the smell of his fingers, our son-in-law.'

Q: Why are women like condoms?

A: They spend 90 per cent of their time in your wallet and the other 10 per cent on your dick.

Smells fishy ...

A man is fishing at his local pool when a fellow angler sets up beside him. After a while spent chatting, the newcomer reveals he got married the day before and is on his honeymoon with his new wife.

'So why are you fishing and not with your new wife?' says the first man.

'I just love fishing,' comes the reply. 'So far I've been fishing all day and all night. I love it.'

'Well, it's nothing to do with me,' says the first man, 'but aren't you missing out on fantastic sex with your new bride at home?'

'I was going to, but she's got gonorrhoea,' he answers.

'Well it is your honeymoon – couldn't you give her one up the arse?'

'I was going to, but she's got diarrhoea.'

'In that case,' says the first, 'she could at least give you a blow job.'

'I was going to ask her but she's got cold sores and warts all over her mouth,' comes the answer.

The first man is confused: 'Gonorrhoea, diarrhoea, cold sores and warts – Jesus, why the hell did you marry her?'

'Great maggots,' comes the reply.

Hear about the blonde...

... who got an AM radio?

It took her a month to realise she could play it at night.

Keep your hat on

On his daily beat, a policeman notices an old lady standing on a corner as a wind whistles through the street. She's clutching her hat firmly to her head as the wind lifts her skirt, showing her pants to the world.

'Look lady,' the cop says, 'while you're holding on to your bonnet, you're showing the whole world your package down there.'

'Listen, sonny,' the unctuous old mare says to the copper. 'What they're getting an eyeful of is 90 years old. This hat, however, is brand new.'

Why do Scotsmen...

...wear kilts?

Because sheep can hear a zipper a mile away.

Safe sex

A beautiful woman is driving back to the city when her sports car breaks down. Desperate, she wanders over the fields and spies a farmhouse, where she knocks on the door.

'Oh, thank God,' she says, after the farmer answers. 'My car's broken down – could I stay the night until someone comes out tomorrow?'

The farmer eyes her suspiciously.

'Well, okay,' he says. 'But don't mess with my two sons, Jed and Jake.'

Behind him, two strapping young men appear, smiling sheepishly. The woman agrees, but after going to the guest-room, she can't stop thinking about the two young bucks in the next room. Throwing caution to the wind, she quietly tip-toes across.

'Jake! Jed!' she whispers. 'Would you like me to teach you the ways of the world?'

'Huh?' comes the reply.

'The only thing is,' says the woman, 'I don't want to get pregnant – so you'll have to wear these condoms.' Beaming, the boys agree – and soon embark on a glorious night of three-way passion.

Forty years later, Jed and Luke are sitting on their front porch, fondly remembering their erotic experience.

'It was fantastic,' says Jed. 'But I do have one question.'

'Oh?' says Jake.

His brother frowned. 'Well, do you really care if that woman gets pregnant?'

'Nope,' says Jake, thoughtfully. 'I reckon not.'

'Me neither,' says Jed. 'Let's take these things off.'

Q: What did Adam say to Eve when he got his first erection?

A: 'Stand back! I don't know how big this thing is going to get!'

Eyecatching

Worried that it might be raining, a bloke in an apartment complex sticks his head out the window to check. As he does so a glass eye falls into his hand. He looks up in time to see a beautiful young woman looking down.

'Is this yours?' he asks.

'Yes,' she replied, 'would you bring it up for me?' The man agrees.

Upon his arrival she is profuse in her thanks and offers him a drink. They sit and chat for a couple of hours, before she says:

'I'm about to have dinner. There's plenty – would you care to join me?'

The man leaps at the offer and has a fantastic meal. As they carry their dishes to the kitchen the woman says, 'I've had a marvellous evening. Would you like to spend the night with me?'

The man hesitates, then asks, 'Do you act like this with every man you meet?'

'No,' she replies, 'only with those who catch my eye.'

Why do female paratroopers...

...wear jockstraps?

So they don't whistle on the way down.

Flat out

An embarrassed man visits the doctor and confesses that he fears he has something wrong with his sexual organs. He takes out his knob, which is covered with scabby sores, dead skin and a weeping yellow discharge.

The doctor winces, but after examining him thoroughly, he sighs and tells the man he has GASH.

'GASH, doctor? What the hell's that?' says the man.

'It's a combination of Gonorrhoea, AIDS, Syphilis and Herpes.'

'Oh, God,' the young man says, 'Is there anything that can be done for me?'

'Yes,' replies the doctor, 'but it involves immediate hospitalization, and feeding you a special diet of Dover sole, pizza and pancakes.'

'Dover sole, pizza and pancakes? Why those in particular?'

'Because it's the only things we can get under the door.'

Sucking a lemon

Distraught and guilty, a woman goes to her priest to seek forgiveness. 'Forgive me father,' she says, 'for I have sinned.'

'What is it you have done, my child?' asks the priest.

'Last night my boyfriend made love to me seven times,' the young lassie says.

'You must go home,' says the priest, 'and suck the juice from seven lemons.'

'Will that cleanse me of my sins?' the girl asks.

'No,' the holy man replies, 'but it'll wipe that smug grin off your face.'

Pillow talk

A man comes home after a hard day's work, looking forward to relaxing. He pours himself a glass of wine, eats a delicious meal cooked by his wife and goes upstairs to his bedroom, where he and his wife have separate beds. His wife follows him up a minutes later.

'Honey-woney,' the man says, 'I just want to thank you for fixing me such a delicious meal. I am blessed to have such a wife as you.'

He then turns out the light and tries to sleep.

After several minutes he finds he can't nod off.

'Sweetie pie,' he calls out, 'I'm lonely.' His wife gets out of bed and makes her way across the room, but she slips, falls and bangs her nose.

'Did my little bunny fall and hurt her nosey-wosey?' the man asks, as his wife climbs into bed with him. There follows a three-hour session of hardcore sex.

When the couple have finished, the wife heads back over to her own bed, and as she goes she slips up a second time.

'Clumsy bitch,' the man mutters.

Q: How many times does 59 go into 21?

A: I dunno, ask Woody Allen.

Silver service

The Lone Ranger and Tonto are enjoying a quiet beer or two in the Dead Gulch Saloon one afternoon when a man bursts through the swinging doors. 'Which one of you men owns that white horse outside?' the panting stranger asks the pair.

'I do,' says the Lone Ranger. 'Why do you ask, hombre?'

'The animal's collapsed,' the man says. 'I think he might be dead.'

The three men rush outside and see that Silver is, indeed, lying in the red dirt of Main Street. The Lone Ranger drips water into the poor horse's mouth, and Silver appears to perk up a little bit.

'It's just heat exhaustion,' the Lone Ranger says. 'Tonto, will you run in circles around Silver for a while? I think the breeze will help to get him back on his feet.'

Tonto begins sprinting around the horse, and the Lone Ranger goes back into the saloon to finish his beer. But just a few minutes later, another man comes bursting through the swinging doors.

'Who owns that white horse outside?' the man asks.

'Oh, dammit,' the Lone Ranger says. 'What's wrong with him now?'

'Nothing partner,' the man says. 'It's just that you left your injun running.'

No way to win

A guy receives a phone call from his local surgery telling him there's been a terrible mix-up with his wife's medical tests. 'We don't know if she's the one with herpes or a heart condition,' apologizes the doctor.

'Oh my god, what can I do?' asks the guy.

'Well,' suggests the doctor, 'send her out jogging and if she comes back don't fuck her!'

Q: When is a pixie not a pixie?

A: When she's got her head down an elf's pants: then she's a goblin.

Natural reaction

On walking into his local, Dave sees his mate Jeff looking depressed at the bar, and asks him what's wrong.

'Well,' replies Jeff, 'You know that gorgeous girl at work? The one who gives me an erection every time I saw her?'

'Yes,' replies Dave with a smile.

'Well,' says Jeff, straightening up, 'I finally plucked up the courage to ask her out, and she agreed.'

'That's great!' says Dave, 'when are you going out?'

'I went to meet her this evening,' continues Jeff. 'I was worried about getting a hard-on so I taped my todger to my leg, so it wouldn't show. But when I got to her house she was wearing the sheerest tiniest dress you ever saw.'

'And what happened then?' asked Dave.

Jeff huddles over the bar again. 'I kicked her in the face.'

Cheese explained

What do you call cheese that isn't yours?

Nacho cheese.

Tough Decision

Jim is walking down the street when his mate Dave rides up on a shiny new bicycle.

'Where did you get such a fantastic bike?' he asks him.

Dave replies, 'Well, yesterday I was walking along minding my own business when a beautiful woman rode up on this bike. She threw the bike to the ground, took of all her clothes and said, "Take what you want." So I did.'

Jim nods: 'Good choice – I don't think the clothes would have fitted.'

What's the similarity...

...between the KGB and oral sex?

One slip of the tongue and you're in the shit.

Lassie learns a lesson

This dog walks into the butcher's shop one afternoon, with a large basket in his mouth. He jumps up onto the counter, puts the basket down and pulls a neatly folded note from within. The butcher opens the note. It reads: 'Please give the dog 1 lb of Cumberland sausages, 1 lb of smoky back bacon, half a dozen lamb chops, 2 lb of rump steak and three slices of gala pie.'

The butcher weighs out the goods and puts them in the basket.

'That'll be £16.54, please,' he says to the dog, who takes a purse from the basket and counts out the exact money with his mouth. The dog then nods his head in thanks, takes the basket back in his mouth, and leaves the shop.

The butcher is stunned by the brilliance of this display – and even more so a week later, when the same thing happens. A further week passes, and the same thing happens again, but this time the butcher shuts up the shop and follows the clever little dog as he trots through the streets. He keeps behind the hound as he makes his way across busy intersections, always observing the Highway Code, until finally the dog walks up to a house, places the basket on the ground and knocks on the door with his paw. The butcher is stunned by the intelligence of the canine.

The door opens and a man in a stained wife-beater vest comes out and starts kicking the dog all over the pavement. The butcher is horrified and runs to restrain the man.

'Stop!' he cries. 'Why are you beating such a clever little animal?'

'He has to learn,' the man replies. 'This is the third time this month he's forgotten his keys.'

Teaching her the ropes

A Texan and his bride ask the hotel desk clerk for a room, telling him they just got married that morning.

'Congratulations!' says the clerk. 'Luckily, all our suites are still available. Would you like the bridal?'

'Naw thanks,' says the cowboy. 'I reckon I'll just hold her by the ears till she gets the hang of it.'

The zebra and the bull

A farmer goes to a livestock auction, but hasn't bought anything by the time the last lot comes up. Not wanting to go home empty-handed, he buys the beast, a female zebra, takes her home and sticks her in a field, not really knowing what to do with the animal. The zebra herself is also fairly bemused. She walks up to a chicken and asks the bird what it does around the farm.

'Oh, I just peck at the loose corn on the ground,' the chicken says. 'And lay eggs for the farmer.'

'I can't do that,' the zebra says, and walks off to talk to the pig.

'What do you do?' the zebra asks the pig.

'Well,' the pig says, 'I eat rotting vegetables and sit in the mud getting fat all day.'

'I don't fancy that much,' says the zebra, and trots off to talk to the bull, who's sporting a massive erection.

'And what exactly do you do around here?' the zebra asks the excited bull.

'Well,' the bull says, 'take your pyjamas off and I'll show you.'

Intake healthy

How do you know you have a high sperm count?

Your girlfriend chews before swallowing.

The wheelbarrow

Months of sexual frustration force a couple to seek advice from a counsellor. After a brief chat with the pair to find out the source of their anguish, the therapist suggests some new sex positions to spice up their nights. 'For example, he suggests, 'why not try the barrow? Lift her by the legs, penetrate and off you go.'

The couple then head off home. Champing at the bit, the husband suggests trying the barrow.

'Okay,' the wife agrees, 'but on two conditions. First, if it hurts you have to stop. And second, promise we won't go past mother's.'

Out for the count

Depressed, a boxer wanders into a doctor's surgery.

'Doc, you've got to help me,' he moans. 'My insomnia is terrible. I just can't get to sleep at night.'

The doctor peers over his glasses. 'Have you tried counting sheep?' he asks.

The boxer sighs. 'That's no good at all,' he moans. 'Every time I reach nine, I get up.'

Read all about it!

This gorilla is swinging through the jungle, when he gets to a waterhole and sees a lion bending down having a drink. The gorilla thinks 'I'll have a bit of that', leaps down and shags the lion right up the arse.

Not surprisingly the lion goes beserk. He turns round, roaring savagely. The gorilla shoots off through the jungle with the lion in hot pursuit. Using the branches and creepers to his advantage, the gorilla builds up a bit of a lead and manages to swing into a clearing some 100 yards ahead.

Sitting in the clearing is an old-style hunter with a pith helmet and Don Estelle shorts, leaning back in a deckchair and reading a newspaper. The gorilla whacks him round the head and knocks him out of his chair, before climbing in and hiding behind the newspaper.

The lion comes roaring into the clearing and bounds up to the chair.

'Have you just seen a gorilla?' he asks the figure in the chair.

'What, the one that just fucked a lion up the arse by the waterhole?' replies the gorilla.

'Oh shit,' says the lion. 'It's not in the papers already, is it?'

Car trouble

A middle-aged lady is in a supermarket when she notices a handsome muscular young man bagging up shopping at one of the checkouts. Making sure she goes through his line, she asks if he'll carry her groceries to her car. 'Sure lady,' he replies cheerfully.

But they're no sooner out of the store, when she beckons him closer. 'You know,' she whispers seductively, 'I have an itchy pussy.'

'You'll have to point it out to me, ma'am. 'All those Japanese cars look alike.'

Love me, love my dog

Feeling very depressed, a man walks into a pub and orders a triple scotch. 'You know,' says the barman, pouring him the drink. 'That's quite a heavy poison. Is something wrong?'

'Well,' says the man, downing the shots in one. 'I got home and found my wife in bed with my best friend.'

'Wow!' exclaims the bartender. 'No wonder you need a stiff drink – the next one's on the house. So what did you do?'

'I walked over to my wife', the man replies, 'and told her that we were through. I told her to get the hell out.'

'That makes sense', says the bartender, nodding. 'But what about your best friend?'

'Well,' slurs the man, tears in his eyes. 'I walked over to him, looked him right in the eye, and said "Bad dog!"'

Q: What's the definition of an Italian virgin?

A: A girl who can run faster than her brother.

Dumb and Dumber

Jim comes home early from work one day, to hear groaning sounds coming from upstairs. Investigating, he finds a bloke in bed humping his wife.

'What the hell's going on here?' he shouts.

His wife turns to her lover, and rolls her eyes.

'See? I told you,' she says, 'He's as thick as pigshit.'

What's the worst thing...

...about being a test-tube baby?

You know your dad's a wanker.

Tit for tat

Saddam Hussein and George Bush meet up in Baghdad for a round of talks in a new peace process. When George sits down, he notices three buttons on the side of Hussein's chair. They begin talking, and after five minutes Saddam presses the first button. A boxing glove springs out of a box on the desk and punches Bush in the face.

Confused, Bush carries on talking, as Saddam falls about laughing. A few minutes later the second button is pressed, and this time a big boot comes out and kicks Bush in the shin. Again, Hussein laughs, and again Bush carries on talking, not wanting to be put off the bigger issue.

But when the third button is pressed and another boot comes out and kicks Dubya in the balls, he's finally had enough.

'I'm going back home!' he tells the Iraqi. 'We'll finish the talks in two weeks.'

A fortnight passes and Saddam flies to the States for talks. As the two men sit down, Hussein notices three buttons on George's chair and prepares himself for the Yank's revenge. They begin talking and George presses the first button. Saddam ducks, but nothing happens. Bush sniggers.

A few seconds later button two is pressed. Saddam jumps up, but again nothing happens. Bush roars with laughter. When the third button is pressed Saddam jumps up again, and again nothing happens. Bush falls on the floor in a fit of hysterics.

'Sod this,' Saddam says, 'I'm going back to Baghdad.'

'Baghdad?' Bush says through tears of laughter. 'What Baghdad?'

What do prawns and women...

...have in common?

Three pink bits that taste nice, but the heads are full of shit.

The Australian virgin

A rich young heiress decided one day she was fed up with all the men she'd ever slept with, as none of them had been a virgin. For once she wanted to bed a man who'd never had sex with anyone in their entire life, so she summoned her flunkies and told them to find her a virgin.

With money no object, her staff searched the planet, finally locating a young man from the Australian outback. Flown back to the UK, the young Aussie was bathed and scrubbed, before finally being allowed into the heiress's bedroom. But when he walked in he ignored the beautiful young woman lying on the bed; instead he put his weight behind the wardrobe and shunted it into the hallway, then rolled up the rug and tore down the curtains.

'What are you doing?' the woman asked, dumbfounded.

'It's true, I've never screwed a woman before,' replied the Aussie. 'But if it's anything like screwing a kangaroo, I'll be needing plenty of room.'

How many blondes...

...does it take to make chocolate chip cookies?

Six. One to stir the mixture, five to peel the Smarties.

The dozy parishioner

A woman who is constantly embarrassed by her husband falling asleep in church goes to the priest to ask for help. The priest says, 'Look love, if he falls asleep again, poke him with this hat pin. I'll nod to you as a signal if I see him dropping off.' The woman agrees to the plan.

So Sunday rolls around and sure enough, good old Mr Jones nods off again.

The priest notices and asks, 'Who is our saviour?' then nods to Mrs Jones.

She pokes her husband and he wakes up and shouts, 'Jesus Christ!'

The priest, pretending to be impressed, says,
'Very good!'

A full three minutes later, Mr Jones is asleep again. The priest again notices and asks, 'What is the name of Jesus's father?' before nodding at Mrs Jones.

She pokes her husband, who screams, 'GOD!' at the top of his lungs. The priest again congratulates Mr Jones on his alertness and continues preaching. However, during the sermon, he begins nodding enthusiastically, which Mrs Jones mistakes for a poking signal. The priest then says, 'And what did Eve say to Adam after she gave him his 99th child?'

Mistakenly Mrs Jones pokes her husband, who shouts, 'If you poke that damn thing into me one more time, I'll snap it in half and shove it up your arse!'

What do you call...

...an anorexic with a yeast infection?

A quarterpounder with cheese.

On the house

A barman walks over to a waiting customer and asks, 'What'll it be, sir?'

'Make it a large Scotch,' says the man.

'No problem,' replies the bartender, handing over the drink. 'That'll be £4.80.'

'Actually,' says the man, 'I don't owe you anything.'

Overhearing the comment, a lawyer sat nearby wanders over. 'You know, he's got you there,' he explains to the barman. 'In the original offer – which constitutes a binding contract upon acceptance – there was no stipulation of remuneration.'

The bartender is unimpressed, but gives in. 'Okay, you beat me this time... but don't let me catch either of you in here again.'

The following day, the same man strolls into the bar. 'What the hell are you doing?' shouts the barman, 'I thought I told you not to come back?'

'I think you've mistaken me for someone else,' replies the man, somewhat bewildered, 'I've never been here before in my life.'

'My apologies... but it's uncanny,' explains the barman, 'you must have a double.'

'Well,' says the man, 'if you insist – make it a large Scotch.'

How pies are made

A young man and his naive girlfriend were taking a leisurely stroll through the countryside when they happened across a huge bull shagging a cow. 'What are they doing?' asked the young woman.

The man, not knowing what to say, replied, 'They're making pies, my sweet.'

They carried on walking, the girl seeming satisfied with the answer. A few miles further on they stumbled across a great big ram shagging a small sheep. 'And what are they doing?' asked the young woman.

To this the man replied, 'They too are making pies.'

Again they carried on, and as they walked the man spotted a deserted barn. All this rambling had made him incredibly randy and, turning to his girlfriend, he enquired as to whether she would like to 'make pies'.

'Okay,' she replied, and they disappeared into the barn, where the man shagged his girlfriend for dear life. Having finished, they carried on walking back to town. After a while the girl turned to the man and said, 'I think the pies are done.'

The man was confused. 'Why's that, dear?'

'Because the gravy has just run down my leg.'

A man walks into a bar...

...holding a newt. 'A pint of lager for me,' he says, 'and a glass of cola for my pet, Tiny.'

The bartender frowns at the man, puzzled. 'Of all things, why d'you call him Tiny?' he asks.

'Well,' says the man. 'He is my newt.'

Q: Why do farts smell?

A: So that deaf people can enjoy them too.

The novelty soap dispenser

Two priests are off to the showers late one night. They undress and step into the cubicles, before they realise there's no soap. Father

John says he has soap in his room and goes to get it, not bothering to dress. He grabs two bars of soap and heads back to the showers, but is only halfway down the hall when he sees three nuns heading his way. Having no place to hide he stands against the wall and freezes like he's a statue.

The nuns stop and comment on how lifelike he looks. The first nun suddenly reaches out and pulls his dick. Startled, he drops a bar of soap. 'Oh look,' says the second nun, 'a soap dispenser!'

To test her theory the second nun also pulls his dick and sure enough he drops the second bar of soap. The third nun then pulls, once, twice, three times, but still nothing happens. So she tries once more, and delightedly yells, 'Look – hand cream!'

Why aren't blondes...

...good cattle herders?

Because they can't even keep two calves together.

The drums! The drums!

Deep in the Amazonian rain forest, an explorer is leading a party of tourists when the native bearers suddenly pull up at the distant sound of drumming. At the next village, the leader asks one of the local inhabitants to explain the bearers' reaction.

'It's bad,' the local man says, 'very, very bad when the drumming stops.'

Then the man runs off into the forest.

The drumming continues and the now desperate trek leader asks another local man to explain the drumming.

'Oh my God!' the man cries. 'It will be terrible when the drumming stops.'

And this man, too, runs away.

Finally, in terror, the leader grabs a third man and asks him to explain the drumming. As he holds the quaking man, the drumming stops.

'Oh no!' the distressed native cries. 'It's very bad! Now the bass solo starts!'

The mechanic's confession

A motor mechanic was working late alone in the garage and was under a car when some brake fluid dripped into his mouth. 'Wow!' he said to himself. 'This stuff doesn't taste too bad.'

The next day he told his buddy about supping on the fluid. 'It's not bad,' he said. 'Got a bit of a kick to it. Think I'll have a bit more today.' His friend was a little concerned but didn't say anything.

The following day the mechanic confessed to drinking a cupful of brake fluid. 'Great stuff! Think I'll have some more today.' And so he did.

A week later the mechanic was up to a bottle a day, and his friend was now really worried. 'Brake fluid's poisonous,' he told his pal. 'You'd better lay off the stuff.'

'Hey, no problem,' the mechanic replied. 'I can stop any time.'

Death by chocolate

A policeman is pounding the beat when he gets an urgent message on his radio telling him a dead body has been found in an ice-cream van, just down the road. He rushes to the scene, where he discovers the body: it's a man with chocolate flakes up each nostril, raspberry sauce all over his head and covered from head to toe in hundreds and thousands.

A puzzled onlooker asks the policeman what he thinks has happened.

'Looks like he topped himself,' says the copper.

Man juice misdirected

There were two sperm swimming in a pink wonderland. One said to the other, 'How far are we from the uterus?'

The other replies, 'Ages, mate. We've only just passed the tonsils.'

Two ducks check into a hotel...

...for a dirty weekend. They can't wait to get up to their room, but then discover they've forgotten the condoms. 'No problem,' quacks the drake, 'I'll just call down to room service and get them to bring a johnny up.'

A few minutes later, room service is knocking at the door. The male duck waddles over, takes the condom and tips the lad.

'Sir,' asks the flunky, 'should I put that on your bill?'

'Christ, no!' quacks the duck, startled. 'What do you think I am, some kind of pervert?'

The archbishop's lunch

A vicar is walking along the riverbank, when he sees Frank loading his rod and tackle into his boat. 'Fancy fishing, Vicar?' calls Frank.

'I can't today – I've got the archbishop coming to lunch,' explains the vicar.

'Oh go on, just for an hour,' cajoles Frank.

'All right then, but just for a short while.' So the vicar and Frank push off and start fishing. Within minutes, Frank's got a massive bite and he spends the next half hour wrestling a huge fish aboard. 'Look at the size of that fucker!' says Frank when the monster finally lies defeated on the floor of the boat.

'Frank,' tuts the vicar, 'it really is a prize specimen but the use of such language is unforgivable.'

'You don't understand, Vicar,' replies Frank, thinking fast. 'This fish really is called a Fucker. Er... why don't you take it home for the archbishop's lunch?'

'Why thank you,' says the man of God, 'I'll clean it up and head home now.'

Back at the vicarage, the churchman plonks the fish on the table. 'Look at the size of this Fucker!' he says to his housekeeper.

She's shocked. 'A fine fish it is but I can't believe you would use such language in the vicarage!' The vicar explains how that's the name of the fish so, slightly happier, she goes into the kitchen to start cooking.

Soon the archbishop arrives, and sits down to lunch with the vicar. In comes the housekeeper with the cooked fish. 'Look at the size of this, archbishop,' she says. 'Frank caught the Fucker, the vicar cleaned the Fucker up and I cooked the Fucker for your lunch!' The archbishop beams, takes off his shoes, puts up his feet and starts to roll a joint. 'You know,' he says, 'you bastards are all right.'

What you can get for a tenner

A man is walking down the street when he notices that a brothel has opened up, so he decides to go in. As soon as he enters, the madam sidles up to him. He explains that he's extremely horny but because he didn't realise the knocking shop had opened he only has five quid with him.

She snatches the money from his hand and promises that she has the solution to his problem. Then she leads him down a hall and into a small room. Expecting to find a woman waiting there, the man can see only a chicken, clucking and pecking at the floor. He figures he was ripped off, so he paces around the room in frustration – but when his wood won't go down he decides to make love to the chicken, chasing the bird around the room before finally catching it.

Perhaps it is the thrill of the chase, but the sex is amazing. Unsurprisingly, the man returns to the brothel a week later, this time with a tenner in his pocket. He explains to the madam that he enjoyed himself so much before that he'd like to double his pleasure.

Once again the madam grabs his money and leads him down another hallway and into a room, where a group of people are sitting around, staring through a window. He joins them and gazes in amazement at the sight of a couple at it like rabbits on the other side of what appears to be a two-way mirror. Obviously the love-makers can't see the audience, which the man finds incredibly arousing. He turns to the bloke next to him and exclaims: 'This is the most amazing thing I've ever seen in my life!'

The man responds, 'That's nothing. You should have been here last week – we watched some sicko have it off with a chicken.'

What's the similarity...

...between a rural jog and Delia Smith?

One's a pant in the country...

How can you tell...

...if it's your turn to do the washing up?

Look down your trousers. If you've got a dick, it's not your turn.

A man walks into a bar...

...and orders 12 shots of whisky. The bartender lines up a dozen shot glasses on the bar and fills them with Scotch. Quickly the man downs one after the other, until he's finished all 12.

'Well,' says the bartender, 'what are you celebrating?'

'My first blow job,' says the man.

'In that case,' says the bartender, smiling, 'let me buy you one more!'

'No thanks,' replies the man. 'If 12 won't get the taste out of my mouth, nothing will.'

The whistling salesman

One day a farmer caught a travelling salesman making love to his youngest daughter. 'You son of a bitch!' he yelled, as he shot the amorous rep in the groin with a 12-gauge shotgun.

The screaming salesman quickly took off for town to find a doctor. He found one, but the physician took one look at the man's dick and told him that nothing could be done for him. 'Please do something,' begged the salesman. 'I'm a rich man and can pay you whatever you ask.'

'Sorry, son,' said the doctor. 'It's beyond my ability. However, there's a man across the street who might be able to help.'

'Is he a specialist?' gasped the salesman.

'No,' said the doctor, 'he's a piccolo player. He'll teach you how to hold your dick without pissing in your face.'

Tough trucker

After three weeks on the road, a trucker pulls in at a local brothel and bangs $500 on the counter. 'Listen, lady,' he says to the madam, 'I want a really tough, overcooked steak and the ugliest woman you've got.'

'What's your problem?' cries the madam. 'For that sort of money I could give you a five-course, cordon bleu meal and the most beautiful girl in the place for the night.'

The trucker glowers at her. 'Listen, sweetheart,' he snarls, 'I'm not feeling horny, I'm feeling homesick.'

Not a pretty sight

A man strolls into a lingerie shop and asks the assistant: 'Do you have a see-through negligée, size 46-48-52?'

The assistant looks bewildered. 'What the hell would you want to see through that for?'

Cheeky lad

A mother and her young son are having a bath together one night, when the son points in between his ma's legs and asks, 'Mum, what's that?'

His mum replies, 'Oh... that's where, er, God hit me with an axe.'

'That was a good shot,' her son replies. 'Right in the cunt.'

You get what you pay for

Eager to earn herself a little extra income, a blonde girl decided to hire herself out as a handyman-type and began canvassing a wealthy neighbourhood. The owner of a lavish mansion soon agreed to use her. 'You could paint my porch – how much do you charge?' he asked.

The girl thought for a moment: 'How about £50?'

The man duly agreed and informed his new employee that the paint and ladders she'd need were in the garage, then left her to get on with it. An uncomfortably short time later, the doorbell rang.

'I've finished!' beamed the blonde girl proudly, 'that'll be £50, please!'

'You've finished already?' asked the man, astounded by the girl's efficiency.

'Of course,' answered the blonde, 'I even gave it two coats, just to be sure!'

Impressed, the man handed her a crisp £50 note.

'Oh, and by the way, silly,' the blonde added, 'that's not a Porsche, it's a Ferrari.'

Passion ignited!

Desperate to rekindle the spark in his marriage, a man returns home from work, finds his wife asleep in bed and plans a surprise. In he jumps, diving under the covers and pleasuring his lady with the most energetic oral sex he's ever given.

After a few minutes of squirming, slurping and moaning, her body spasms with ecstasy and she enjoys an incredible climax. Satisfied with his effort, the man goes to brush his teeth in the bathroom. In he goes... and there before him? His wife shaving her legs. 'What the fuck are you doing in here?' he screams.

'Shh...' she replies, pointing to the bed, 'you'll wake your mother!'

What's the difference...
...between Israeli soldiers and Dwight Yorke?

Israeli soldiers knew when to pull out of Jordan.

He never forgets
In his last days on Earth, Bob Hope accepts an invitation to go on Surprise, Surprise, where he brags to Cilla that, despite his 97 years of age, he could still have sex three times a night. After the show, Cilla wanders over. 'Look Bob,' she purrs, 'I hope I'm not being too forward, but I'd love to have sex with an older man.'

Smiling, the pair go back to her place and have great sex. Afterwards, Bob turns to the Liverpudlian loudhailer. 'If you think that was good,' he grins, 'let me sleep for half an hour, and we'll do it again. But while I'm sleeping, hold my testicles in your left hand and my penis in your right hand.'

Perplexed, Cilla nevertheless agrees – and after 30 minutes' kip Bob wakes up and, again, makes love like an athletic 25-year-old. As before, Bob then turns to the Mersey motormouth. 'Cilla, that was wonderful,' he smiles. 'But if you let me sleep for an hour – again while holding my genitals – we can have the best sex yet.'

But Cilla is curious. 'Bob, tell me,' she asks. 'Does my holding your testicles in my left hand and your penis in my right stimulate you while you're sleeping?'

Bob shakes his head. 'No,' he replies, 'it's just that the last time I slept with a Scouser, she stole my wallet.'

What's in a name?

A Native American boy asks his father, 'How did you pick names for us kids, Pop?'

'Well,' the chief replies, 'when your older brother was born, the first thing I saw when I came out of the teepee was an eagle soaring high in the sky. So I named him Flying Eagle. And when your little sister was born, the first thing I saw was a deer running away, so I named her Running Deer. Why do you ask, Fucking Dog?'

Suicide blonde

A blonde suspects her husband of fooling around. She follows him to his girlfriend's house one day, busts open the door and puts the gun to her own head.

The husband pipes up, 'Honey! Don't do this!'

'Shut up!' she says. 'You're next.'

The deaf bear

It's spring, and baby bear staggers out of his cave. His knees are wobbling, paws shaking – he's a wreck, all skin and bones with big circles under his eyes. 'Junior!' his mother says. 'Did you hibernate all winter like you were supposed to?'

'Hibernate?' he says. 'I thought you said masturbate!'

Dead or alive

A primary school pupil tells his teacher that he's just found a cat at the side of the road. 'It's dead,' he reveals.

'How do you know it's dead?' asks the teacher.

'Easy,' says the child, 'because I pissed in its ear and it didn't move.'

'You did what?!' the teacher shouts.

'You know,' explained the boy, 'I leant over, went "Pssst!" and it didn't move.'

Q: Why did the pervert cross the road?

A: He couldn't get his knob out of the chicken!

Which service...?

A Glaswegian woman dials 999 and requests an ambulance, telling the operator that she is pregnant.

'Madam, you can't have an ambulance simply because you're pregnant,' explains the operator. 'This line is for emergencies only.'

'Och, ah know,' says the woman, 'but ma waaters have broke!'

'Oh – that's a different matter,' says the operator. 'Where are you ringing from?'

'Christ,' the woman replies, 'from ma fanny tae ma feet.'

How the other half live

A rich man and his wife are being served dinner by their chef. 'You know, dear,' says the man, looking up from his soup, 'if you could cook, we could fire the chef.'

'That's true, darling,' the wife responds. 'And if you could fuck, we could fire the chauffeur.'

A three-legged dog...

...walks into a wild west saloon. He sidles up to the bar and announces, 'I'm looking for the man who shot my paw.'

The lezzer's exam

A lesbian goes to see her GP for her annual check-up. The doc does an internal and says, 'My, you're looking pretty clean these days.'

'I should be,' the lesbian replies. 'I have a woman in three times a week.'

A sweet story

Smartie and Polo are enjoying a quiet drink in a bar when the doors open and in walks Humbug. 'Oh shit,' mutters Polo, diving underneath the table.

'What are you doing?' asks Smartie.

'Humbug always slaps me around whenever I see him, so I'm hiding,' explains Polo.

'You should stand up to him,' says Smartie. 'He'll respect you if you do.'

As predicted, Humbug walks straight over and gives the mint a smack. 'Piss off you stripy twat, or I'll knock your glazing off!' snarls Polo.

'Oh, right...' says Humbug. 'Sorry mate, I'll leave it.'

Next night, Polo and Smartie are once again sitting in the bar, when Humbug walks in with his friend, Tune. 'Oh shit,' says Smartie, diving for the floor.

'What are you doing?' asks Polo.

'I know I told you to stand up to bullies, but Humbug's with Tune!' hisses Smartie from under the table.

'So?' says Polo.

'He's fucking menthol!' says Smartie.

The blonde's audition

Hoping for a part in a seedy sex show, a stunning blonde presents herself at an agent's office. 'What do you do, honey?' the agent asks.

'I play the harmonica with my fanny,' she replies. The blonde then gives a demonstration of her special talent. 'Fantastic,' enthuses the agent, reaching for the telephone. 'Keep on playing while I phone the producer of the show.'

Holding the phone out towards the performing blonde, the agent gets the producer on the line. 'What do you think of this?' he shouts over the performance.

'What the hell are you playing at?' bellows the producer.

'You drag me out of bed just to hear some cunt play the harmonica?'

The wedding anniversary

An elderly couple are having an elegant dinner to celebrate their 75th wedding anniversary. The old man leans forward and says softly to his wife, 'Dear, there's something I must ask you. It's always bothered me that our tenth child never quite looked like the rest of our children. Now, I want to assure you that these 75 years have been the most wonderful experience I could have ever hoped for, and your answer cannot take all that away. But I must know – did he have a different father?'

The wife drops her head, unable to look her husband in the eye. She pauses for a moment and then confesses, 'Yes. Yes he did.'

The old man is shaken – the reality of what his wife is admitting hits him harder than he had expected. With a tear in his eye he asks, 'Who? Who was the father?'

Again the old woman drops her head, saying nothing at first as she tries to muster the courage to tell her husband the truth. Then, finally, she says, 'You.'

Woof!

Three heavily pregnant women meet on a maternity ward. The first woman says, 'I was on my back during conception, so I'm going to have a girl.'

The second one says, 'Well, I was riding on top at conception, so I'm going to have a boy.'

The third one looks horrified. 'Oh shit,' she says. 'I'm going to have puppies!'

What qualifications do you need...

...to be a road sweeper?

None. You just pick it up as you go along.

Unlucky purchase

A young man walks into a chemist's and asks for a pack of condoms. 'Hot date?' says the pharmacist.

'You betcha,' says the horny youngster. 'My new girl and I are driving to the lake tonight – gonna steam up some windows!'

When he goes to pick up his date, she invites him in to meet the parents. After the usual stilted pleased to meet yous, the young man tells his date, 'Hey – instead of going out tonight, why don't we just play Monopoly?'

She's puzzled but agrees, so the young couple sit down with the parents and play board games until midnight. When it's time to leave, the girl takes her date aside and whispers to him, 'Why didn't you tell me you wanted to stay in tonight?'

'Why didn't you tell me your dad works in the chemist's?' the lad replies.

Dyslexics on the piste

Two dyslexics decide to go skiing. They're just about to start up the mountain when the first one asks, 'How do we get down? Do we zag-zig or zig-zag?'

'How the hell do I know?' replies the other.

So they walk up the mountain. When they reach the top they still haven't decided how to get down, so they ask a bloke: 'How do we get down the mountain? Do we zig-zag or zag-zig?'

'I don't know,' the man replies. 'I'm a tobogganist.'

'Oh, right,' says the first dyslexic. 'Can I have 20 B&H then?'

Doctor baffled

A man goes to see his doctor. 'What seems to be the problem?' the medic asks.

'It's my penis,' says the man. 'I'd like you to take a look at it.'

'Hop up onto the bed and whip it out,' says the doc, 'and I'll examine it.'

So the man jumps onto the bed and produces a 12-incher from his underpants. After about five minutes peering and prodding it, the bemused doctor says, 'I have to say, I can't see anything wrong with it.'

To which the man replies, 'I know – isn't it a beauty!'

The Buddhist's toothache

Did you hear about the Buddhist who refused the offer of Novocain during his root canal work?

He wanted to transcend dental medication.

What did the blonde...

...get on her IQ test?

Nail varnish.

The mark of the master

Standing at a urinal, one man turns to another. 'Excuse me,' he says, 'but I couldn't help noticing that you've been circumcised.'

'Er, yes,' says the second man, baffled. 'I'm Jewish, so I was circumcised at birth.'

'I guessed,' says the first. 'And your surgeon was Dr Abraham Winklehock – no doubt about it.'

'You're right!' cries the second man, amazed.

'How did you know? It was 30 years ago!'

'Bastard never could cut straight,' says the first man. 'And you're pissing on my shoe.'

Anatomy lessons

What have the clitoris and the Antarctic got in common?

Most men know it's down there somewhere, but really don't care.

The big brew

An Irishman goes for a job on a building site as an odd-job man.
The foreman asks him what he can do.

'I can do anything,' says the Irishman.

'Can you make tea?' asks the foreman.

'Jesus, yes,' replies the Irishman. 'I can make a great cup of tea.'

'Can you drive a forklift?' asks the foreman.

'Mother of God!' replies the Irishman. 'How big is the teapot?'

Doc's new career

A gynaecologist decided on a career change and signed up for a motor
mechanic's course, where greasy-fingered tutors taught him how to
take an engine apart and put it back together again. Following his final
practical exam, the former doc anxiously awaited his results – and
was pleasantly surprised when he was awarded a mark of 200%.

Upon asking his examiner how this was possible, he was told
that his stripping and reassemble had been perfect, earning him
100%. The additional 100% had been awarded for doing it all
through the exhaust pipe.

Q: Why can't you have driving lessons and receive sex education on the same day in Iraq?

A: It wears out the camel.

The legless parrot

A man is not getting along very well with his wife, so he goes to a
pet shop, hoping that having an animal to care for will bring the
couple closer together. After mooching around the store he spots a
parrot on a little perch. It doesn't have any feet or legs.

'I wonder what happened to you, little fella?' the man says to
himself.

To his surprise, the parrot answers. 'I was born this way!' the
bird squawks. 'I'm a defective parrot.'

The man is flabbergasted. 'Are you telling me you understood
what I said?' he asks.

'Every word,' replies the parrot. 'I am a highly intelligent, thoroughly educated bird.'

'Oh yeah?' says the man. 'Then answer me this: how do you hang onto your perch without any feet?'

'Well,' the parrot says, 'this is a little embarrassing, but since you asked... I wrap my twisty parrot penis around this wooden bar, like a little hook. You can't see it because of my feathers.'

'Wow,' the man says. 'You really can understand and answer, can't you?'

'Of course. I speak both Spanish and English. I can converse with reasonable competence on almost any subject: politics, religion, sports, physics, philosophy – and I'm especially hot on ornithology. You ought to buy me. I'm a great companion!'

The man looks at the price tag. '£200!' he says. 'I can't afford that!'

'Listen,' the parrot hisses, motioning the guy closer with a wing. 'Nobody wants me 'cause I don't have any feet. You can get me for £20, just make an offer.'

So the man offers the shopkeeper £20 and walks out with the parrot. Weeks go by. The bird is sensational. He's funny, he's interesting, he's a great pal, he understands everything, sympathises, gives good advice. The man is delighted – until one day, when he comes home from work and is beckoned over by his multicoloured friend.

'I don't know if I should tell you this or not,' whispers the parrot, 'but it's about your wife and the postman...'

'What?' says the man.

'Well,' the parrot says, 'when postie came to the door today, your wife greeted him in a negligée and kissed him on the mouth.'

'What happened then?' asks the man.

'Then the postman came into the house and lifted up the negligée and began fondling her naked body,' reports the parrot.

'Oh no!' the man says. 'Then what?'

'Then he got down on his knees and began kissing her, starting with her breasts and slowly going down and down...'

The parrot pauses. 'Then what happened? What happened?' says the man, frantically.

'I don't know,' says the parrot. 'That's when I fell off my perch.'

Should have read the small print

After years of milking cows with the traditional stool-and-squirt method, Farmer Giles eventually orders a high-tech milking machine. The equipment arrives a few days later and, realising his wife is out for the day, he decides to test the machine on himself first.

After setting it up, the farmer quickly eases his beef bayonet into the equipment and flicks the switch. The sucking teat pleasures him better than his wife ever could but, when it's over, the machine will not release his member. In desperation, the farmer calls the Customer Service Hotline. 'Hello,' he winces, 'I've just bought a milking machine from your company. It works great but, er, how do I remove it from the cow's udder?'

'Don't worry,' replies the rep. 'The machine will release automatically once it's collected two gallons.'

Paid in kind

An old lady walks into a hardware store and asks the male assistant if she can purchase a painting hung up on the wall.

The man replies, 'Would you like a screw for that?'

She thinks for a moment. 'No,' she says, 'but I'll give you a blow job for a cooker.'

What's in a name?

A burglar is quietly going about his illegal work one night, when he hears a voice: 'Jesus is watching you.'

He looks around but there's no-one there, so he carries on piling swag into his bag. Then the voice speaks again: 'Jesus is watching you.'

Again he looks around, and this time he sees a parrot in a cage. He walks up to the cage and says: 'A talking parrot, that's fantastic – are you Jesus?'

'No,' replies the bird, 'I'm Moses.'

The thief laughs. 'What kind of people would name a parrot Moses?!'

'The same people who'd call a Rottweiler Jesus,' replies the bird.

Q: Did you hear about the paranoid with low self-esteem?

A: He thought that nobody important was out to get him.

Ask a stupid question...

Steve was in a terrible accident at work: he fell through a hole in the floor and ripped off both his ears. Since he was permanently disfigured, he settled with the company for a rather large sum of money and went on his way. Steve decided to invest his money in a small, but growing, telecom business. After weeks of negotiations, he bought the company outright. It was only after signing on the dotted line, however, that it dawned on him that he knew nothing about running such a business – so he set out to hire someone who could do that for him.

The next day he set up three interviews. The first guy was great. He knew everything he needed to and was very interesting. At the end of the interview, Steve asked him, 'Do you notice anything different about me?'

'Why yes,' the candidate answered. 'I couldn't help but notice you have no ears.' Steve got very angry and threw him out.

The second interview was with a woman, and she was even better than the first guy. He asked her the same question: 'Do you notice anything different about me?'

'Well...' she replied, 'you have no ears.' Steve tossed her out.

The third and last interview, with a young man fresh from university, was the best of all three. He was smart. He was confident. And he seemed to be a better businessman than the first two put together. Steve was anxious, but went ahead and asked the young man the same question: 'Do you notice anything different about me?'

To his surprise, the young man said what he wanted to hear. 'Why yes – you wear contact lenses.'

Steve was shocked. 'What an incredibly observant young man,' he said. 'How in the world did you know that?'

'Well, it's hard to wear glasses with no fucking ears,' replied the young man.

The randy cheapskate

A man is wandering through a red light district when he spies a
brothel advertising the best whores in town. Walking up to the front
desk, he asks for the cheapest girl available and is led into a
darkened room. There, he finds a woman lying on the bed – but as
soon as he climbs on top and starts pumping, she repeatedly spits in
his eye.

Furious, he sprints down to the front desk. 'That bitch spat in
my eye!' he screams at the receptionist.

The woman behind the desk calmly turns around to a bunch of
men playing cards. 'Get to it boys. The corpse is full.'

What do you call...

...a ferret on ecstasy....

Madferret.

The rooster race

A farmer decides it is time to get a new rooster for his hens. The
current rooster is still doing an okay job, but he is getting on in
years, so the farmer buys a young cock from the local poultry
emporium and turns him loose in the barnyard.

The old rooster sees the young one strutting around and he
gets a little worried. So he walks up to the new bird and says,
'You're the new stud in town? I bet you think you're hot stuff.
Well I'm not ready for the chopping block yet. I'm still the better
bird. And to prove it, I challenge you to a race around the hen
house. Ten laps, and whoever finishes first gets to have all the
hens for himself.'

The young rooster is a proud bird, and definitely a match for the
old guy. 'You're on,' says the young rooster. 'And since I know I'm
so great, I'll even give you a head start of half a lap.'

So the two roosters start racing, with all the hens watching and
cheering the two birds on. After the first lap, the old rooster is still
maintaining his lead. After the second lap, the old guy's lead has
slipped a little but he's still hanging in there. By the fifth lap he's
barely in front of his young challenger.

By now the farmer has heard all the commotion. Thinking a fox must have broken in, he grabs his shotgun and runs into the barnyard. When he gets there, the two roosters are rounding the hen house, with the old rooster still slightly in the lead. He immediately takes aim, fires and blows the young rooster away.

'Damn!' he curses to himself. 'That's the third gay rooster I've bought this month.'

What do men with two left feet...

...wear on the beach?

Flip-flips.

The samurai tournament

In need of a new chief samurai, the Emperor calls together all the great dojo masters. After a huge and glorious tournament, just three champions are left: a Chinese samurai, a Japanese samurai and a Jewish samurai. In one final test, the Emperor asks the trio to prove their swordsmanship. Immediately, the Chinese samurai steps forward, unsheathes his mighty sword and it scythes through the air with a 'whoosh'. The onlookers gasp as a single fly falls to the floor, sliced in two.

The Japanese samurai is not impressed. Wielding his own shiny blade, he also clefts the air, and with a quick 'swish' another fly falls – this time in four, precise pieces. The crowd goes wild.

Finally, it's the turn of the Jewish samurai. Smiling, he pulls out his weapon as another fly buzzes past, and there's a flurry of thrusts. The fly, however, glides happily away and out of a nearby window.

'Shame on you,' grumbles the Emperor. 'You failed to kill the fly.'

'True,' says the Jewish samurai, 'but circumcision is not meant to kill.'

Two cannibals were eating a clown...

...when one said to the other, 'Here – does this taste funny to you?'

Simple economics

A man comes home from work to find his wife in the bedroom, packing her suitcase. 'What the hell are you doing?' he asks.

'I'm leaving you for a better life,' she replies. 'I'm going to Las Vegas – I hear they pay $400 for a blow job out there.'

The man thinks for a minute, then gets his suitcase out and starts packing. 'I'm going to Las Vegas, too,' he tells her. 'I want to see how you live on $800 a year.'

He knows all

A Christian was wandering around town, thinking about how good his wife had been to him and how fortunate he was to have her. 'God – why did you make her so kind-hearted?' he asked the Creator.

'So you could love her, my son,' the Lord responded.

'Why did you make her so good-looking?'

'So you could love her, my son.'

'Why did you make her such a good cook?'

'So you could love her, my son.'

The man thought about all this, then he said: 'I don't mean to seem ungrateful or anything, but... why did you make her so stupid?'

'So she could love you, my son.'

Kid logic

Little Billy walked into his parents' bedroom one day, only to catch his dad sitting on the side of his bed sliding a condom onto his penis in preparation for making love to his wife.

Billy's father, in an attempt to hide his raging, condom-tipped hard-on, bent over as if he were looking under the bed. 'What are you doing, dad?' asked little Billy.

'I thought I saw a rat go under the bed...' his father quickly replied.

'So what are you going to do?' said Billy. 'Fuck it to death?'

The deaf newlyweds

Two deaf people get married. However, during the honeymoon, they find they're unable to communicate in the bedroom when they turn off the lights because they can't see each other using sign language. After several nights of fumbling and misunderstandings, the wife decides on a solution.

'Honey,' she signs, 'why don't we agree on some simple signals? For instance, at night, if you want to have sex with me, reach over and squeeze my left breast once. If you don't want to have sex, reach over and squeeze my right breast once.'

The husband thinks this is a great idea and signs back to his wife, 'Very clever. Now, if you want to have sex with me, reach over and pull on my penis once. If you don't want to have sex, reach over and pull on my penis... 50 times.'

Bad dog!

A man is stopped by an angry neighbour. 'I'd just left the house this morning to collect my newspaper when that evil Doberman of yours went for me!'

'I'm astounded,' said the dog's owner. 'I've been feeding that fleabag for seven years and it's never got the bloody paper for me.'

Soaks debate hobby

Two alcoholics are sat in a bar. One says to the other, 'If you had the choice, which disease would you rather be struck down by – Alzheimer's or Parkinson's?'

'That's a good one,' slurs his chum. 'It would have to be Parkinson's. I'd rather lose half my pint than forget where I put it in the first place.'

Love Down Under

An Australian is walking down a country road in New Zealand, when he happens to glance over the fence and see a farmer going at it with a sheep. The Aussie is quite taken aback by this, so he vaults the fence and walks over to the farmer. Tapping him on the shoulder, he says, 'You know, mate, back home we shear those.'

The New Zealander looks round frantically. 'Get lost, mate!' he says. 'I'm not shearing this with no-one!'

The odd couple

Attracting more than a few raised eyebrows, a 70-year-old groom and his beautiful 25-year-old bride check into a resort hotel. Next morning at 8am sharp, the groom wanders down to breakfast whistling a happy tune. He sits at a table and, with a beaming smile to the waitress, orders bacon and eggs.

Fifteen minutes later the young bride gingerly trudges into the dining room with bowed legs – her face drawn and her hair tangled. Such is her appearance that a waitress rushes to her aid. 'My God, honey, what happened?' she cries. 'Here you are – a young bride with an elderly husband. But you look like you've had a fight with wild dogs.'

'That bastard double-crossed me,' sighs the bride. 'He told me he'd saved up for 50 years. I thought he was talking about money.'

Q: What is the cleverest thing to have come from a woman's mouth?

A: Einstein's dick.

The bodybuilder's tale

A man was sitting at a bar when he noticed another patron a few stools away. The guy had a body like Charles Atlas but his head was the size of a thimble. 'Excuse me for staring,' said the first man, 'but I can't help but be curious as to why your body is so well developed but your head is so small.' The bodybuilder said, 'Buy me a drink and I'll tell you.' So drinks were ordered and the story began. 'I was in the navy and my ship was sunk by a torpedo. I was the only survivor and managed to make it to a desert island.

'I was sitting on the beach one day, trying to catch a fish so I would have something to eat, when I saw a beautiful mermaid sunning herself on a nearby rock. She swam over and informed me that she was a magical mermaid and could grant me three wishes. "Great," I said. "I'd like to be rescued." So she slapped the water with her tail and a ship appeared, sailing straight for my island.

'Next I asked for a body like Charles Atlas. Another slap of the tail and here it is. 'Then, noticing how beautiful she was and with all my other wishes fulfilled, I asked if I could make love to her. She said no – it just wouldn't work, her being half-fish and all. So I asked her for a little head.'

The businessman's gamble

A blonde and a businessman are seated next to each other on a flight. 'Let's play a game,' proposes the man. 'I ask you a question. If you don't know the answer, you pay me £5, and vice versa.'

The blonde isn't interested, instead preferring just to nap.

'Okay, okay,' insists the businessman, 'you don't know the answer, you pay me £5, I don't know, I pay you £500!'

Sensing no end, the blonde agrees. The businessman asks the first question: 'What is the distance from the Earth to the moon?'

Without even thinking, the blonde reaches into her purse, pulls out a fiver and hands it over. 'Cool,' says the businessman, 'your turn!'

'What goes up a hill with three legs and comes down with four?'

Puzzled, the businessman takes out his laptop and searches the internet for an answer. No luck. Frustrated, he sends e-mails to all his friends and co-workers, to no avail. After an hour, he wakes the blonde and hands her £500. The blonde thanks him, turns over and shuts her eyes.

'Well,' says the businessman, miffed, 'you could at least tell me the answer.'

Without a word, the blonde reaches into her purse, hands over £5 to the businessman and happily drifts back to sleep.

Q: How long does a pubic hair stay on the toilet seat?

A: Until it gets pissed off.

The Good Samaritan

A man comes into work on a Monday with a black eye. His fellow workers ask him what happened. 'I was in church yesterday,' says the man, 'when a young woman came in wearing a summer dress and sat in the seat in front of me. When she stood up the dress was caught between the cheeks of her bum, so I leaned forward and plucked it out. And she hit me!'

The next Monday he comes in with two black eyes. 'I was in church yesterday,' he explains, 'and the same young woman in the same dress sat in front of me. When she stood up her dress was caught between the cheeks of her bum again, and the man beside me leaned forward and plucked it out. I knew she didn't like that, though, so I pushed it in again...'

Too literal

A teenage boy and his dad are alone in the house when there's a knock at the door. The boy answers it. 'Dad,' he says, 'there's a girl at the door. She wants to come in. Shall I let her?'

'Yes, son.'

'Dad, this girl wants to go upstairs. Shall I let her?'

'Yes, son.'

'Dad, this girl wants to get into bed with me. Shall I let her?'

'Yes, son.'

'Dad, what should I do?'

'Well – stick your hairy bit into her hairy bit.'

There is a muffled scream. 'Dad! My head's stuck!'

The coach party

A coachload of Scousers goes screaming into a sharp bend on an icy night and everyone dies. At the Pearly Gates, Saint Peter opens up – and is horrified to see 40 of Liverpool's finest wanting to come in.

'I can't just let you all in – I've got to tell the boss,' he explains, and goes to check with God if it's okay.

Imagining halos being used as frisbees, angels with missing wings and worse, the Lord tells Peter: 'Send 'em all back but, if you must, let the first five in.'

Ten minutes later, Saint Peter returns in a panic. 'God,' he shouts, 'they've gone!'

'What, all 40?' asks the Almighty.

'No,' says Peter, 'the gates!'

Man cops eyeful

A man approaches a stunning, voluptuous young woman while out shopping in the supermarket. 'I'm terribly sorry,' he says, 'I've lost my wife – I don't suppose you'd mind talking to me for a couple of minutes, would you?'

The woman is bewildered. 'Why?' she asks.

'Well,' replies the man, 'every time I talk to a woman with tits like yours, the old bat just seems to appear out of nowhere.'

Prudent farmer

A young man was driving past a farm when he spied a pig with a wooden leg. Puzzled, he pulled in and approached the farmer: 'What's the story with the pig, there?' he asked.

'That pig can recognise 100 different commands, work out mathematical equations in the dirt and speak 25 words,' said the farmer.

'So what's with the wooden leg?' asked the man.

'Well,' replied the farmer, 'when a pig's that special, you just don't eat him all at once.'

What do you call...

...two skunks having a 69?

Odour eaters.

Cruel cream

A little blind girl goes up to her mum. 'Mummy,' she says, sadly, 'when will I be able to see?'

Smiling kindly, her mum replies, 'I'll tell you what, I'll take you to the chemist and get you some special cream for your eyes. You should be able to see by tomorrow morning.'

With the little girl jumping around excitedly, the two head into town. They return with the cream, and that evening the mother rubs the balm onto her little girl's eyes. 'Aah, mummy!' cries the girl. 'It stings!'

'Be brave,' consoles her mother, and wraps her head in bandages before putting her to bed.

The next morning, the little girl stumbles into her mum's bedroom. 'Quick mummy,' she insists eagerly, 'take off the bandage!'

So, very slowly, the mother peels off the bandages, while her daughter braces herself for the magic moment. 'But mummy,' says the girl once the final bandage is removed, 'I still can't see.'

Her mother grins at her sympathetically. 'Yes dear,' she replies. 'April fool.'

Blonde stumped

Deep into a game of Trivial Pursuit, it was once again the young blonde's turn to throw. She picked up the die, threw a six and landed on Science & Nature. 'If you're in a vacuum and someone calls your name,' asked her friend, 'can you hear it?'

She thought for a moment. 'Right...' she replied, 'is it on or off?'

Desert dilemma

After a ghastly plane crash in the desert, only two men survive. They stumble across the sands for days, sunburnt and thirsty, before sighting three tents in the distance. Not knowing whether they're real or a mirage, they run towards the vision anyway.

They're real! Stumbling into the first tent, they're confronted by an Arab salesman. 'Water, please!' the men croak. 'Do you have water?'

'Sorry, I've only got whipped cream,' replies the desert-dweller.

The men tumble into the next tent and again ask for water. 'Sorry, I only have custard,' says the Arab sitting within.

They go into the last tent and ask for water, but again are told, 'I've only got jelly. Sorry.'

As the men resume their desert trek, one goes to the other, 'That was weird – all that food and no water.'

'Yes,' comes the reply. 'It was a trifle bazaar.'

One-upmanship

A pro-am golf competition is taking place in Wicklow, and two amateurs are having a conversation on the first tee. The first, in a very posh voice, says, 'I've reserved a rather lovely suite in the Grand Hotel. Where are you staying for the duration, old boy?'

'Jaysus,' says the second amateur, 'Oi'm sleepin' in the back of me Morris Minor in the Golf Club car-park.'

'Really?' says the toff.

'That must be rather uncomfortable.'

'No, not a bit of it. Oi've a lovely king-sized double bed in the back.'

'Good Lord! Really? I have a colour TV and a bar in the back of my Rolls, but no bed.'

'Well, ye'd want to get one! They're the business!' says the other fellow.

A year later, back at the pro-am competition in Wicklow, the toff glides up in his Rolls-Royce and enters the clubhouse looking for the chap in the Morris Minor. The steward directs him to the far corner of the car park. There he finds the old grey Morris, windows steamed up, rocking back and forth frenetically on its springs. Politely, the toff taps on the window. A moment later the window is wound down and the other fellow appears, looking sweaty and dishevelled.

'Hello, old boy!' says the toff. 'I just popped by to tell you I've had a bed fitted in the back of the Roller.'

The other fellow looks at him in disbelief and says, 'You got me out of the Jacuzzi to tell me that?'

Emergency call

A man phones up the vet in the middle of the night to tell him his pet dog has swallowed a condom. 'You've got to help,' he cries. 'I don't know what to do.'

'It is rather late,' says the vet. 'But as it's an emergency, I'll be there as soon as I can.'

'What should I do in the meantime,' says the owner.

'Just keep the dog as still as you can,' says the vet.

'I won't be long.'

After an hour, the vet is still driving when his mobile rings. 'I phoned earlier,' says the caller. 'My dog swallowed a condom.'

'Yes, I know,' says the vet. 'I'm going as fast as I can, but I'm stuck in traffic.'

'You needn't bother,' says the dog owner. 'It's okay now. We've found another one in the drawer.'

Bloody kids

A kid is watching his grandfather take a piss. 'Hey, Grandpa,' he says. 'My dad has got two of those things.'

'What do you mean, son?' says the old man.

'Well, he's got a wobbly one like that for pissing through, and a long, hard one for cleaning mummy's teeth.'

Bad day

An Englishman, an Irishman and a Scotsman were in a pub, talking about their sons. 'My son was born on St George's Day,' commented the Englishman. 'So we called him George.' 'That's a real coincidence,' remarked the Scot. 'My son was born on St Andrew's Day, so we called him Andrew.' 'My God, that's amazing,' said the Irishman. 'The same thing happened with my son Pancake.'

Mixed blessings

A police officer on a motorcycle pulls alongside a man driving around the M25 in an open-topped sports car and flags him down.

The policeman solemnly approaches the car. 'Sir, I'm sorry to tell you your wife fell out a mile back,' he says.

'Oh, thank God,' the man replies. 'I thought I was going deaf.'

How do you make...

...a cat go woof?

Cover it in petrol.

Literary complaint

A man visits his doctor: 'Doc, I think I'm losing it,' he says, 'I'm forever dreaming I wrote Lord Of The Rings.'

'Hmm. One moment,' replies the doctor, consulting his medical book.

'Ah yes, now I see... you've been Tolkien in your sleep.'

Always finish the story

A man is very suspicious of his wife's activities, so he asks his seven-year-old son to look out for any strange men calling at the house during the day. First thing when he gets back from work, he asks his son to tell him all about what mummy has been up to. 'Well,' says the son, 'Mr Jones from next door came round and mummy started to kiss him.'

'And what happened next?' asks daddy, warming to the conversation.

'Then mummy took off all of her clothes.'

'Okay, that's far enough,' he says. 'You can finish off the story on Saturday, when all the family are coming around.'

So Saturday arrives and in the middle of the main course the man turns to his son and tells him to tell his story to everyone. 'Well,' says the son, 'Mr Jones came round the other day and started to kiss mummy, then mummy took off her clothes and her and Mr Jones went into the bedroom.'

'Yes,' says the father, 'now tell everyone what happened then.'

'So,' says the son, 'Mr Jones and mummy got on the bed and started playing that funny old game you play with Aunt Maureen.'

A farmer takes his driving test...

'Can you make a u-turn?' asks the instructor.

'You betcha,' the farmer replies. 'I can make its fucking eyes water.'

The busman and the banana

Ted's a bus conductor, until one fateful morning when he tells the driver to pull away as a frail old lady is boarding. Tragically, she's killed. Ted is convicted of manslaughter and, residing in Texas, faces death by the electric chair. 'Any last requests?' asks the executioner.

'Well,' says Ted, 'I see you've an unripe banana there. Mind if I have it?'

The executioner agrees, Ted polishes off the fruit and the switch is flipped – but when the smoke clears Ted is still very much alive. The authorities set him free and before long he's back on the buses... then disaster. The same accident befalls another commuter. Ted is once more sent to the chair, once more gobbles down an unripe banana and once more survives.

He returns to society, and disaster strikes again: three children are pulled under the bus and it's back to the chair. Come last request time the executioner produces an unripe banana and, a few minutes later, Ted's ready. The switch is thrown, all the prison lights go out... and there's Ted, fit as a fiddle.

'Why won't you die!' screams the executioner. 'It's that banana, isn't it?'

'Not at all,' whimpers Ted. 'I'm just a really bad conductor.'

Bride-to-be sets out stall

After a brief, sex-free relationship, an elderly couple finally decide to marry. Before the wedding, they have a long conversation about how things might change in married life, discussing finances and living arrangements, before eventually the old man enquires about doing the wild thing.

'How do you feel about sex?' he asks, rather hopefully.

'Well,' thinks his partner, 'I'd have to say I like it infrequently.'

The old man pauses. 'I see,' he says, 'just to clarify, was that one word or two?'

Bursting!

Linford Christie is walking around town when he finds himself dying for a piss. Wandering over to the nearest public loo, he finds it's closed for repairs. He jogs over to McDonald's – but their dunnies are for paying customers only. Becoming ever more anxious, he trots over to a petrol station, but their shitters are being cleaned.

By now, the situation is getting critical for the Olympic medal winner, so Linford starts sprinting up the High Street looking for relief. Finally, he spies a hidden public bog, and dashes inside. Letting out a huge sigh of relief as he drains his bladder, he grins to the man in the next urinal. 'Phew! Just made it!'

'Christ!' says his neighbour, glancing down, 'can you make me one too?'

Underfoot crime

The authorities were called to a local housing estate last night after a man was shot in a row over a carpet.

Police suspect it was rug related.

Man accompanies victim

A man is walking down the High Street when suddenly a nearby wall collapses, burying him in rubble. It's ten minutes before another passer-by – a smartly dressed man – happens to wander past. 'Christ! Are you okay mate?' he cries. 'Has anyone called an ambulance?'

'Uh... no,' comes the agonised reply.

'Right. Has anyone called the police?' asks the second man.

'No,' moans the injured man.

'Okay... has the compensation board been informed?'

By now the injured man is groggily angry, 'Look – you're the first one here!'

The smart man thinks for a minute. 'All right,' he says, shifting some rubble. 'Move over, then.'

Englishman hails fire chief

While on a visit to New York, an Englishman decides to take a trip to Ground Zero. Spotting the local Fire Chief, he takes the opportunity to pass on his admiration and support for their excellent work. 'Thank you very much,' replies the fireman. 'So where do you hail from?'

'Wolverhampton,' replies the Englishman.

'And what state is that in?' enquires the Fire Chief.

'Oh – pretty much the same as this.'

What's the difference...

...between toast and women?

You can make soldiers out of toast.

Salesman gets cocky

A little old lady answers a knock at her door, where a well-dressed young man carrying a vacuum cleaner greets her. 'Good morning,' he says, 'if I could have two minutes of your time, I shall demonstrate the latest in high-powered suction.'

'Bugger off,' replies the old lady, moving to slam the door shut, 'I haven't got any money!'

Quick as a flash, the salesman wedges his foot in and pushes the door wide open. 'Now don't be too hasty, madam,' he pleads, 'at least see my demonstration!' And with that, he empties a bucket of manure all over her carpet. 'If this vacuum cleaner doesn't remove all traces of this muck from your carpet, I'll eat the remainder.'

'Then I hope you've got a bloody good appetite,' says the woman, 'the electricity was cut off this morning.'

Q: What did the cannibal do after he dumped his girlfriend?

A: He wiped his arse.

The Irish pilots

Paddy and Mick rent a private plane for the day, and are doing fine until it's time to land. Paddy concentrates on the instrument readings and finally gets the plane down, but he has to screech to a stop to avoid running onto the grass.

'Boy, that's a short runway,' Mick says, wiping the sweat from his forehead.

'Yeah,' says Paddy. 'But look how wide it is.'

The johnny stand

A boy and his dad are at the chemist's. As they walk past the condom display the boy asks, 'Dad – what are those for?'

'Son,' the man replies, 'they're for safe sex.'

The little boy then asks why one box has only three condoms. The dad answers, 'Because that is for sixth-form boys. One for Friday night, one for Saturday night and one for Sunday night.'

The boy then inquires why another box has six condoms. The dad explains that it is for college boys: two for Friday night, two for Saturday night and two for Sunday night.

Then the boy sees a 12-pack. 'Son, that's for married men,' the father explains. 'One for January, one for February...'

OAP gets ideas

A Salvation Army band is merrily knocking out hymns in the local square. Soon the captain walks round with the collection box, approaching an old dear sat on the bench. 'Would you like to make a donation?' he asks.

'Oh yes, of course,' smiles the old lady, popping a pound into the collection.

'And for that, madam,' insists the captain, 'how about you select one of our hymns for yourself?'

'Ooh, really?' says the woman, delighted. 'Right, I'll have him, then – the stud with the trombone.'

The dog walkers

Two men walking their dogs pass each other in a graveyard. The first man says to the second, 'Morning.'

'No,' says the second man. 'Just walking the dog.'

Guess the vegetable

One day a teacher brought in a bulging paper bag. 'Now class,' she said, 'I'm going to reach into the bag and describe a vegetable, and you tell me what I'm talking about. Okay, first: it's round, plump and red.'

Of course, Johnny raised his hand high, but the teacher wisely ignored him and picked Deborah, who promptly answered: 'An apple.'

'No, Deborah, it's a beetroot, but I like your thinking. Now for the second. It's soft, fuzzy, and coloured red and brownish...'

Johnny was hopping up and down in his seat, trying to get the teacher to call on him, but she skipped him again and called on Billy. 'Is it a peach?'

'No, Billy, I'm afraid it's a potato. But I like your thinking. Here's another: it's long, yellow and fairly hard.'

By now Johnny was about to explode as he waved his hand frantically. But the teacher skipped him again and called on Sally. 'A banana,' she said. 'No,' the teacher replied, 'it's a squash, but I like your thinking.'

Johnny was pretty pissed off by now, so he spoke up. 'I've got one for you, ma'am. Let me put my hand in my pocket. Okay, I've got it: it's round, hard and it's got a head on it.'

'Johnny!' she cried. 'That's disgusting!'

'No,' said Johnny, 'it's a ten-pence piece – but I like your thinking.'

Did you hear about...

...the paraplegic juggler?

He dropped all the paraplegics.

The bells! The bells!

A fireman comes home from work one day and tells his wife, 'You know, we have a wonderful system at the fire station. Bell One rings and we all put on our jackets. Bell Two rings and we all slide down the pole. Bell Three rings and we're ready to go on the engines.'

'That's super, dear,' says his old lady.

'From now on,' continues the firefighter, 'we're going to run this house the same way. When I say Bell One, I want you to strip naked. When I say Bell Two, I want you to jump into bed. When I say Bell Three, we're going to screw all night.'

So the next night the fireman comes home from work and yells, 'Bell One!' and his wife takes off all her clothes. 'Bell Two!' he shouts, and she jumps into bed. 'Bell Three!' he barks, and they begin to screw.

But after just a couple of minutes, his wife yells, 'Bell Four!'

'What's this Bell Four?' the husband asks.

'More hose!' she replies. 'You're nowhere near the fire!'

Why do women...

...have small feet?

To get closer to the oven.

The crash survivor

A plane crashes over some desolate mountainous terrain. The only survivor is a Scotsman, who manages to stumble out of the wreckage and crawl, hungry and exhausted, for several miles before finding shelter in a cave. A Red Cross search party soon arrives and begins combing the mountains, looking for survivors. After a few hours, they spot the cave entrance. 'Is anyone alive in there?' shouts the group leader.

'Who's that?' squawks the reply.

'Red Cross,' answers the leader.

'Thank you,' comes the response, 'but I've already donated.'

The brush of doom

An army major pops in to a field hospital to visit three sick troopers. He goes up to the first private and asks, 'What's your problem, soldier?'

'Chronic syphilis, sir.'

'And what treatment are you getting?'

'Five minutes with the wire brush each day.'

'What's your ambition?'

'To get back to the front, sir.'

'Good man,' says the major, and moves on to the next bed. 'What's your problem, soldier?'

'Chronic piles, sir.'

'And what treatment are you getting?'

'Five minutes with the wire brush each day.'

'What's your ambition?'

'To get back to the front, sir.'

'Good man,' says the major, and he goes to the next bed. 'What's your problem, soldier?'

'Chronic gum disease, sir.'

'And what treatment are you getting?'

'Five minutes with the wire brush each day.'

'What's your ambition?'

'To get the wire brush before the other two, sir.'

Old fogey aids golfer

After returning from the local golf course, an old man is moaning to his wife about his game. 'You see, I was driving the ball pretty well,' he laments, 'but my eyesight's got so bad that I couldn't see where the blasted thing went.'

'You're 75, Jack!' tuts his wife. 'Why don't you take your brother Geoff along?'

'But he's 85 and doesn't play golf any more,' replies Jack.

'Well, he does have perfect eyesight,' his wife points out. 'He could watch where the ball goes.'

So the next day, Jack takes his brother down to the course. With

Geoff looking on, his first swing sends the ball shooting down the middle of the fairway. 'Did you see it?' asks Jack.

'Yup,' comes the reply, 'clear as a bell.'

'Well, where did it go?' asks Jack, squinting into the distance.

Geoff looks at the ground. 'Uh,' he coughs, 'I forgot.'

Meeting the parents

A lad meets a girl whom he really, really likes, and soon he's invited round to meet her parents. Sitting outside their house in the car, the girl says, 'Look, there's something I better warn you about. My parents are both deaf and dumb, and they have their own special way of communicating. I just don't want you to be shocked, okay?'

So it's with some trepidation that the couple enter the kitchen. Nothing could have prepared the lad for what he sees. There is the girl's mother, skirt up around her hips, shoving a bottle into her fanny, while the father is standing with his bollocks on the table and his eyes pinned open by matchsticks.

'What on earth's going on!' stutters the lad.

'I suppose I ought to translate,' says the girl. 'My mother's saying, "Get the beers in, you cunt," and my father's reply is, "Bollocks, I'm watching the match."'

The magic Coke machine

A blonde walks up to a Coke machine in a Las Vegas casino, puts in a few coins and out pops her fizzy pop. She puts some more coins into the machine, and another can of Coke pops out. She keeps putting in coins, and cans of Coke keep coming out.

A guy comes up behind her and asks to use the machine. 'Piss off,' she hisses. 'Can't you see I'm winning?'

An inventor was trying to...

...sell his new computerised crystal ball to a marketing executive. As expected, the executive was highly sceptical. 'Tell you what,' said the inventor, 'why don't you type in a question?'

The executive tapped out: 'Where is my father?'

The crystal ball bleeped and blooped, then finally returned an answer: 'Your father is fishing in Scotland.'

'Ha!' laughed the executive, 'I knew this thing was rubbish – my father's been dead 15 years!'

The inventor was puzzled. 'This can't be right – try asking the question in a different way.'

The executive again began typing: 'Where is my mother's husband?'

A short bleep later and the crystal ball returned its answer, 'Your mother's husband has been dead for 15 years. Your father just landed an eight-pound trout.'

Q: Why don't worms have balls?

A: Because they can't dance.

Almost got away with it

After watching a car weave in and out of the lanes, a police officer pulls over the driver and asks him to blow into a breathalyser. 'Sorry officer,' says the driver, 'I can't do that – I'm an asthmatic, and I may have an attack.'

'Okay, fine,' replies the rozzer, 'but you'll have to come down to the station for a blood sample.'

The driver shakes his head.

'I can't do that either. I'm a haemophiliac, so I might bleed to death.'

'Well, then, we need a urine sample.'

'Nope, no can do – I'm also a diabetic, I'm afraid. If I do that, I'll get really low blood sugar.'

Exasperated, the officer pulls open the door. 'All right then,' he shouts. 'I'll need you to come out here and walk the white line.'

'But I can't do that, officer,' replies the man.

'And why the hell not?'

The man furrows his brow. 'Because I'm really pissed.'

Just the one pill

A man goes to see his GP. 'Doc, you've got to help me,' he says. 'My wife just isn't interested in sex any more. Haven't you got a pill or something I can give her?'

'Look,' says the doc, 'I can't prescribe...'

'We've been friends for years!' pleads the patient. 'Have you ever seen me this upset? I'm desperate! I can't think, I can't concentrate, my life is going to hell! You've got to help me!'

So the doctor opens his desk drawer and removes a small bottle of pills. 'Ordinarily,

I wouldn't do this,' he explains. 'These are experimental, and the tests so far indicate they're very powerful. Don't give her more than one, understand? Just one.'

'I don't know, doc – she's awfully cold...'

'One. No more. In her coffee. Okay?'

'Um... okay.' So our hero heads off for home, where his wife has dinner waiting. When dinner is finished, she goes to the kitchen to fetch the pudding. The man, in fumbling haste, pulls the pills from his pocket and drops one into his wife's coffee. He reflects for a moment, hesitates, then drops in a second pill. Now he begins to worry – the doctor did say they were powerful. Then inspiration strikes: he drops one pill into his own coffee.

His wife returns with a crumble and they enjoy their dessert and coffee, our hero with a poorly concealed look of anticipation. Sure enough, a few minutes after they finish, his wife shudders a little, sighs deeply and heavily, and a strange smoky look enters her eyes. In a deep, throaty, near whisper, in a tone of voice he has never heard her use before, she says, 'I... need... a man.'

His eyes glitter and his hands tremble as he replies, 'Me... too.'

What is an Essex girl's...

...idea of safe sex?

Putting the handbrake on.

Public transport

A man with no arms or legs is waiting at a bus stop when his mate pulls up, driving a bus. 'All right, Dave!' says the driver as he opens the door. 'How are you getting on?'

What do you get...

...if you cross a Rottweiler with a Labrador?

A dog that scares the shit out of you then runs off with the bog roll.

Second time lucky

A young couple are cuddling on the bed, when the boyfriend tries his luck on his loved one. But she turns round and says, 'Sorry dear, but tomorrow I'm going to the gynaecologist and I want to smell fresh and nice.'

At this the boyfriend turns his back, peeved at her rejection. After a short while he rolls back and taps her on the shoulder. 'You don't have a dentist's appointment as well, do you?' he whispers.

What's white...

...and wiggles slowly across a disco floor?

Come dancing.

Love potion abused

A man walks into the chemist's and tells the pharmacist, 'Listen, I've got two girls coming over this weekend and they're hot, hot,

hot. Would you have something to keep me going all night? It's going to be one hell of a party.'

The pharmacist smiles and disappears into the back room, returning with a dusty old bottle. 'This stuff is potent,' he says. 'Drink only one ounce of it, and I guarantee you'll be doing the wild thing all night. Let me know how it goes!'

The weekend passes and on Monday morning the pharmacist arrives at work to find the same guy waiting for him on the doorstep. 'So?' says the chemist. 'How was your weekend?'

The man replies, 'Quick, I need pain relief!'

The pharmacist, knowing what the guy had been doing all weekend, says, 'Are you crazy? You can't put that on your penis. The skin is way too sensitive.'

'It's not for that,' says the man. 'It's for my arm.'

'What happened?'

'Well... I drank the whole bottle of your potion,' the man admits. 'Then the girls never showed up.'

Q: Why couldn't Mozart find his music teacher?

A: He was Haydn.

Dangerous driving

An old lady, slightly mad, is wandering round the old folks home with her Zimmer on wheels. Another loony stops her in the corridor and says, 'Show me your driving licence.'

The old woman fiddles about in her pocket and pulls out a sweet wrapper. He checks it and lets her go on her way.

Then a second man stops her and demands to see her tax disc. She presents a drinks coaster, which the lunatic checks before letting her pass on.

She carries on until she sees a third man standing with his penis hanging out. 'Oh no,' she mutters to herself. 'Not the bloody breathalyser again.'

The passenger's revenge

A man gets ripped off by a taxi driver one night, so he decides to get his own back whenever he next gets the chance. Soon after, he sees the same taxi driver, third in the cab rank. The man goes up to the first cab in the rank, gets in and tells the driver he has no money – but if he gives him a lift home he'll get a blow job in payment. The taxi driver freaks and kicks the guy out.

He then goes to the second cab and makes the same offer: a blow job for a lift home. The second taxi driver also refuses, and again he gets kicked out.

So he gets into the third cab – the guy who ripped him off – and asks to be dropped off round the corner. The driver complies and drives off. As he passes the two other cabs in the rank, the passenger smiles at the other drivers and gives them both a big thumbs-up.

Dying footie fan makes last request

Having followed Manchester City his entire life, an old man lay on his death-bed with his son at his side. 'Is there anything you would like me to do for you, father?' asks the son.

'Well, son,' coughs his old man, 'there is one thing... go and buy me a Manchester United shirt.'

'But dad,' protests the bloke, 'after all these years as a loyal Blue, how can you turn now?'

'Trust me, son,' explains his father, 'far better one of them buggers dies, than one of us.'

Q: What's the difference between erotic and kinky?

A: Erotic, you use a feather. Kinky, you use the whole chicken.

Mistaken identity

A Jewish captain and a Chinese first officer are flying together for the first time. After half-an-hour's strained silence, the captain speaks. 'I don't like the Chinese.'

'You don't like the Chinese?' replies the first officer. 'Why?'

'Well, it was you lot who bombed Pearl Harbor.'

The Chinese officer shakes his head. 'We didn't bomb Pearl Harbor – that was the Japanese!' he cries.

The captain laughs, 'Chinese, Japanese, Vietnamese... they're all the same to me.'

There's a painful silence, before the Chinese pilot pipes up. 'I don't like Jews.'

'What's wrong with Jews?' growls the captain.

'Well,' says the Chinese officer, 'Jews sank the Titanic.'

'No, no,' corrects the captain. 'The Jews didn't sink the Titanic. That was an iceberg.'

The Oriental looks back at him. 'Iceberg, Goldberg, Rosenberg... they're all same to me.'

The power of advertising

An old lady is walking down the High Street when she stops outside a pet shop. As she curiously studies the window, she notices a poster saying, 'Fanny-licking frog inside.'

Excited by the prospect of this, the old lady ventures inside and asks the tall, dark-haired gentleman behind the counter for more details of this mouth-watering offer.

'Bonjour, Madame,' replies the shopkeeper, smiling.

Hard time

A mild-mannered accountant finds himself imprisoned for tax fraud, and on his first night is escorted to his cell. When the door opens he's confronted by a six-foot skinhead covered in tattoos, staring at him from the top bunk. Terrified, the accountant curls up in the bottom bunk. After a few minutes' silence, the skinhead whispers down, 'Hey, new fish – when the lights go out tonight, you and me are going to have a little game of Mummies And Daddies.'

'O-o-o-okay,' stammers the tax dodger.

'Which do you want to be?' hisses the skinhead. 'Mummy or daddy?'

Gasping for breath, the bean counter thinks fast. 'I'll be daddy.'

'Guess who's sucking mummy's cock tonight...' whispers the skinhead.

Pub grub

A bloke walks into a pub and sees a sign hanging over the bar which reads: cheese sandwich £1.50, chicken sandwich £2.50, hand job £10. Checking his wallet for the necessary payment, he walks up to the bar and beckons to one of the three exceptionally attractive wenches serving drinks to an eager-looking group of men.

'Yes?' she enquires with a knowing smile, 'can I help you?'

'I was wondering,' whispers the man, 'are you the one who gives the hand jobs?'

'Yes,' she purrs, 'indeed I am.'

The man replies, 'Wash your hands, would you? I want a cheese sandwich.'

Pal reprimanded

Fred arrives home from work and hears strange noises coming from the bedroom. He runs upstairs only to burst in and find his best mate pumping away with Fred's rather ugly wife.

He looks at the pair in utter disgust before turning to his friend. 'Honestly, Dave,' he says. 'I have to, but you?'

What goes...

...'Oooooo'?

A cow with no lips.

Divorcee annoys

A judge is questioning a woman over her pending separation. 'And the grounds for your divorce, madam?'

'Ooh,' she replies, 'about four acres, with a small stream running by...'

'No,' says the judge, 'I mean what is the foundation of this case?'

'Oh right,' the woman continues, 'well it's mainly concrete, brick and mortar...'

'No, no,' the judge reiterates, 'what are your relations like?'

'I have an aunt and uncle living here in town,' smiles the woman, 'and my husband's parents aren't far from us either.'

'Dear God,' pleads the judge, 'let's try this as simply as we can. Do you have a grudge?'

'Oh no,' says the woman, 'we have a huge driveway – we've never needed one to be honest.'

'Is there any infidelity in your marriage?' asks the judge, now tiring.

'Both my son and daughter have stereo sets,' explains the woman, 'they're always blaring out music!'

'Madam,' asks the judge, sick to the back teeth, 'does your husband ever beat you up?'

'Occasionally,' she replies, 'about twice a week he gets up about 20 minutes before me.'

'That's it!' screams the judge, 'why do you want a divorce?'

'Oh, I don't want a divorce,' she replies, still smiling away, 'my husband does – he says he can't communicate with me.'

God plays golf

A man and his local vicar were playing golf. The man had a terrible time on the green and kept missing crucial three-foot putts. The third time he missed one, he exclaimed, 'Fuck, missed!'

'You should curb your language, my son,' the vicar commented, 'or God will strike you down.'

At the next hole the man missed another sitter, and again cried, 'Fuck, missed!' The vicar again warned the man about the virtues of an unclean tongue.

At the next hole the man missed yet another three-footer. 'Fuck!' he wailed. 'Missed!'

The vicar was livid. 'May God have mercy upon your soul, my son, for surely the Lord will strike you down.' As he was speaking, dark clouds built up over the green, and no sooner had the vicar fallen silent than an enormous bolt of lightning forked down... and turned the vicar to ash.

'Fuck!' came a booming voice from the heavens. 'Missed!'

What's the difference...

...between a 16-stone woman and a 16-year-old girl?
  One is trying to diet...

Patient troubled

After experiencing an itchy, red rash on his forehead, a man goes to
see his doctor, who immediately takes a swab of the area and sends
it to the lab. 'They're extremely unusual results,' says the doctor.
'The sample contained genital DNA – basically, you have a very
rare condition where a penis is growing on your forehead.'

  Aghast, the man breaks down. 'Oh my Lord, what am I going to
do?' he sobs. 'I'll have to give up my job... my girlfriend will leave
me... and... how can I ever look in the mirror again?'

  'Oh, I wouldn't worry about that,' says the doctor.

  'Really?' cries the man, with new hope.

  'Oh yes,' replies the physician. 'You won't see a thing with those
bollocks over your eyes.'

What did the leper...

...say to his mother while riding his bike?
  'Look mum, no hands!'

The dreams of death

A man goes into his young son's bedroom to check he's all right.
The lad is having a nightmare, so the man wakes him. The boy says
he dreamt that Aunt Susie had died. The father assures the son that
Aunt Susie is fine, and sends him back to bed. The next day,
however, Aunt Susie dies.

  A week later, the lad has another nightmare
– this time that his granddad had died. The father assures his
son that granddad is fine and sends him to bed, but sure enough,
the next day granddad keels over and dies.

  One week later, it's nightmare time once more – and this time
the boy says he dreamt his daddy had died. The father assures the
son that he's okay and sends the boy to bed.

The next day, the father awakes, petrified. He's sure he's going to die.

After dressing, he drives cautiously to work, fearful of a collision. He doesn't eat lunch because he's scared of food poisoning. He avoids everyone, for sure that he'll somehow be killed, jumping at every noise, starting at every movement and hiding under his desk.

Upon getting home at the end of the day, he has to unburden himself to his wife. 'I've just had the worst day of my entire life!' he exclaims.

'You think your day was bad?' his wife replies. 'The milkman dropped dead on the doorstep this morning.'

What have parsley...

...and pubic hair got in common?

You just push it to the side and carry on eating.

The overenthusiastic doctor

A husband and wife are on a nudist beach when suddenly a wasp buzzes into the wife's business end. Naturally enough, she panics. The husband is also quite shaken, but manages to put a coat on her, pull up his shorts and carries her to the car. Then he makes a mad dash to the doctor.

The doctor, after examining her, says that the wasp is too far in to remove with forceps. The husband will have to try and entice it out by putting honey on his dick and withdrawing as soon as he feels the wasp.

The honey is duly smeared, but because of his wife's screaming and his frantic dash to the doctor and general panic, he just can't rise to the occasion. So the doctor says he'll perform the deed if the husband and wife don't object. Naturally both agree, for fear the wasp will do some damage, so the doctor quickly undresses, smears the honey on and instantly gets an erection, at which time he begins to plug the wife. Only he doesn't stop and withdraw but continues with vigour.

The husband shouts, 'What the hell's happening?'

To which the doctor replies, 'Change of plan. I'm going to drown the little bastard!'

Q: Why should blondes not be given coffee breaks?

A: It takes too long to retrain them.

Best feet forward

A single man wanted help with the household chores, so he decided to get a pet to help out. At the pet store, he asked the owner for advice on a suitable animal. The owner suggested a dog, but the man said, 'No – dogs can't do dishes.'

The owner then suggested a cat, but the man said, 'No – cats can't do the ironing.'

Finally the owner suggested a centipede. 'This is the perfect pet for you,' he explained. 'It can do anything!' Okay, the man thought, I'll give it a try, so he bought it. Once home he told the centipede to wash the dishes. The centipede glanced over and saw piles and piles of dirty dishes. Five minutes later, all the crockery was washed, dried and put away.

Great, thought the man. Next he told the centipede to do the dusting and vacuuming. Fifteen minutes later the house was spotless.

Wow, thought the man, deciding to push his luck. 'Go down to the shop and get me the evening paper,' he told the centipede, and off it went. Fifteen minutes later, the centipede hadn't returned. Thirty minutes later and still no centipede. Forty-five minutes and the man got sick of waiting, so he went out to look for the centipede.

As he opened the front door, there on the step was the centipede. 'Hey, what are you doing there?' he said.

'I sent you out for the paper 45 minutes ago!'

'Hold your horses,' said the centipede. 'I'm still putting on my boots.'

Think about it...

What does DNA stand for?

National Dyslexic Association.

Kid too honest

A small child is out shopping with his dad one day, when in the madness of the sales, the two become separated. Knowing what to do, as told a thousand times before by his parents, the boy locates a shop assistant for help. 'Don't worry, little fella...' the assistant happily reassures the boy, 'now, what's daddy like?'

'Well...' the boy thinks for a moment, 'necking lager, shagging mummy and saying "bollocks" a lot.'

Hunter mislays mate

A group of friends go deer hunting, separating into pairs for the day. As a huge thunderstorm rolls in, the group return to the ranch – only to spy Bill returning alone, staggering under a huge buck. 'Where's Harry?' asks another hunter.

'He fainted a couple of miles up the trail,' Bill replies.

'You left him lying there alone and carried the deer back?'

Bill nods. 'It was a tough decision,' he says, 'but I figured no-one is going to steal Harry.'

The super salesman

A man was handing down the family hardware store to his son. 'Now Jim,' the father said, 'just watch as I deal with this customer.'

A man entered the shop and asked for a packet of grass seed. The father handed it to him and asked if he needed a lawn mower, too. 'Why would I need one of those?' said the man.

'Simple,' the father said, 'these grass seeds grow really fast.' The man accepted the deal and left £80 worse off.

Now the son of the shopkeeper took over at the counter. Another customer walked in. 'Could I possibly have a packet of Tampax, please,' he requested.

'Certainly, sir,' the young boy said. 'And will you want a lawn mower with that?'

The stunned man retorted, 'Why?'

'Well, sir,' the boy said, 'you'll be doing bugger all else this weekend, so you might as well cut the grass.'

Q: What's the difference between a light bulb and a pregnant woman?
A: You can unscrew the light bulb.

Mugged by a midget
Standing at a urinal, a man notices that he's being watched by a midget. Although the little fellow is staring at him intently, the man doesn't feel uncomfortable until the midget drags a small stepladder over to him, climbs it, and proceeds to admire his privates at close range. 'Wow!' says the dwarf. 'Those are the nicest balls I've ever seen!'

Surprised and flattered, the man thanks the midget and starts to move away.

But the little man stops him. 'Listen, I know this is a rather strange request,' says the pygmy, 'but would you mind if I touched your balls?'

'Er, I suppose there's no harm in it,' says the gent, glancing around.

Quickly, the midget reaches out, and tightly grips the man's testicles. 'Okay,' he shouts. 'Now hand over your wallet or I'll jump...'

Patient troubled 2
A man walks into a surgery. 'Doctor!' he cries. 'I think I'm shrinking!'

'I'm sorry, sir, there are no appointments at the moment,' says the physician. 'You'll just have to be a little patient.'

The tight-lipped colonel
A crusty old US Air Force Colonel finds himself at a gala event hosted by a local arts college. There is no shortage of young, idealistic ladies in attendance, one of whom approaches the Colonel for conversation. 'Excuse me,' says the student, 'but you seem to be a very serious man. Is something bothering you?'

'No,' the Colonel says, 'I'm just serious by nature, ma'am.'

The young lady looks at his awards and decorations and says, 'It looks like you've seen a lot of action.'

'Yeah, lot of action,' replies the soldier.

'Look,' cries the girl, angry at his taciturn nature. 'You should lighten up a little. Relax. Enjoy yourself.'

When the Colonel replies that he's already relaxed, the girl snaps. 'Stop being so formal!' she shouts. 'I mean, when was the last time you had sex?'

The Colonel looks at her. 'Well, that would be 1955,' he replies.

The girl cackles in triumph. 'That's it,' she laughs. 'You've got a hang-up about sex. You need to chill out! No sex since 1955! Isn't that a little extreme?'

'Oh, I don't know,' says the Colonel, glancing at his watch. 'It's only 2130 now.'

The big question

What have a staff toilet's lavatory seat and a fanny got in common?

They're usually warm and comfortable, except you can't help wondering who's been there before you.

Wash day

A happily married couple decide that instead of mentioning sex in front of their children, they would refer to the dirty deed as 'doing the laundry'. One evening after dinner the husband says to his wife, 'Let's go upstairs and do the laundry.'

'Not now,' the wife replies. 'I've got a headache.'

Later on whilst watching telly, the wife says: 'Darling – let's go do the laundry now.'

'It's okay, honey,' the man replies. 'I only had a half load so I did it earlier by hand.'

Closet economics

A married woman is having an affair, and whenever her lover
comes over, she puts her nine-year-old son in the closet. One
day, when her and her man are hard at it, the woman hears her
husband's car in the driveway – so she shoves her lover in the
closet as well.

'It's dark in here, isn't it?' says her little boy.

'Yes, it is,' the man replies.

'Do you want to buy my cricket ball?' the little boy asks.

'No thanks,' the man replies.

'Oh, I think you do,' the little extortionist continues.

'Okay, okay,' the man replies after considering the position he's in.
'How much?'

'Twenty-five pounds,' the little boy replies.

'Twenty-five quid!' the man repeats incredulously, but has no
choice but to comply.

The following week the lover is back with the woman when she
hears a car in the driveway, and again he finds himself in the closet
with her little boy. 'It's dark in here, isn't it?' the boy starts off.

'Yes, it is,' replies the man.

'Want to buy a cricket glove?' the little boy asks.

'Okay, okay,' the hiding lover responds, acknowledging his
disadvantage. 'How much?'

'Fifty pounds,' the boy replies and the transaction is completed.

The next weekend, the little boy's father says, 'Hey, son. Go get
your cricket gear and we'll get some practice.'

'I can't,' replies the little boy. 'I sold them.'

'How much did you get?' asks the father, expecting to hear the
profit in terms of snails and sweeties.

'Seventy-five pounds,' the little boy says.

'How much? That's extortionate! I'm taking you to the church
right now!' the father explains as he hauls the child away. 'You
must confess your sin and ask for forgiveness.'

At the church the little boy goes into the confessional box,
draws the curtain, sits down and says, 'It's dark in here, isn't it?'

'Don't you start that shit in here,' the priest replies.

The blonde trackers

Two blondes were walking through the woods when they came to some tracks. The first blonde said, 'These look like deer tracks.'

'No,' said the other one, 'they look like moose tracks.'

They argued for quite a while. In fact, they were still arguing when the train hit them.

The Brummie elephant

During his travels through the African jungle, Tarzan discovers an elephants' graveyard, where he spies one of the mighty beasts wandering around. Noticing it's an Indian elephant, Tarzan tries to make conversation. 'So... you're not from around these parts, are you?' he says.

'Actually,' the pachyderm replies, 'I'm from Birmingham Zoo, in England.'

Tarzan is amazed. 'That's a hell of a long way to come to die,' he says.

The elephant looks at him. 'Oh no,' he responds, shaking his huge head. 'I got here yesterday.'

What do you call...

...a judge with no thumbs?

Justice Fingers.

The baby-maker

An attractive young woman goes to the IVF clinic for a course of artificial insemination. The doctor tells her to go behind the screen, take all her clothes off and lie on the examination table.

A few minutes later the doc joins the woman behind the screen and starts removing all of his clothes. At this the woman is obviously a little worried, so she asks what's going on.

'I'm afraid we've run out of the bottled stuff,' the doctor replies. 'You're going to have to have draught.'

Q: What does an accountant do when he's constipated?
A: Works it out with a pencil.

Beaten by Bill
Snow White, Arnold Schwarzenegger and Quasimodo are having a conversation. Snow White says, 'Everybody tells me I am the most beautiful, divine woman that any man has ever laid his eyes on, but how do I know?'

Arnie says, 'I sympathise. Everybody tells me I am the most muscular, hunky man that has ever lived, but how do I know?'

Quasimodo says, 'Everybody tells me I'm the most disgusting, despicable, grotesque creature that has ever roamed the Earth, but how do I know?'

Snow White says, 'Let's go and see the wise man!' So off they trot. Snow White goes in first, and five minutes later she comes out and says, 'It's true. I am the most beautiful, divine woman that any man has ever laid his eyes on.'

Arnie goes in, and five minutes later he comes out and says, 'It's true. I am the most muscular, hunky man that has ever lived.'

Quasimodo goes in, and five minutes later he comes out and says, 'Who's this Bill Gates character, then?'

Magic dad
For his homework, little Johnny is asked to write a story about a member of his family who is utterly amazing. The following day, Johnny returns to class and tells everybody his dad can eat light bulbs!

'Have you any proof, young man?' asks his teacher, somewhat disbelievingly.

'Oh yes, I heard him say it,' replies Johnny. 'He was in the bedroom last night with mum when he said, "If you turn out the light, I'll eat that bloody thing..."'

What does a blonde...

...put behind her ears to make her more attractive?

Her ankles.

The red-headed whore

A red-headed hooker decided she was doing pretty well for herself, so put on a special offer. On the inside of her left thigh she had a tattoo done of Osama Bin Laden, and on the inside of her right thigh one of George Bush, then told her clients that whoever could name these two men could pork her for free.

The next day she went out on the streets and was approached by an Arab gentleman. 'If you can name these two blokes on the inside of my thighs, I'm free,' she told the man as she opened her legs.

'Well, the one on the left is Osama, but I don't know who the other guy is,' he confessed, so he had to pay.

A little later on, an American gentleman came over. She took him to her room, stripped, opened her legs and said, 'Name these two guys and you can have me for free.'

'Well, the one on the right is Dubya, but I haven't a clue who the other guy is...' the man said, so he had to pay.

A couple of days later a German propositioned the hooker. So she took him up to her love nest, stripped and spread her legs on the bed. 'Name these two men and you can shag me for free,' she told him.

The German sat there for a moment before replying, 'I don't know who the guys are on the inside of your thighs, but the one in the middle with big lips and red hair is Boris Becker.'

What do you call...

...a breakdancer with no arms or legs?

Clever dick.

Supersonic!

Two aeronautic workers are painting a Concorde late one night. One man notices that the paint smells like vodka, and dares the other to take a swig. His co-worker does so and realises that the paint has some alcohol effect. Thirty pots later, the two men are pissed and stagger off their separate ways.

The next morning one of the men wakes up with the most incredible hangover. Easing himself out of bed, he finds himself being hurled halfway across the room.

'What the hell!' he exclaims, as he sees wheels on his feet. He skates to the bathroom and looks in the mirror. He has grown a long pointy nose, his shoulders have moved back and his arms have grown long and thin.

At this point the phone rings – it's his drinking buddy from the day before. 'What's going on?' he blurts down the line. 'I've got wheels on my feet, wings instead of arms, and my head looks like a cockpit!'

'I know,' says his mate. 'And here's a word of warning: whatever you do, don't fart. I'm calling from America.'

Q: What did the agoraphobic skinhead say?

A: 'Oi – inside!'

Doctors get fruity

A man and woman are enjoying a few drinks at a bar. They soon realise they're both doctors, and after several more drinks the man decides to try his luck. 'Listen,' he says, 'how about we go back to mine and do the wild thing tonight?'

The woman agrees, and they leave. Back at the house, the woman strips off, walks to the bathroom and starts scrubbing up like she's about to conduct major surgery. Ten minutes later she's done, and she returns to the room where the pair have sex.

'You're a surgeon, aren't you?' says the man just moments after finishing.

'I am,' replies the woman. 'How did you know?'

'It was the scrubbing up before we started,' he says.

'Makes sense,' says the woman. 'You're an anaesthetist, aren't you?'

'Wow,' says the man, 'how on Earth did you know?'

'I didn't feel a thing...'

Bearly funny

A grizzly bear walks into a pub and says, 'Can I have a pint of lager... and a packet of crisps please.'

To which the barman replies, 'Why the big paws?'

Organ confusion

A man walks into his local chiropodist and plants his cock on to the table. 'That's not a foot,' says the chiropodist.

'I know,' replies the man, 'but it's a good 11 inches!'

Golf is like sex

A husband and wife love to go golfing together, but neither of them are playing like they want to, so they decide to take some private lessons. The husband has his lesson first. After the pro sees his swing, he says, 'No, no, no – you're gripping the club way too hard!'

'Well, what should I do?' the man asks.

'Hold the club gently,' the pro replies, 'just like you'd hold your wife's breast.' So the man heeds the advice, takes a swing and pow! He hits the ball 250 yards straight up the fairway.

The man goes back to his wife with the good news, and the next day the wife goes for her first lesson. The pro watches her swing and says, 'No, no, no – you're gripping the club way too hard.'

'What can I do?' asks the wife.

'Hold the club gently, just like you'd hold your husband's penis.'

The wife listens carefully to the pro's advice, takes a swing, and thump! The ball goes straight down the fairway... for about 15 feet.

'That was great,' the pro says. 'Now take the club out of your mouth and try it again.'

The stutterer's complaint

After years of stuttering, Jim finally goes to the doctor to see if he can be cured. The doctor thoroughly examines him, and finally asks him to drop his pants – whereupon Jim's massive cock thuds onto the table. 'Hmm,' says the physician. 'I see the problem – because of gravity, your penis's weight is putting a strain on the vocal chords in your neck.'

'B-b-but wh-what c-c-can b-be d-d-done ab-b-bout i-it?' asks Jim. The doctor smiles.

'Don't worry. Modern surgery can work miracles. We can replace your dick with one of normal size and the stuttering will instantly disappear.'

Convinced, Jim agrees to the op – and, as the doctor promised, his stuttering completely stops afterwards. Three months later, however, he returns to the doctor's surgery. 'Doc, I'm still grateful for what you did,' he says, 'but my wife really misses my big dick. So I've decided I'll live with stuttering for the rest of my life, and get my old dick back.'

The doctor shakes his head, sadly. 'Hey,' he says, 'A d-d-d-deal's a d-d-deal.'

Blondes in space

An experimental shuttle mission blasts off for the moon with just three crew members on board: two monkeys and a blonde. As they reach orbit, Mission Control radios the craft. 'Monkey No 1! Monkey No 1! Go to the control console and complete your launch checks.' Quickly, the ape swings over and sits down to follow the instructions: he releases the pressure in the payload bay, lowers the temperature in engine four and balances the oxygen ratio in the reactors.

Moments later, Mission Control calls again. 'Monkey No 2! Monkey No 2! Go to the control console and complete your orbital tasks.'

The primate knuckles over and does what he's told – launching a key weather satellite and analysing solar radiation readings.

An hour into the journey, Mission Control calls again: 'Woman!

Please go to the console.' As she sits at the blinking screen, the speaker barks again. 'Please complete your...'

'I know...' she moans. 'Just feed the monkeys, don't touch anything.'

Multiple birth

A young lady in a maternity ward is asked by the midwife if she would like her husband to be present at the birth. 'I'm afraid I don't have a husband,' she replies.

'Okay – do you have a boyfriend?' asks the midwife.

'No, no boyfriend either.'

'Do you have a partner then?'

'No, I'm unattached, I'll be having my baby on my own.'

After the birth the midwife again speaks to the young woman. 'You have a healthy bouncing baby girl, but I must warn you before you see her that the baby is black.'

'Well,' replies the girl. 'I was very down on my luck, with no money and nowhere to live, and so I accepted a job in a porno movie. The lead man was black.'

'I see,' says the midwife. 'I'm sorry that I have to ask you these awkward questions, but I must also tell you that the baby has blonde hair.'

'Well yes,' the girl replies. 'You see, there was this Swedish guy also involved in the movie. I needed the money – what else could I do?'

'Oh, I'm sorry,' the midwife says. 'That's really none of my business. I hate to pry further, but your baby has Oriental eyes.'

'Well yes,' continues the girl. 'I was incredibly hard up and there was a Chinese man also in the movie. I really had no choice.'

At this the midwife again apologises, collects the baby and presents her to the girl, who immediately gives the baby a slap on the bum. The baby starts crying and the mother exclaims, 'Thank God for that!'

'What do you mean?' asks the midwife, shocked.

'Well,' says the girl, extremely relieved, 'I had this horrible feeling that the little bastard was going to bark.'

What's in a name?

A bloke is on an aeroplane when he sees a beautiful woman sitting across the aisle. He notices that she's reading a magazine article about penis size, so he decides he'd better introduce himself. He walks across and says, 'What you reading?'

'Well,' she says, 'it says here that Native Americans have the thickest cocks of all men. And it also says that Polish men have the longest cocks of all men. Oh, I'm sorry, I didn't get your name...'

'Tonto Kowalski,' he smiles.

Sex education

Sammy came running into the house and asked, 'Mummy, can little girls have babies?'

'No,' said his mum, 'of course not.'

So he ran back outside. 'It's okay,' his mum heard him say to the girl next door. 'We can play that game again!'

Fly killer on ball

A lady walks into the kitchen where her husband is busy killing flies with the swatter. 'Any luck?' she asks.

'A bit,' he replies, 'I've killed three males and two females.'

Intrigued, she asks how he could possibly know the sex.

'Easy,' he responds, 'three were sitting on my beer can and the other two were on the phone.'

Did you hear about...

... the dyslexic pimp?

He bought a warehouse.

Mutt enjoys flick

A man visits his local cinema. Throughout the film, he notices that a young chap in front has brought his dog along – and what's more the hound is laughing and crying at all the relevant places. The film finishes and, gripped by curiosity, the man wanders over to the pair.

'I couldn't help but notice,' he says to the chap, 'but your dog laughed at all the funny bits and cried at all the sad bits... it's amazing! I just can't believe it!'

'I can't believe it either,' replies the man, 'he hated the book.'

What does a tornado...

...have in common with a white trash divorce?

Someone's always losing a trailer.

The prodigal sons

Four middle-aged men are telling stories in a bar. While one has gone for a piss, the first guy says, 'I was worried that my son was going to be a loser, because his first proper job was washing cars on a garage forecourt. But it turns out he got a break, they made him a salesman, and he sold so many motors that he bought the dealership! In fact, he's so successful that he just gave his best friend a new Mercedes for his birthday.'

The second man says, 'I was worried about my son too, because he started out tidying gardens for a lettings agency. Turns out he got a break, they made him a salesman, and he eventually bought the firm. In fact he's so successful that he just gave his best friend a new house for his birthday.'

The third guy says, 'I hear what you're saying. My son started out sweeping floors in a bank. He got a break, they made him a trader, and now he owns the company. In fact, he's so rich that he just gave his best friend £1m in shares for his birthday.'

The fourth bloke comes back from the toilet. The first three explain that they are telling stories about their sons, so he says, 'Well, I'm embarrassed to admit that my son is a major disappointment. He started out as a hairdresser – and is still a hairdresser after 15 years! In fact I just found out that he's gay and has several boyfriends. But I try to look on the bright side: his boyfriends just bought him a new Mercedes, a new house and £1m in shares for his birthday.'

Why did the...

...leprechaun wear two condoms?

To be sure, to be sure.

The three ducks

A farmer walks into a pub with his three favourite ducks. He says to the barman, 'I'll have a pint of Guinness please.'

So the barman starts to pour the farmer's pint. Whilst it's settling the farmer says to the barman, 'If I show you a trick, can I have my pint for free.'

The barman looks at the farmer and says, 'Well, it'll have to be something special for a free pint.'

'Just go and talk to my three ducks and you'll see how special it is,' says the farmer. So the barman walks over to the ducks.

'Hello, first duck, what's your name?'

'My name's Stanley,' replies the first duck.

'And what have you been up to today, Stanley?'

'It's been raining all day and I've been jumping in and out of puddles. It's been great.'

'And what's your name, second duck?' asks the barman.

'My name is Jeremy,' replies the second duck.

'And how are you, Jeremy?'

'Fine, thank you – it's been raining all day and I've been jumping in and out of puddles.'

The barman approaches the third duck, noticing that he doesn't look as happy as Stanley and Jeremy. 'Hello, third duck,' he says. 'And what's your name?'

'Puddles,' says the duck. 'Don't ask.'

MD makes choice

To cut costs, a managing director is forced to sack an employee. After much thought, he narrows it down to just two people: young Debbie and young Jack.

Both have near identical performance records and it's a tough decision. After hours of deliberation, he's still undecided, so he makes it simple on himself. The first person to the water cooler on Monday morning gets the sack.

Monday arrives and Debbie walks in with a monstrous hangover. After a few minutes she's at the water cooler. Slowly, the MD wanders over: 'Debbie, I'm so sorry,' he says, 'I've never had to do this before but due to powers beyond my control, I've got to lay you or Jack off.'

'I see,' says Deborah,

'could you jack off then? I've an awful headache this morning...'

Q: What's white and fluffy and lives in trees?

A: A meringue-utan.

The clumsy lumberjack

Sam and John were out chopping wood when John cut his arm off. Sam wrapped the severed arm in a plastic bag, then drove it and his bleeding buddy to the nearest surgeon. 'You're in luck!' the surgeon exclaimed. 'I'm an expert at reattaching limbs – come back in four hours.'

When Sam returned the surgeon said, 'I got it done faster than I expected to. John's down the pub.' Overjoyed, Sam ran to the pub, where John was fit and well and playing darts.

A few weeks later Sam and John were out again, and this time John chopped his leg off. Sam put the leg in a plastic bag and took it and John back to the surgeon. 'Legs are a little tougher,' said the medic. 'Come back in six hours.'

Sam returned at the allotted time and the surgeon said, 'I finished early – John's down the park.' Sam headed off and there was John, playing football, good as new.

A few weeks later, John had a terrible accident and cut his head off. Sam put the head in a plastic bag and drove it and the rest of John to the surgeon. 'Heads are really tough,' said the bone-cutter. 'Come back in 12 hours.'

When Sam returned, he was met by a glum-faced surgeon. 'I'm sorry,' he said, 'John died.'

'I understand,' said Sam, 'heads must be tough.'

'No, the surgery went fine,' explained the doc. 'But he suffocated in that plastic bag.'

What do you call...

...a hotel lobby full of chess experts bragging about how good they are?

Chess nuts boasting by the hotel foyer.

The sailor's parcel

Just after getting married, a sailor is informed his next naval posting will be a remote Pacific island. A few weeks after arriving, he begins to miss his new wife, and so writes her a letter. 'My love,' he writes, 'we will be apart for a year – far too long. Already I'm missing you and there's really not much to do here. Worse, we're constantly surrounded by young, nubile native girls. Do you think if I had a hobby of some kind I would not be tempted?'

A few weeks later, a parcel arrives from his wife, containing a harmonica and a note, saying, 'Why don't you learn to play this?'

Several months later, his tour of duty ends and he rushes back to his wife. 'Darling,' he cries, 'I can't wait to get you into bed so that we can make passionate love!'

The wife frowns at him. 'First things first,' she replies. 'I want to see you play that harmonica.'

The holy round

God and Saint Peter are playing golf, and it's level pegging as they reach the 18th hole. God steps up to the tee and belts his ball. It hooks wide into the trees... but a few seconds later a rabbit runs out onto the fairway with God's ball in its mouth, attempting to eat it.

While the rabbit is chewing at the ball, a hawk flies overhead and swoops down on the bunny, picking it up with its claws and flying back up again. From a hut just inside the woods runs a hunter, who loads his weapon, aims and shoots the hawk out of the sky. The hawk's crumpled body falls out of the sky, still holding onto the rabbit, and lands right next to the 18th hole. The ball rolls out of the deceased rabbit's mouth to give God a hole in one.

'Are we here to play golf,' asks Saint Peter, 'or are You just going to fuck around?'

On top of the tower

Three pissed-up blokes stood on top of the Eiffel tower. The first one said, 'I bet you I could jump off this tower and bounce all the way back up.'

The second bloke said that it was impossible and taunted the first to have a go. With that the first bloke leapt off the tower, fell to the bottom and bounced back up.

The second bloke was amazed, and said he'd try it for himself. So he leapt from the tower... and fell to his death on the cobbles below. With that the third bloke turned to the first and said, 'You're a right bastard when you're pissed, Superman.'

How do you make...

...five pounds of fat look good?

Put a nipple on it.

Ask a silly question...

After getting a job at the income tax office, a young financial hotshot is given his first assignment: auditing a rabbi. Arriving at the synagogue, he decides to have some fun. 'Rabbi,' he begins. 'What do you do with the drippings from the candles?'

'Well,' the elderly rabbi replies, startled, 'we send them to the candle factory, and every once in a while they send us a free candle.'

'And what do you do with the crumbs from your table?' asks the taxman.

The rabbi looks at him, surprised. 'Well, we send them to the matzo ball factory, and every once in a while they send us a free box of matzo balls.'

Nodding, the young hotshot turns to his final question. 'So tell me,' he asks, steepling his fingers, 'what do you do with the foreskins from circumcisions?'

By now, the rabbi's had enough. 'Well, we send them to the income tax office,' he answers patiently. 'And every once in a while they send us a little prick like you.'

How do you get...
...a one-handed Irishman out of a tree?

Wave to him.

The newlyweds' rules
Two newlyweds are in their honeymoon suite, when the groom decides to let the bride know where she stands right from the start of the marriage. He proceeds to take off his trousers and throw them at her. 'Put those on,' he says.

The bride replies, 'I can't wear your trousers.'

He replies, 'And don't forget it! I'll always wear the trousers in this family!'

So the bride takes her knickers off and throws them at him with the same request, 'Try those on!'

'I can't get into your knickers,' he says.

'And you never bloody will,' she snorts, 'if you don't change your attitude.'

Why can't Miss Piggy...
...count to 70?

Because every time she gets to 69 she gets a frog in her throat.

A busy day in Heaven
Three men were standing in line to get into Heaven. It had been a pretty busy day, however, so Saint Peter had to tell the first one: 'Heaven's getting pretty close to full and I've been asked to admit only people who have had particularly horrible deaths. What's your story?'

The first man replied: 'For a while I've suspected my wife has been cheating on me, so today I came home early and tried to catch her red-handed. As I came into our 25th-floor flat, I could tell something was wrong, but all my searching around didn't reveal where this other guy could have been hiding. Finally, I went out to the balcony, and sure enough there was this man hanging off the railing, 25 floors above ground! By now I was really mad, so I started beating him and kicking him, but wouldn't you know it, he wouldn't fall off. So finally I went back into my apartment and got a hammer and starting hammering on his fingers. Of course, he couldn't stand that for long, so he let go and fell – but he landed in the bushes, stunned but okay.

I couldn't stand it any more, so I ran into the kitchen, grabbed the fridge and threw it over the edge, where it landed on him, killing him instantly. But all the stress and anger got to me. I had a heart attack and died there on the balcony.'

'That sounds like a pretty bad day to me,' said Peter, and let the man in.

The second man came up and Peter explained to him about Heaven being nearly full, and again asked for his story. 'It's been a very strange day,' he began. 'You see, I live on the 26th floor of a building, and every morning I do my exercises out on my balcony. Well, this morning I must have slipped or something, because I fell over the edge. But I got lucky, and caught the railing of the balcony on the floor below me. I knew I couldn't hang on for very long, when suddenly this man burst onto the balcony. I thought I was saved, but he started beating me and kicking me!

I held on for as long as I could, until he ran into the flat, grabbed a hammer and started pounding on my hands. Finally I just let go, but again I got lucky and fell into the bushes, stunned but all right. Just when I was thinking I was going to be okay, this refrigerator comes falling out of the sky and crushes me instantly, and now I'm here.'

Once again, Peter had to concede that that sounded like a pretty horrible death, and in he went.

Then the third man came to the front of the line, and again the whole process was repeated.

'Picture this,' said the third man. 'I'm hiding naked inside a refrigerator...'

What have Arsenal and a three-pin plug...
...got in common?

They're both useless in Europe.

Why do doctors...
...spank babies when they're born?
    To knock the dicks off the dumb ones.

Quickie pays off handsomely

A teenage girl confesses to her mother that she's missed her period for two months running. They immediately purchase a home pregnancy test, and the result's confirmed – she's up the duff. 'Bring me the pig who did this to you!' screams her incandescent mother.

'I want to see him, now!'

The girl quickly makes a phone call to her lover, and half an hour later a gleaming, brand new Ferrari pulls up outside the house. Out steps a mature and distinguished gentleman, handsome and impeccably dressed. He enters the house and sits down in the living room with the father, mother and the girl.

'Good afternoon,' he politely greets the family, 'your daughter has informed me of the situation. I am unable to marry her due to my personal family circumstances, but rest assured, I'll take full responsibility. If a girl is born, I'll bequeath her three of my shops, two townhouses, a beach house and a £1m bank account. If it's a boy, my legacy will be two factories and a £2m bank account. If it's twins, a single factory and £500,000 each. However, if there is a miscarriage...'

The father, breaking his stunned silence, places a hand firmly on the man's shoulder: 'You'll shag her again, right?'

Q: Why couldn't Dracula's wife get to sleep?
A: Because of his coffin.

Should have listened

A secretary answers the phone in a busy office. 'Good morning, Nottingham Parachute Club,' she says.

There's a sharp intake of breath. 'Excuse me,' says a man on the other end of the line, obviously startled. 'But don't you mean the Nottingham Prostitute Club?'

'Oh no, sir,' laughs the secretary, 'it's definitely a parachute club.'

'Damn!' says the man. 'Last week your salesman called and signed me up for two jumps a week.'

Did you hear about...

...the new blonde paint?

It's cheap and it spreads easily.

A man walks into a bar...

...with an ostrich and a cat. The man buys the first round, the ostrich buys the second round, but when it's the cat's round the moggie refuses to pay.

The bartender asks the man what the problem is. 'I met a genie and he gave me one wish,' explains the man, sourly. 'So I wished for a bird with long legs and a tight pussy.'

Did you hear about...

...the guy with five dicks?

His pants fit him like a glove.

A wig and a turd...

...walk into a bar, where the wig orders two pints of lager. When the barman refuses to serve him, the wig asks why.

'Because you're off your head,' replies the barman, 'and your mate's steaming.'

Why does an elephant...

...have four feet?

Because six inches isn't long enough.

Q: How do you castrate a priest?

A: Kick the altar boy in the back of the head.

The potato daughters

One evening, the women in the Potato Head family were getting dinner ready – mother Potato Head and her three daughters. Midway through the preparation of the meal, the eldest daughter spoke up. 'Mother?' she said. 'I have an announcement to make.'

'And what might that be?' said mother, seeing the obvious excitement in her eldest daughter's eyes.

'Well,' replied the daughter, 'I'm getting married!'

The other Potato daughters squealed with surprise as Ma Potato exclaimed, 'Married! That's wonderful! And who are you marrying, eldest daughter?'

'I'm marrying a Russet!'

'A Russet!' replied mother Potato with pride. 'Oh, a Russet is a fine tater, a fine tater indeed!'

As they got back into preparing dinner, the middle daughter spoke up. 'Mother? I, too, have an announcement.'

'And what might that be?' encouraged mother Potato.

The middle daughter paused, then said with conviction, 'I, too, am getting married!'

'You, too!' mother Potato said with joy. 'That's wonderful! Twice the good news in one evening! And who are you marrying, middle daughter?'

'I'm marrying a King Edward!' beamed the middle daughter.

'A King Edward!' said mother Potato with joy. 'Oh, a King Edward is a fine tater, a fine tater indeed!'

Once again the kitchen came alive with laughter and excited plans for the future, when the youngest Potato daughter interrupted. 'Mother? Umm... I, too, have an announcement to make.'

'Yes?' said mother Potato with great anticipation.

'Well,' said the youngest Potato daughter with the same sheepish grin as her sisters before her, 'I hope this doesn't come as a shock to you, but I am getting married as well!'

'That's wonderful. Who are you marrying?' asked mother Potato Head.

'I'm marrying John Motson!' the youngest Potato daughter replied. 'John Motson!' shrieked mother Potato. 'But he's just a common tater!'

How do you call...
...all the squirrels in the world?
'Calling all squirrels, calling all squirrels...'

Refugees assisted
A driver spies a refugee eating grass along a stretch of motorway. He pulls over. 'Hey, don't eat that,' he shouts, 'it's filthy! Full of dog shit, road grit, all sorts. If you're hungry, come along home with me!'

The refugee looks up and replies: 'I have a wife also...'

'No problem,' says the man, 'bring her as well, the more the merrier!'

'I also have eight children, two grandchildren and many cousins,' the refugee continues.

'Now wait a minute,' shouts the man, readying his engine, 'just how big do you think my bloody lawn is!'

The three hookers
Three tarts are sitting up at the bar. The first prossie says, 'I bet you a fiver I can put my three fingers up my fanny.'

The second hooker pipes up, 'I've had so much sex, I bet I can put a whole fist up mine.'

The third says nothing and simply slides down the bar-stool.

The thirsty grasshopper
A grasshopper walks into a pub and asks for a pint. As the landlord is pulling the beer he says to the grasshopper, 'We've got a cocktail named after you here.'

'What?' says the grasshopper. 'You've got a cocktail called Steve?'

Did you hear about...
...the dumb terrorist who tried to blow up a bus?

He burnt his lips on the exhaust.

The mystery of the tunnel
An Irishman, an Englishman and Claudia Schiffer were sitting in a train carriage when the loco plunged into a tunnel. As it was an old-style train, there were no lights in the carriages, and it went completely dark. Then there was a kissing noise, followed by the sound of a really loud slap.

When the train came out of the tunnel, Claudia Schiffer and the Irishman were sitting as if nothing had happened. The Englishman, however, had his hand against his reddening cheek.

The Englishman was thinking: 'The Irish fella must have kissed Claudia Schiffer, but she missed him and slapped me instead.'

Claudia Schiffer was thinking: 'The English fella must have tried to kiss me and actually kissed the Irishman, and got slapped for it.'

And the Irishman was thinking: 'This is great. The next time the train goes through a tunnel, I'll make another kissing noise and slap that English bastard again.'

New shoe range
Have you heard about 'Dike', the new running shoe for lesbians?

It has an extra long tongue and only takes one finger to get off.

The oldsters' breakfast
An elderly couple had been married for 50 years. They were sitting at the breakfast table one morning when the old gentleman said to his wife, 'Just think, darling, we've been married for half a century.'

'Yes, dear,' she replied. 'Just think, 50 years ago we were sitting here at this breakfast table together.'

'I know,' the old man said. 'And we were probably sitting here naked, too.'

'Well,' granny snickered, 'what do you say? Should we get naked again?' Whereupon the pair stripped to the buff and sat back at the table.

'How does that feel?' asked the man.

'You know, sweetheart,' the little old lady replied, breathlessly, 'my nipples are as hot for you today as they were 50 years ago.'

'I'm not surprised,' replied gramps. 'One's in your coffee and the other's in your porridge.'

Twice is nice

Two old men are comparing their sex lives. 'I can still do it twice!' claims the first man.

'Which time do you enjoy the most?' inquires the second.

'I think the winter,' he replies.

What's the difference...

...between a bumpy road and a prostitute?

A bumpy road knackers your tyres...

The quick thinking explorer

Two polar explorers are walking in the Arctic when all of a sudden a ferocious polar bear comes charging towards them. 'Oh shit!' says the first explorer, panicking. 'What are we going to do?'

The second explorer says nothing, but calmly takes off his backpack, puts on a sweat-band and shorts, takes off his snow-shoes and slips on a pair of trainers. The first explorer turns to him and gabbles, 'You're mad! There's no way you'll outrun a polar bear!'

'You're right,' replies the second man. 'But I'll sure outrun you.'

Q: How do you blind a woman?

A: Put a windshield in front of her.

The three nutters

The Queen visits a mental hospital. Walking into the first ward, she's greeted by a patient sitting up in bed. With his left hand he seems to be grabbing something from the air.

'What are you doing, young man?' asks Her Maj.

'I'm taking the stars from the sky!' replies the patient.

Moving swiftly on, the Queen walks over to the second patient. He too is sitting bolt upright in bed, but this time he seems to be inserting something into the air.

'What are you doing, young man?' asks the regent, politely.

'I'm putting the stars back in the sky!' babbles the second patient.

Chastened, she reaches the third patient. He's sitting up, gripping an imaginary steering wheel and making high-speed noises.

'And what exactly are you doing?' asks the Queen, wearily.

'I'm trying to get away from those two nutters,' the patient gabbles. 'They're mental!'

The absent brothers

An Irishman walks into a pub and orders three pints of Guinness, taking a sip out of each pint in turn. The barman says to him, 'A pint goes flat after I pull it – it'd be better if you bought one at a time.'

The Irishman replies, 'Well, I have two brothers, one in America and the other in Australia. We promised we'd all drink this way to remember the days we supped together.'

Over the weeks the Irishman becomes a regular and always buys his drinks three at a time, until one day, when he orders just two pints. The other drinkers fall silent.

'I don't want to intrude on your grief,' says the barman when the Irishman comes back for a second round, 'but I wanted to say I'm sorry about your loss.'

'Oh, no,' says the Irishman, 'my brothers are fit and well. It's just that I've given up drinking.'

Thanks for the advice

Barely 20 minutes after teeing off, a woman stumbles into the golf course clubhouse, grimacing in pain. 'What happened?' the club pro asks.

'I got stung by a bee,' she replies.

'Where?'

'Between the first and second holes.'

'Hmmm,' murmurs the pro. 'Sounds like your stance was a little too wide.'

Did you hear about the crab...

...who went to the disco? He pulled a muscle.

Footballer enjoys welcome

After finally negotiating a professional contract, a striker arrives for his first match at his new Premiership club. 'I'll tell you what,' says the coach. 'As it's your first game, you can play for 45 minutes then I'll pull you off at half-time.'

'That's not bad,' the lad replies. 'I only got half an orange at my old place.'

The dyslexic redneck

In a tiny shack in Louisiana, Mary-Jo has gone into labour – and the baby is coming fast. Her husband Billy Bob dials 911 and asks for help. 'Certainly,' says the emergency operator, 'we'll send the paramedics straight out to you. Just tell me where you live.'

Billy Bob thinks for a second. 'On Eucalyptus Drive,' he drawls.

'Can you spell that for me?' asks the operator.

There's a long pause. 'Tell ya what,' Billy Bob says, furrowing his brow, 'I'll drag her onto Oak Street. Pick her up from there.'

The Barbie pricelist

A man walks into Toys-R-Us and says to the sales assistant, 'Could you show me your Barbie dolls, please?'

'Certainly, sir,' she says. 'Here, we have Fashion Barbie at £15.95, Vacation Barbie, also £15.95, Housewife Barbie – that's £15.95 too – and Divorcee Barbie, at £215.95.'

The man is astonished. 'Why's Divorcee Barbie so much?' he asks. 'She looks the same as the others to me.'

'Well, sir,' says the assistant, 'that's because Divorcee Barbie comes complete with Ken's car, Ken's house, Ken's furniture, Ken's dog...'

Q: What does a postcard from a blonde on holiday say?

A: 'Having a great time. Where am I?'

The life of Jesus

A Sunday School teacher was concerned that his young students might be a little confused about the life of Jesus Christ. He wanted to make sure they understood that the birth of Jesus occurred a long time ago, so he asked his class, 'Where is Jesus today?'

Little Stevie raised his hand and said, 'He's in Heaven.'

Mary was called on and answered, 'He's in my heart.'

Johnny, waving his hand furiously, blurted out, 'I know! I know! He's in our bathroom!'

The whole class went very quiet, looked at the teacher and waited for a response. The teacher was at a loss for a few very long seconds. Finally, he gathered his wits and asked Johnny how he knew this.

'Well, every morning my dad gets up, bangs on the bathroom door and yells, "Jesus Christ! Are you still in there?"'

OJ's collection

A man is driving along the freeway in Los Angeles. As he reaches the downtown area he finds himself in the middle of a massive traffic jam, blocking up five different freeways and sending lines of cars back for miles in all directions. After a while, he notices a guy walking from car to car down the freeway, stopping and talking to people.

When the guy reaches him he rolls down his window and says, 'Hey! What's causing all this delay?'

The pedestrian says, 'Well, you're not going to believe this, but OJ Simpson has sat down in the middle of the freeway intersection up there, and he's totally distraught. He says there's no way he can ever pay the $35 million he owes the Goldmans and the Browns, so he's threatened to douse himself in gasoline and set himself alight if people don't give money sufficient to cover the cost of the judgement. I've taken up a collection to try to end the traffic jam.'

'How much have you got so far?' asks the motorist.

'About ten gallons.'

Kids – bless 'em

A little boy walks into the bathroom as his dad is just about to get into the shower. He looks up and points at his father's waist and says, 'Daddy, daddy, what's that?'

To which his father replies, 'Oh, er... that's my hedgehog, son.'

The kid thinks for a moment, then says, 'Wow! He's got a big cock, hasn't he?'

What do you give a man...

...who's got everything?

Penicillin.

Sporting condition

While out jogging in the park, a young chap happens upon a brand new tennis ball. Seeing nobody around to claim it, he slips it into the pocket of his shorts and continues on.

A few roads from home, he reaches a pedestrian crossing. Waiting for the traffic to stop, a young lady standing next to him can't help but notice the considerable bulge in his shorts. 'Oh my,' she gasps, 'whatever is that in your shorts?'

'Tennis ball,' replies the man, still breathless from exercise.

'Oh, poor you,' sympathises the woman. 'I once had tennis elbow.'

What do you call...

...a Teletubbie that's been burgled ?

Tubbie.

Fergie accosted

Sir Alex Ferguson is a guest of honour at the Miss World contest. During the interval, the judges and contestants are mingling over drinks when Sir Alex is besieged by the voluptuous Miss Venezuela. 'Sir Alex, I admire your management skills and all you have achieved and the trophies you have won,' the beauty says. Sir Alex is flattered, then bowled over as the Venezuelan belle lowers a shoulder strap, revealing her left breast. 'Would you autograph this please?'

Bemused, Sir Alex nevertheless duly obliges, makes his excuses and wanders off. Moments later, the equally beautiful Miss Croatia approaches him. 'Sir Alex,' she blushes, 'I so admire the way you play mind games with your opponents even before you meet them on the pitch.' Acknowledging the compliment, Sir Alex is about to thank the girl when she lowers a strap and presents her right breast to him: 'Would you be so kind as to autograph this?'

Sir Alex again obliges, mumbles an excuse and makes for the bar – where Miss Argentina taps him on the shoulder. 'Oh, Sir Alex, how I admire the way you motivate your players and shield them like they're your own sons,' she gushes. But before Sir Alex can do or say anything, the South American ups her dress, pulls aside her knickers and asks, 'Would you do me the honour of signing this?'

'You must be joking, hen!' laughs Sir Alex. 'The last time I signed an Argentinian twat, it cost me £28 million!'

The magic diddle

A little boy is casually walking along the upstairs landing when he happens to see his older sister's door partially open. Glancing inside he notices his sister moaning in the throes of ecstasy whilst fingering herself, uttering the words, 'I want a man!' over and over again.

The little boy hastily goes downstairs to watch television, slightly confused by the incident.

A couple of hours later he's disturbed by groaning and grunting noises from the landing. He dashes upstairs and sees through the crack in his sister's door that her boyfriend is banging her senseless.

On seeing this, the little boy dashes into the bathroom, pulls down his kecks and starts pulling away, muttering to himself, 'I want a bike, I want a bike!'

Pirate in the wars

A pirate walks into a tavern. 'Haven't seen you in a while,' says the barman, 'what happened? You look terrible!'

'What do you mean?' replies the pirate.

'Well, you never had the wooden leg before,' says the barman.

'Oh... we were in a battle and I got hit on the knee by a cannonball,' says the pirate.

'Well what about that hook?' asks the barman.

'Another battle,' says the pirate. 'Enemy captain came at me with a sword and cut it clean off. So I got this hook.'

'I see,' says the barman, 'and the eye-patch?'

'A bird flew over and shat in my eye,' replies the pirate.

'You're kidding!' roars the bartender. 'You lost an eye from a bird shitting in it?'

'Not quite,' says the pirate. 'It was my first day with the hook.'

What do you have...

...if you've got a green ball in one hand and a green ball in the other?

Complete control of Kermit the frog.

Child ponders human biology

A young boy was feeling inquisitive. 'Mum, is it true that people can be taken apart like machines?'

'Of course not, sweetie,' she replied, 'where on Earth did you hear such nonsense?'

'From daddy,' said the boy. 'He was talking to someone on the phone the other day and said he was screwing the arse off his secretary.'

Moscow table manners...

What does a Russian use to wipe his mouth after dinner?

A Soviet.

Fear the pretzel!

It's the final of the wrestling at the Olympics, and the field has been narrowed down to a Russian and an American competing for the gold medal. Before the bout, the American wrestler's trainer gives him a pep talk. 'Don't forget all the research we've done on this Russian,' says the trainer. 'The guy's never lost a match because of this "pretzel" hold he has. Whatever you do, don't let him get you in this hold! If he does, you're finished.'

The American wrestler nods in agreement, and the match begins. The combatants warily circle each other, looking for an opening, when all of a sudden the Russian lunges forward, grabs the American and wraps him up in the dreaded pretzel hold! A sigh of disappointment goes up from the crowd while the trainer buries his face in his hands – he knows all is lost.

Suddenly there's a scream, followed by a cheer from the crowd. The trainer raises his eyes just in time to see the Russian flying up in the air. His back hits the mat with a thud; the American weakly flops on top of him, gets the pin and wins the match.

The trainer's astounded! Rushing forward with a towel he throws it over his boy, then hisses, 'How did you ever get out of that hold? No-one's ever done it before!'

'Well, I was ready to give up,' the wrestler explains, 'but at the last moment I opened my eyes and saw this pair of balls hanging right in front of my face! I thought I had nothing to lose, so with my last ounce of strength I stretched out my neck and chomped down on those plums just as hard as I could.'

'And that worked!' says the trainer.

'Oh yes,' replies the wrestler. 'You'd be amazed how strong you get when you bite your own balls.'

The drowning presidents

Richard Nixon, Jimmy Carter and Bill Clinton are on the Titanic. When it starts to sink, Carter yells, 'Quick! Save the women and children first!'

Nixon shouts, 'Fuck the women and children!'

To which Bill replies, 'Do we have time?'

Library causes pain

A man is horribly run over by a mobile library. The van screeches to a halt, the man still screaming in agony with his limbs torn apart. The driver's door opens, a woman steps out, runs over to the victim, leans down and whispers, 'Ssshhhhh...'

Q: What's an Australian's idea of a balanced diet?

A: A pint in each hand.

Doc tests oldies

The senior house doctor is doing his weekly rounds at the nursing home. As usual, he conducts a memory test with three elderly residents, asking the first lady what three times three is.

'Hmm....' thinks the old girl, 'ah, I know – 274!'

The doctor sighs, shakes his head and proceeds to the next woman in the line. 'Can you tell me what three times three is, please?' he asks.

'Sure can!' says the lady, 'Tuesday!'

The doc moves on. 'Okay,' he says, finally arriving at the third patient, 'three times three – what's the answer?'

'Nine,' comes the reply, sharp as a knife.

'Blimey!' says the doc, impressed, 'how did you arrive at the answer?'

'Easy,' she replies, 'I just subtracted 274 from Tuesday.'

What do you call...

...a condom strolling down the street?

Johnny Walker.

The prying priest

A priest in a small village is walking down the street one evening when he hears music and laughter coming from one of the houses. He decides to knock on the door and find out what's going on. 'Hello there, Father,' replies an old lady. 'And how are you on this fine evening ?'

'Actually I was wondering what was going on,' says the reverend. 'Are you having a party ?'

'Yes, we are,' says the biddy. 'Perhaps you'd like to join in? All the young folk in the village are here playing a game.'

'And what game is that?' asks the priest.

'Well,' goes the lady, 'all the boys get naked and so do all the girls.'

'My God!' shrieks the priest. 'What kind of party is this?'

'I'm not finished,' explains the old bag. 'Then the girls all put on blindfolds and have to go up to each boy, feel his bits and pieces and guess which boy it is.'

'Stop, stop!' screams the priest. 'I can't hear any more! Do you really believe that I would be involved in such an event?'

'Well actually, Father, your name has come up a few times...'

Two - stroke penalty

A man staggers into an A&E with a golf club wrapped around his throat. Concerned, the doctor asks what happened. 'Well,' begins the man, 'I was having a quiet round of golf with the wife when she sliced her ball into a field full of cows. We went to look for it and while I was rooting around I noticed one of these cows had something small and white in its backside. I walked over, lifted up its tail and, sure enough, there was the wife's golf ball lodged right in the middle of its arse... and that's when I made my mistake.'

'What did you do?' asks the doc.

'I yelled to my wife: "Hey! This looks like yours!"'

Blonde pipes up

A class of aspiring female psychiatrists attend their first lecture, on emotional extremes. 'To establish some parameters,' says the professor, 'what is the opposite of joy?'

'Sadness,' replies a brunette.

'And the opposite of depression?'

'Elation,' blurts out another brunette.

'Very good. And you, young lady,' he says, pointing to a blonde at the back, 'what about the opposite of woe?'

'Easy,' she says, 'giddy up!'

How do you spot...

...a blind man in a nudist camp?

It's not hard.

The first day at school

Four-year-old Billy is about to start his first day at school. Just before he leaves, however, his dad goes up to him and tells him, 'Right, Billy – since you are now starting school, from now on you're to speak only proper English. No more "choo-choo train" or childish phrases like that.'

Billy agrees and makes his way to school. A few hours later, the lad arrives back home to be greeted by his dad. 'Hi, son! How was your first day at school?'

'Okay,' Billy replies.

'Did you do anything exciting?' says his dad.

'Yes, I read a book.'

'Well done!' his dad exclaims. 'And what book did you read?'

'Winnie the Shit.'

The sweary tots

Little Timmy and Little Bobby go to visit their grandmother in the country. They've been brought up in a fairly ill-disciplined household and are prone to swearing. Anyway, after about a solid week of cursing and swearing their grandmother can't take it any more, so she goes to see her friend Maude to get some advice.

'What can I do about them swearing?' says the grandmother.

'As far as I'm concerned there is only really one thing you can do,' says Maude. 'Next time they swear, just hit 'em good and hard and they won't do it again.'

'I can't do that!' says grandma, shocked at the thought. 'They're my grandchildren!'

'Look,' says Maude, 'It'll teach 'em a good lesson, mark my words.' So grandma leaves and goes home. The next morning Timmy and Bobby go downstairs to have breakfast. Grandma says to Bobby, 'And what would you like for breakfast?'

To which Bobby replies, 'Give me some of them fucking cornflakes!'

Grandma lashes out with this big swing and knocks Bobby clean out of his chair. He sits on the ground, looking shocked. Next

Grandma turns to Timmy: 'And what would you like for breakfast, little Timmy?'

Timmy looks at his brother, then back to his grandmother, and says, 'I don't know – but you can bet your sweet arse it won't be fucking cornflakes.'

Birds of a feather

Two men are standing on the edge of a cliff. One has a budgie on each shoulder, the other has a parrot on one shoulder. The first jumps off the cliff and, halfway down, the budgies fly off. He hits the ground with a wet splat. Barely alive, he rolls around, groaning.

Now the second man jumps off the cliff. Halfway down the parrot flies off, so the man reaches into his jacket and pulls out a shotgun. He shoots the parrot... just before landing on the rocks with a sickening thud.

As they both lie there in pain, the first man comments: 'I don't think much of this budgie jumping.'

The second replies, 'I don't think much of this free-fall parrot-shooting, either.'

Patient reprimanded

A guy goes to the doctor and is confronted by the receptionist. 'What's wrong?' she asks.

'It's my knob!' exclaims the bloke. The receptionist complains to the doctor and when he sees the patient he tells him not to be so specific and to stop shocking everyone in the waiting room.

A few weeks go past and the guy shows up again. 'What's the problem?' asks the receptionist.

'It's my ear,' says the guy.

'What's wrong with it?' she asks.

'I can't piss out of it,' mumbles the man.

The skiving builders

An Englishman, a Scotsman and an Irishman are on a building site when the foreman says, 'I'm going off-site for an hour – anyone leaves here and they're fired!'

Naturally, the moment he's gone the Englishman says, 'To hell with this – if he's off then I'm going down the boozer.'

'Too right,' says the Scotsman. 'I'm going down the bookies.'

'I'm off to see the missus,' says the Irishman, and he goes home. As he opens the front door, however, he hears panting and groaning from upstairs, so he goes to investigate. As he peeks through the bedroom door, what does he see but the foreman shagging his wife, so he scampers downstairs and back to the building site.

The next day at the site the foreman once again says he's going off for an hour, and that anybody leaving the site will be fired. Immediately the Englishman announces that he's sloping off to the pub and the Scotsman says he's off to the bookies but, when asked, the Irishman says that he's going to stay and get on with his work.

The Englishman and Scotsman are shocked. 'Why don't you go home?' asks the Englishman.

'You must be joking,' says the Irishman. 'I nearly got caught yesterday!'

Who invented football?

Jesus. He went up for the cross but was nailed by two defenders.

Lucky Linda

A man goes down for breakfast, where it's quite obvious his wife has the hump with him. He asks what's the matter. She replies, 'Last night you were talking in your sleep. I want to know exactly who "Linda" is!'

Thinking quickly, he tells her that he was dreaming of 'Lucky Linda' – a horse he'd bet on and that had won him £40.

The wife seems quite happy with the explanation and he goes off to work, but when he gets home that night his wife has the hump with him once again.

'What is it now, my love?' the man enquires.

'Your horse phoned,' she growls.

How do you make your girlfriend scream...

...after an orgasm?

Wipe your dick on the curtains.

The nuns' interrogation

Three nuns died in a car crash and found themselves standing before the Pearly Gates. Saint Peter greeted them and said they would have to answer one question each before being admitted into the Kingdom of Heaven. Sister Mary said,

'Saint Peter, I'm ready for my question.'

Peter consulted a heavy volume and read out, 'Your question is: Who was the first man on Earth?'

The nun replied, 'Why, it was Adam.' And the lights flashed, the bells tolled and the gates of Heaven opened.

Sister Bernadette stepped forward for her question and Peter intoned, 'Who was the first woman on Earth?'

'Eve,' the nun replied. And the lights flashed, the bells tolled and the gates of Heaven opened.

Mother Superior stepped forward and said, 'I'm ready, Saint Peter!'

Peter turned to his book for a third time, before reading out, 'And what was the first thing Eve said to Adam?'

The nun was shocked. 'My goodness,' she said, 'that's a hard one.' And the lights flashed, the bells tolled and the gates of Heaven opened.

The big kiss

At the back of the cinema, a girl and a boy are kissing passionately – until they finally stop and come up for air. 'Look,' pants the boy, 'I really love kissing you, but do you mind not passing me your chewing gum?'

'Oh, that's not chewing gum,' replies the girl. 'I've got bronchitis.'

The freezer of punishment

A man buys a parrot for his kids, but the bird is simply obnoxious. He uses bad language and no-one can handle it without getting pinched, until finally one day when the bird insults the man's wife. He grabs the parrot and tosses it cursing and flapping into the freezer, slamming the door behind it.

After a few seconds, all goes quiet. The man opens the door and the parrot meekly walks out. 'I realise I've offended you and I'm sorry and humbly beg your forgiveness,' says the potty-mouthed pet.

The man is touched.

'That's okay,' he says. You're forgiven.'

'Good' says the parrot. 'Now, if I might ask: what did the chicken do?'

How do you make...

...a dog drink?

Put it in a liquidiser.

Man of God offers solace

Mary pulls aside the Father following his Sunday morning service. She's in tears, and the priest is worried, 'What could possibly be bothering you, Mary my dear?'

'Oh, Father,' sobs Mary, ' I've terrible news – my husband passed away last night!'

'Oh sweet Jesus, Mary,' says the Father, 'that's terrible! Tell me, Mary, did he have any last requests?'

'That he did, Father,' replies Mary, 'that he did... he screamed, "Please Mary, put down that damn gun!"'

The lucky punter

A bloke is walking along the street and he finds a little oil lamp in the gutter. So he picks it up, gives it a rub and out pops a genie. 'I grant you one wish,' the genie says.

The bloke thinks for a while, and eventually requests that he be incredibly lucky for the day. 'So be it!' says the genie, and disappears in a puff of smoke. So the man's walking along the road, wishing he had some cash so he could go down to the bookies to test the theory out, when all of a sudden he sees a spanking new £50 note in the gutter.

'How lucky,' he says to himself as he sets off for the bookies. Having placed the whole £50 on the nose on a 400-1 long-shot, he waits for the race. Eventually his horse comes in second. What a shame. All of a sudden there's an announcement – there has been a steward's enquiry and the winner has been disqualified, making his horse the winner! 'How lucky,' he thinks to himself.

He decides to celebrate with a drink and wanders off to his local. As he walks through the door hundreds of lights start flashing and a siren sounds. 'Congratulations, sir!' says the landlord. 'You're our one-millionth customer – free drinks for you all night!'

'How lucky,' he thinks to himself.

So he sits down with his mates and tells them about the day's events. None of them believe him, so they set a challenge. The Indian barmaid is sexy as hell – but none of them has managed to bed her yet. That is his challenge. So he goes up to the Indian barmaid and starts chatting. They're getting on superbly, when the next thing he knows he's giving her a good seeing to in the pub toilets. 'How lucky,' he thinks to himself.

However, after a couple of minutes he stops. 'Look, I'm sorry,' he says, 'I know it's a religious thing, but I can't take my eyes off that red dot on your forehead. It's ruining my concentration.'

'Don't worry,' she says,

'it's just a bit of paint – scratch it off.'

So he scratches at the spot. 'Bugger me, I've won a car!'

The voodoo dick

A businessman was going on a long trip abroad so thought he'd get his wife something to keep her occupied while he was gone. He went to a sex shop and explained the situation to the man behind the counter.

'Well, sir, I don't usually mention this, but there is the "voodoo dick".' The man reached under the counter and pulled out an ornate wooden box. He opened it, and there lay a very ordinary-looking dildo.

The man pointed to a door and said, 'Voodoo dick, the door.' The voodoo dick rose out of its box, darted over to the door, and started screwing the keyhole. The whole door shook with the vibrations and a crack developed down the middle. The man said, 'Voodoo dick, get back in your box!' The voodoo dick stopped and floated back to its box. 'I'll take it!' said the businessman.

When he gave it to his wife he explained that it was a special dildo and that to use it, all she had to do was say, 'Voodoo dick, my pussy.' Then he left for his trip.

After he'd been gone a few days, the wife found herself unbearably horny, so she got the voodoo dick out and said, 'Voodoo dick, my pussy!' The voodoo dick shot to her crotch and started pumping. It was like nothing she'd ever experienced before. After three orgasms, however, she decided she'd had enough and tried to pull it out – but it was stuck. Her husband had forgotten to tell her how to shut it off, so she drove to the hospital to see if they could help. On the way, another orgasm nearly made her swerve off the road, and she was pulled over by a policeman. He demanded her licence, then asked how much she'd had to drink. She explained she hadn't been drinking, but that a voodoo dick was stuck in her fanny.

The officer said, 'Yeah, right. Voodoo dick, my arse.'

Canine contraceptives

Two dogs, walking down the road. One dog says, 'Do you use a condom when you're making love?'

The other dog replies, 'Durex.'

'No,' says dog number one. 'I asked you first.'

The shipwreck survivor

A cruise liner sinks and the sole survivor finds himself on a deserted island. For the next four months he eats nothing but bananas and drinks coconut milk. One day he sees a rowboat, and in it is the most gorgeous woman he's ever seen. 'How did you get here?' gasps the man.

'I rowed from the other side of the island,' says the woman. 'I washed up there when my ship sank.' 'Amazing,' says the man. 'You were lucky to have a rowboat wash up with you!'

'The rowboat didn't wash up,' says the woman.'I made it from gum branches, palm branches and a eucalyptus.'

'But,' stutters the man, 'you had no tools.'

'Oh, that was no problem,' replies the woman. 'The island is littered with an alluvial rock. When I fired it to a certain temperature in my kiln, it melted into ductile iron. I used that to make tools. Why don't we row over to my place now?' says the woman. After a journey of a few minutes, she docks the boat at a small wharf. In front of them is an exquisite bungalow. The man can only stare, dumbstruck. 'Would you like a drink?' asks the woman.

'I'm sick of coconut milk,' mutters the man. 'Don't be silly!' the woman replies.

'I have a still. How about a piña colada?'

Trying to hide his amazement, the man accepts, and they sit down to talk. After they've exchanged stories, the woman announces, 'I'm going to slip into something comfortable. Would you like to take a shower and shave?'

The man goes into the bathroom and finds a razor made from bone and cowry shells. He scrapes off his beard and goes back to the living room, where the woman is wearing nothing but vines and smelling faintly of gardenias. She beckons him to sit down next to her. 'Tell me,' she whispers, slithering closer, 'we've been out here for a very long time. You've been lonely. I've been lonely. There's something I'm sure you feel like doing right now, something you've been longing for all these months...' She stares into his eyes.

'You mean...?' he stutters, '...you mean I can check my e-mail from here?'

The nervous parachutist

A young man joined the army and signed up for paratrooper training, and finally went to take his first jump from an aeroplane. The next day, he phoned his father to tell him what had happened.

'So, did you jump?' the father asked.

'Well, we got up in the plane, and the Sergeant opened the door and asked for volunteers. About a dozen men got up and just leapt out the aircraft!'

'Is that when you jumped?' asked the father.

'Um, not yet. Then the Sergeant started to grab the remaining men one at a time and threw them out the door.'

'Did you jump then?' asked the father.

'I'm getting to that,' said the youngster. 'I was the last man left on the plane and told the Sergeant I was too scared to jump. He told me to leap out of the plane or he'd kick my arse.'

'So, did you jump?'

'Not then. I grabbed onto the door and refused to go, so he called over the Jump Master – this great big guy, must have been six-foot five and 17 stone. He said to me, "Boy, are you going to jump or not?" I said, "No, Sir. I'm too scared." So the Jump Master pulled down his zip and took his penis out. I swear, it was ten inches long! He said, "Boy, either you jump out of that door, or I'm sticking this up your arse."'

'So, did you jump?' asked the father.

'Well, a little, at first.'

What's the name...

...of the active ingredient in Viagra?

Mycoxafailin.

The customer's always right

A woman goes into a US sporting goods store to buy a rifle. 'It's for my husband,' she tells the clerk.

'Did he tell you what gauge to get?' asks the clerk.

'Are you kidding?' she says. 'He doesn't even know that I'm going to shoot him!'

Explorers amazed

Paddy and Murphy are strolling through the jungle by a riverbank when they spy a crocodile with a man's head protruding from its mouth.

Paddy turns to Murphy and says, 'Would you look at that flash twat in his Lacoste sleeping bag...'

Thanks, waitress

A couple are dining in a restaurant when the man suddenly slides under the table. A waitress, noticing that the woman is glancing nonchalantly around the room, wanders over to check that there's no funny business going on.

'Excuse me, madam,' she smarms, 'but I think your husband has just slid under the table.'

'No he hasn't,' the woman replies. 'As a matter of fact, he's just walked in.'

Wild west watches

One day in the old west, a rancher was riding along, checking the fence around his property. After a while he came across an Indian, lying in the dirt, completely naked and with a huge erection. 'What the hell are you doing?' asked the rancher.

'I'm telling the time,' said the redskin. He looked at the shadow cast by his penis and said, 'It's one o'clock.'

The rancher kept on riding until, after an hour, he came across another Indian, lying in the dirt completely naked, with a huge hard-on. 'Are you telling the time, too?' asked the rancher.

'Sure am,' said the Indian. Then he looked at the shadow cast by his penis and said, 'It's two o'clock.'

The rancher rode on for another hour until he came to a third Indian, lying in the dirt completely naked and masturbating vigorously. 'Those other two Indians were telling the time,' said the rancher. 'Why the hell are you whacking off like that?'

'I'm winding my watch,' the brave replied.

The Lottery winner

A man wins the Lottery and decides to buy himself a top-of-the-range superbike. The shop's owner warns him to coat the bike in Vaseline every time it looks like raining.

That night he goes and picks his girlfriend up on his new toy and heads over to her parents' house for the first time. As they arrive, she explains to him that when they have dinner, he shouldn't talk. 'It's a family tradition,' she tells him. 'If you say anything, you'll have to do the pots.'

As the girlfriend warned, the family sit down for dinner without anyone saying a word. So the man decides to take advantage of the situation by groping his girlfriend's tits. Not a sound comes from anyone.

So he decides to shag his bird on the table – still, not a word. He then proceeds to do his girlfriend's mum over the table – still, amazingly, not a word.

Suddenly he notices spots of rain on the kitchen window and remembers his precious motorbike, so he reaches into his pocket and gets out the Vaseline, at which point his girlfriend's dad leaps up and shouts, 'Okay, I'll do the pots.'

Bunda!

While out on an expedition, three explorers get caught by a race of brutal savages. The chief goes up to the first explorer and makes him a simple offer. 'Choose,' says the chief. 'Death or bunda?'

The first explorer thinks about this and decides that anything has to be better than death, so he chooses bunda. The chief turns to his followers, shouts, 'Bunda!' and cuts the explorer loose, telling him to run.

The first explorer legs it, hotly pursued by a group of whooping, hollering savages. Moments later, however, he is caught, dragged into some bushes and brutally buggered in every orifice.

The chief turns to the second explorer and asks, 'Death or bunda?'

The second explorer, reckoning he can make a better job of escaping, chooses bunda. Again, the chief turns to his followers, shouts, 'Bunda!' cuts the explorer loose and tells him to run. The second explorer runs even quicker than the first, but eventually he too is caught by the savages and subjected to the most vile of buggerings.

Finally, the chief turns to the third explorer and asks, 'Death or bunda?' The guy thinks about what happened to his colleagues and, taking a deep breath, chooses death.

The chief stares at him with a look of pity in his eyes, turns to his followers and shouts, 'Death! By bunda!'

What's orange...

...and sounds like a parrot?

A carrot.

The priest's bath

It was time for Father John's Saturday night bath.

A young sister, Jane, had prepared the bathwater and towels just the way the old nun instructed. Sister Jane was also told firstly, not to look at Father John's nakedness if she could help it; secondly, do whatever he told her to do; and thirdly, to pray.

The next morning the old nun asked Sister Jane how the bath went. 'Oh, sister,' said the young nun dreamily. 'I've been saved.'

'Saved? And how did that fine thing come about?' asked the old nun.

'Well, while Father John was soaking in the tub, he asked me to wash him. While I was washing him he guided my hand down between his legs, where he said the Lord keeps the key to Heaven!'

'Did he now,' said the old nun, evenly.

Sister Jane continued, 'And Father John said that if the key to Heaven fit my lock, the portals of Heaven would be opened to me and I would be assured of salvation and eternal peace. And then Father John guided his key to Heaven into my lock.'

'Is that a fact?' said the senior nun, even more evenly.

'At first it hurt terribly, but Father John said the pathway to salvation was often painful and that the glory of God would soon swell my heart with ecstasy. And it did! It felt so good being saved!'

'That wicked old devil,' said the old nun. 'He told me it was Gabriel's Horn, and I've been blowing it for 40 years...'

Emergency service

Two hunters are out in the woods when one suddenly cries out and falls to the ground. He doesn't appear to be breathing and his eyes are rolled back in his head, so the friend panics and telephones 999 on his mobile.

'My friend is dead!' he gasps to the operator. 'What can I do?'

The operator, speaking in a soothing voice, calms him down. 'Just take it easy. I can help. First, let's make sure he's dead.'

The line goes silent for a moment, and there's a loud bang before the man comes back on the line. 'Okay,' he says breathlessly, 'now what?'

What do Americans use...

...as contraception?

Their personalities.

An inspector calls

A TV licence inspector knocks at the door as the owner's hurriedly on her way out. 'Just here to check your licence, madam,' he politely asks.

'I'm terribly late already,' explains the woman, 'come back at three and see my husband – tell him it's behind the clock on the mantelpiece.'

At three sharp, the inspector returns. 'Hello, sir, I'm here to see your television licence.'

'I'm awfully sorry,' replies the man, 'I haven't a clue where it is.'

'No problem,' says the inspector, 'it's behind the clock on the mantelpiece...'

'Sweet Jesus,' replies the man, 'I knew your equipment was good, but not that bloody good!'

Q: Did you hear about the dyslexic devil-worshipper?

A: He sold his soul to Santa.

Court of appeal

A man appears in court requesting a divorce. After reviewing the papers, the judge turns to him. 'Please tell me why I should grant this,' he asks.

'Because,' the man replies, 'we live in a two-storey house.'

The judge looks at him sternly. 'What kind of a reason is that? What's the big deal about a two-storey house?'

'Well, your honour,' the man answers, 'one story is "I have a headache," and the other story is "It's that time of the month."'

Elevator etiquette

A man is in the back of a crowded elevator when he yells, 'Ballroom, please!'

The lady in front of him turns around and says, 'Sorry – I didn't know I was crowding you.'

Virgin gets a shock

A virgin gets married to a man who is supposed to be rather well endowed. On the first night of their honeymoon she confesses her fears to her new husband, who tells her that he'll get round the situation by showing her his dick bit by bit.

So the wife is lying in bed when she sees three inches of dick come round the door. 'Are you nervous yet?' asks her husband.

'No, I'm okay,' she replies.

Another six inches of dick comes around the door. 'Are you still okay?' he asks.

'Yes,' she replies. A further foot comes around the door. 'I'm not nervous,' she calls.

'Okay,' her husband replies. 'I'm coming up the stairs.'

Nudist colony #1

Who's the most popular woman in a nudist colony?

The one who can eat the last doughnut.

Loan repaid

Chris goes to see his friend Tony. Tony's wife Sara answers the door and says that Tony has gone shopping, but Chris can wait if he wants. After a few minutes Chris says, 'Sara, you have the greatest breasts I've ever seen. I'd give you £100 if I could just see one.'

Sara thinks about this for a minute and figures what the hell – 100 quid for a flash! So she opens her robe and shows a nork. Chris politely thanks her, pulls two £50 notes from his pocket and throws them on the table. Then Chris says, 'I've just got to see the both of them – I'll give you another 100 notes if I could see the both of them together.'

Sara thinks, 'For £100?' then opens her robe and gives Chris a long look. He throws another £100 on the table, then says he can't wait any longer for Tony and leaves.

A while later Tony arrives home. 'Your weird friend Chris came over,' his wife tells him.

'Great,' says Tony. 'Did he leave the £200 he owes me?'

Q: What's the best thing about having Alzheimer's?

A: You get to meet new people every day.

Blind ambition

A blind man walks into a supermarket. He grabs his guide dog by the tail and swings it around his head.

'What the hell do you think you're doing?' shouts a sales assistant.

'Having a look round,' replies the blind man.

Towel therapy

After marrying a younger woman, a middle-aged man finds that no matter what he does in the sack, she never achieves orgasm. So he visits his doctor for advice. 'Maybe fantasy is the solution,' says the doctor. 'Why not hire a strapping young man and, while you two are making love, have him wave a towel over you?' The doctor smiles. 'Make sure he's totally naked – that way your wife can fantasise her way to a full-blown orgasm.'

Optimistic, he returns home and hires a handsome young escort. But it's no use: even when the stud stands naked, waving the towel, the wife remains unsatisfied. Perplexed, the man returns to his doctor. 'Try reversing it for a while,' says the quack. 'Have the young man make love to your wife and you wave the towel over them.'

And so he returns home to try again – this time, waving the towel as the same escort pumps away enthusiastically. Soon the wife has an enormous, screaming orgasm.

Smiling, the husband drops the towel and taps the young man on the shoulder. 'You see?' he shouts triumphantly. 'That's how you wave a bloody towel.'

What has an old woman got...

...between her tits that a young woman hasn't?

Her belly button.

Skill demonstrated

A young man visits a talent scout, claiming he has an unbelievable act. 'Okay then,' says the scout, 'show me what you can do.'

With that, the man pulls a claw hammer from his pocket and chows it down within seconds – wood, metal, the lot.

'Bravo!' says the talent scout, clapping wildly and rising to his feet. 'Do you do this professionally?'

'Oh no,' replies the man, 'I'm an 'ammer chewer.'

Why do sumo wrestlers...

...shave their legs?

To avoid being mistaken for feminists.

Gramps treats kids

An old man takes his two grandchildren to see the new Scooby-Doo film. When he returns home, his wife asks if he enjoyed himself.

'Well,' he starts, 'if it wasn't for those pesky kids...!'

Did you hear about the monk...

...who got his dick caught in the bell-rope?

He told himself off.

Sexual economics

A couple in their late sixties make an appointment to see a sex therapist, and ask him if they can have sex while he watches. Puzzled, the doctor nevertheless agrees – and sits quietly while the elderly lovers get down to it. After a screaming climax, the physician nods solemnly.

'In my professional opinion,' he says, 'there's nothing wrong with the way you have intercourse.'

Happy, the couple pay the £50 fee and leave – only to return the next week and repeat the exercise. This continues for several weeks, and each time the doctor has to conclude that no matter what the position, the paramour pensioners are perfectly adequate at shagging. Finally, the doctor himself becomes curious. 'Just exactly what are you trying to find out?' he asks.

'Nothing,' says the old man, 'but she's married and we can't go to her house.

I'm married and we can't go to mine.'

'So why come to me?' says the doctor.

The old man grins. 'Well,' he beams, 'the Holiday Inn charges £90. The Hilton charges £108. We do it here for £50 – and I get £43 back from Bupa.'

Why haven't women...

...been to the moon yet?

It doesn't need cleaning.

A bald cat...

...walks onto a bus in Liverpool and goes straight to the back. 'Hey!' shouts the conductor. 'Where's your fur?'

A man walks into a bar...

...with a steering wheel in his underpants.
The barman asks, 'Is that painful?'
The man replies, 'It's driving me nuts!'

The lucky frog

A man is playing a practice round of golf, when he notices a frog sitting next to the green. Thinking nothing of it, he takes out a six iron to play his shot when he hears: 'Ribbit. Nine iron.'

The man looks around. There's no-one in sight, so he lines up his shot once more. 'Ribbit. Nine iron.'

He gives the frog a long look and, putting his other club away, grabs the nine iron. Thwack! He puts the ball ten inches from the hole! 'You must be a lucky frog,' he tells the frog.

'Ribbit. Lucky frog,' the creature replies.

The man picks the frog up and carries him to the next hole. 'What do you think, little fella?' he asks.

'Ribbit. Three wood,' comes the reply.

The man takes out a three wood, and boom! Hole in one. Two hours later, he's played the best round of golf in his life, so he decides to take the frog to Las Vegas. As soon as the plane touches down the frog pipes up, 'Ribbit. Roulette.' As the wheel spins, the frog's there again: 'Ribbit. $3,000, black six.' The man plonks all his money down.

Result! Black six! The man takes his winnings and checks into the best room in the hotel. He says to the frog, 'I don't know how to repay you.'

'Ribbit. Kiss me,' the frog replies. The man puckers up – why not, after all the frog's done for him? And with that kiss, the frog turns into a gorgeous 15-year-old girl.

'And that, Your Honour, is how she ended up in my room.'

What are the three worst things ...

...about being an egg?

You only get laid once, it takes ten minutes to go hard and the only bird to sit on your face is your mum.

Patient request worries staff

A man lies on his hospital bed, desperately ill with an oxygen mask covering his mouth. A young nurse arrives to sponge his face and hands. 'Nurse,' he mumbles, 'are my testicles black?'

Embarrassed, the young nurse explains how she's only there to wash him, and carries on about her business.

'Please nurse,' pleads the man, again, 'I have to know, are my testicles black?'

Again the nurse refuses to check, but duly concerned she summons the ward sister to see what the problem is. 'Sister,' the man mumbles, clearly in pain, 'all I want to know is – are my testicles black?'

With that, the ward sister whips off the sheets, strips him and has a good poke around his clockweights. Nothing.

'There's absolutely nothing wrong with those,' she yells at the man, 'now please leave us to do our job!'

'For Christ's sake,' shouts the man, pulling away the oxygen mask, 'I couldn't give a hoot about my bollocks – I want to know if my test results are back!'

Q: How do you make your wife cry while having sex?

A: Phone her up.

Jim's Nails

A man named Jim owned a small company which manufactured nails. One night he bumped into his old schoolmate, Bob. They got talking and Bob asked Jim what he was doing. 'I own my own nail manufacturing company, called Jim's Nails,' he said. 'What about you?'

'Oh, I make adverts for TV,' said Bob. 'Tell you what, since we were friends at school I'll make you an advert for free.'

So a few days later, Bob phoned him to say that his advert would be on in the middle of Coronation Street. Jim waited for his spot, only to find that the 'advert' was simply a picture of Jesus nailed to a cross with the caption 'Use Jim's Nails' written in large letters.

Being a good Catholic, Jim was outraged. He phoned Bob up and asked him what the hell he thought he was doing. Bob apologised profusely, and offered to shoot another spot to make it up to his old school buddy.

A few days later, in the middle of The Bill, the new ad came on: Jesus was running through the desert with sweat pouring down his brow, obviously running for his life. The camera panned out to reveal two Roman guards about 100 yards behind Jesus, chasing after him. The camera zoomed in on the guards just as one said to the other, 'I told you we should have used Jim's Nails.'

Nudist colony #2

Who is the most popular man in a nudist colony?

The bloke who can hold two cups of coffee and nine doughnuts.

Weevil rivalry

Two boll-weevils grew up in North Carolina. Eventually, one upped and left for Hollywood where it became a famous actor. The other stayed behind, tending to the cotton fields, never amounting to much. This second one, naturally, became known as the lesser of two weevils.

Alien invasion thwarted

Two aliens landed in the Arizona desert near an abandoned gas station. They approached one of the petrol pumps, and one of them said to it, 'Greetings, Earthling. We come in peace. Take us to your leader.'

The petrol pump, of course, didn't respond. The alien repeated the greeting. Again, no response. The alien, annoyed by what he perceived to be the petrol pump's haughty attitude, drew his ray gun and said impatiently, 'Earthling, how dare you ignore us in this way! Take us to your leader or I will fire!'

The other alien shouted to his comrade, 'No, you mustn't anger him!' but before he finished his warning, the first alien fired. There was a huge explosion that blew both of them 200 yards into the desert, where they landed in a heap. When they finally regained consciousness, the one who fired turned to the other one and said, 'What a ferocious creature. It nearly killed us! But how did you know he was so dangerous?'

The other alien answered, 'If there's one thing I've learned during all my travels through the galaxy, it's that if a guy has a penis he can wrap around himself twice and then stick into his own ear, don't mess with him!'

A rural Christmas

Two farmers were leaning over a fence discussing Christmas. The first farmer said that he bought his wife a fur coat and a Mercedes for the festive season.

The second farmer asked why he bought her such expensive presents. The first farmer replied that if she didn't like the coat, she could drive in the Mercedes to take it back.

The second farmer nodded his head, understanding the reasoning behind the answer. The first farmer then asked the second what he got his wife for Christmas. He replied that he bought his wife a pair of slippers and a vibrator. 'Why that combination?' asked the first farmer.

'Well,' said the second, 'if she didn't like the slippers she could go fuck herself.'

Customer complaint

A middle-aged woman walks into a sex shop and asks the shop owner, 'D-d-do you s-s-sell vibrators?'

'Yes madam, we do,' replies the man.

'D-d-do you s-s-sell them th-this big?' the woman asks, holding her hands about 12 inches apart.

'Yes – we sell them that big.'

'D-d-do you s-s-sell them th-this w-wide?' the woman asks, holding her hands about four inches apart.

'Yes, we sell them that wide.'

'D-d-do you ha-have them with b-batteries?'

'Yes we do.'

'W-well, how the f-f-fuck do you t-t-turn them off?!'

Prostitute inflation

Three prostitutes once lived together: a grandmother, mother and daughter. One night the daughter came home looking very upset. 'How did you get on tonight, dear?' asked her mother.

'Not too good,' replied the daughter. 'I only got £20 for a blow job.'

'Wow!' said the mother, 'in my day we gave a blow job for 50p!'

'Good God!' said the grandmother. 'In my day we were just glad to get something warm in our stomachs.'

In-law comes a cropper

A big-game hunter is on safari with his wife and mother-in-law. One night, his wife wakes up to discover her mother is gone, so wakes her husband and insists they search for the old girl. Rifle in hand, he wanders to the edge of the camp where – shock horror – the mother-in-law is backed up against a tree with a huge lion inching towards her. 'Oh no,' screams the wife, 'what are we going to do?'

'Nothing,' replies her husband, 'the lion got himself into this mess, let him get out of it.'

Catholic logic

Two Irishmen were digging a ditch opposite a brothel when they saw a rabbi enter its front door. 'Will you look at that?' the first ditch-digger said. 'What's our world comin' to when men of the cloth are visitin' such places?'

A short time later, a Protestant minister walked up to the door and slipped inside. 'Do you believe that?' the same workman exclaimed. 'Why, 'tis no wonder the young people today are so confused, what with the example clergymen set for them.'

Another hour went by, and the men watched as a Catholic priest quickly entered the whorehouse.

'Ah, what a pity,' the digger said. 'One of the poor lasses must be ill.'

War wounds

Two elderly gents are taking a leak in a public toilet when one notices the other gent is pissing two streams. 'What the hell is that?' he asks.

'War wound,' replies the other. 'I took a revolver bullet in the penis in North Africa, which left a hole.'

'Me too,' says the first – showing he's pissing with three streams. 'War wound, Germany. A high-powered rifle round in the penis – left me with two holes.'

At this point, a young lad stands between them – and squirts 12 streams of amber onto the porcelain.

'My God,' exclaims the second veteran, 'did you get that from a machine gun?'

'No mate,' says the youngster, incredulously. 'My zip's stuck.'

Driver carries no cash

One dismal rainy night, a taxi driver spots an arm waving from the shadows of an alley. Even before he rolls to a stop at the curb, a figure leaps into the cab and slams the door. Checking his mirror as he pulls away, the cabbie is startled to see a dripping wet, naked woman sitting in the back seat. 'Er, where to?' he stammers.

'The station,' answers the woman.

'You got it,' he nods, taking another long glance in the mirror.

Looking up, the woman catches him staring. 'Just what the hell are you looking at, driver?'

The driver coughs politely. 'Well, I'd just noticed that you were completely naked.'

'So?'

'I was just wondering how you'll pay your fare.'

Nodding slowly, the woman spreads her legs and puts her feet up on the front seat headrests. She smiles at the driver. 'Does this answer your question?'

'Bloody hell,' cries the cabbie, still staring in the mirror. 'Got anything smaller?'

Third time unlucky

While admiring the view from her flat on the 20th floor of an apartment building, a young woman slips and falls out of the window. Luckily, she's caught by the ankle a few floors down by a man who happens to be out on his balcony. 'Thank the Lord you were there!' gasps the young woman.

The man simply asks, 'Do you suck?'

'No!' says the horrified young woman. The man immediately drops her. But she only falls a couple more floors when she's once again caught by a man out on his balcony. 'Thank you!' she gasps.

The man simply asks, 'Do you fuck?'

'No!' she exclaims, and he lets her go.

As she falls, she prays for one last chance. And lo and behold, a third man catches her from his balcony. Quickly she blurts out, 'I suck, I fuck!'

'Slut,' he says, and drops her.

Rewarding ramble

A man arrives back from a long business trip and finds that his son has a brand new £500 mountain bike. 'How did you get that, son?'

'By hiking,' replies the boy.

'Hiking?' asks his old man.

'That's right,' says the boy. 'Every night while you were away, your boss came over and mum gave me £20 to take a hike.'

The stranded businessman

A businessman's car broke down on a country lane, so he walked to a nearby farmhouse. When the farmer answered he said, 'May I use your phone? My car has broken down about a mile down the road.'

'I'm afraid we don't have one, but I could give you a tow to town in the morning and you can stay here the night,' the farmer offered.

When it came to bedtime the farmer admitted they only had one bed, so they all went to bed, with the businessman lying in the middle. After a while the businessman got a huge erection. The wife turned to the businessman and said: 'Listen, if you want to sleep with me, pull a hair out of my husband's arse and see if he moves. If he doesn't, then he's asleep.'

So the businessman teased a hair out of the farmer's arse. The old boy didn't move – so he shagged the wife.

Half an hour later, the businessman got another erection. Pleased with her last shag, the wife told the businessman to pull another hair out. Discovering that the farmer was still asleep, they went at it again.

Half an hour later, the businessman got another hard-on. This time, when he pulled a hair out of the farmer's arse, the old boy turned to him and said, 'Look, I don't mind you shagging my wife, but do you have to use my arse as a scoreboard?'

Q: How is a woman like a laxative?

A: They both irritate the shit out of you.

Hooker stressed

Fearing she might be a haemophiliac, a prostitute visits her GP. 'It's awful,' she says, 'every time I get even a small cut, it takes days for the bleeding to stop.'

'Hmmm,' replies the physician, scribbling down notes, 'and roughly how much do you lose when you get your period?'

The woman thinks for a moment. 'About a grand...'

Did you hear about the bloke...

...who tried to flush his Viagra down the loo?

The toilet seat stayed up for a month.

Checkout number three, please!

A man was in a really long queue at the supermarket checkout. After 15 minutes of waiting he finally reached the checkout girl – and only then remembered that he had a hot date that night. Not wanting to line up again, he said to the girl: 'I meant to buy some condoms, er, but I forgot...'

'Do you know what size you are?' asked the girl.

'No.'

'Okay then – drop your pants and I'll tell you what size you are.'

Not being the shy type, the man duly dropped his trousers. The girl had a quick feel with her hand then said into the microphone, 'One packet of large condoms to checkout three, please.'

The man then pulled up his trousers, the condoms were brought to him, he paid the bill and went on his way.

The next customer was a man who thought he'd like to have this nice girl fondling his prick – so said the same thing to her. A similar course of events duly took place, only this time after having a feel she said, 'One packet of medium-sized condoms to checkout three, please.' The condoms were duly brought to him; he paid the bill and went on his way.

Also watching this course of events was a 15-year-old boy, who decided to try the same routine. 'I'd like to buy some condoms please, but I forgot...' he said to the poor sales girl.

'Do you know what size you are?'

'No.'

'Okay, I'll check... mop and bucket to aisle three please.'

Breaking it gently

A middle-aged couple win a holiday in a prize draw, but are dismayed to find it's for just one person. 'If anyone deserves this holiday,' says the husband, 'it's you.'

Tearfully grateful, the wife accepts. A few days later, she phones home to check everything is okay. 'The weather's bad,' says her husband, 'but I'm eating well. Oh – and your cat's dead.'

Predictably, his wife is beside herself with grief. 'That's terrible,' she blubs. 'Why did you break the news so suddenly?'

'What do you mean?' says her husband.

'I don't know,' she laments, 'Er... you could have said the cat's stuck on the roof. Then tomorrow say the fire brigade was trying to get it down. Then the next day say the fireman dropped her, and she's fighting for her life at the vet's. Then, on my last day, tell me she died peacefully in her sleep.'

'I see,' replies her husband. 'Well, you try to enjoy the rest of your holiday.'

So the wife rings off, and tries to cheer herself up.

The next day, she phones again to check in with hubby. 'So how's everything today?' she asks.

'Well,' says her husband, sighing. 'Your mum's stuck on the roof...'

Q: What are the three words you don't want to hear when you're making love?

A: 'Darling, I'm home!'

Heavenly transport

When three men go to Heaven, St Peter says to them, 'How many times have you been unfaithful to your wives?'

The first man says three times, so Peter decrees he must travel round Heaven in a Fiesta. The second man says five times, so Peter makes him travel round Heaven in a Lada.

The third bloke has never been unfaithful, so Peter says, 'Well done! You get to drive a Rolls-Royce in Heaven.'

A while later Peter comes across the man in the Rolls at the side of the road, crying. 'What's the matter?' he asks. 'You have a beautiful car!'

'I know,' says the man, 'but I just saw my wife go past on a skateboard.'

A step too far

A voluptuous woman goes to a gynaecologist, who tells her to undress at once. After she's disrobed, he begins to stroke her thigh. As he does this he says to the woman, 'Do you know what I'm doing?'

'Yes,' she says, 'you're checking for any abrasions or dermatological abnormalities.'

'That is correct,' says the lecherous doctor. He then begins to fondle her breasts. 'Do you know what I'm doing now?' he asks.

'Yes,' says the woman, 'you're checking for any lumps or breast cancer.'

'That's right,' replies the doctor. He then begins to have sexual intercourse with the woman. He says, 'Do you know what I'm doing now?'

'Yes,' she says. 'You're getting herpes.'

Antique valued

A man drags a huge box to Antiques Roadshow, and after a long wait he's finally ushered towards an expert. 'Where did you get this, then?' asks the ageing know-it-all behind the desk.

'It's been in my loft for 40 years,' replies the man.

'I assume it must be some sort of heirloom.'

'I see,' says the expert, looking it over. 'Tell me, do you have it insured?'

'I don't,' says the man, thinking his luck must be in, 'should I?'

'Absolutely,' insists the expert, 'it's your sodding water tank.'

President visits

President Bush is visiting a school where a class is discussing words and their meanings. The teacher asks Dubya if he would like to lead a discussion on the word 'tragedy'. Bush asks if anyone can give him an example of a tragedy, and a boy stands up.

'If my best friend was playing in the street and a car ran him over, that would be a tragedy.'

'No,' says Bush, 'that would be an accident, son.'

A little girl then raises her hand, 'If a school bus carrying 20 children drove off a cliff, killing everyone, that would be a tragedy.'

'I'm afraid not, missy,' explains the President, 'that would be a great loss.'

The room goes quiet. Finally, after an embarrassing silence, way at the back of the room a small boy raises his hand. 'If Air Force One, carrying you and Mrs Bush, were struck by a missile and blown to smithereens by a terrorist, that would be a tragedy.'

'Fantastic,' says Bush, 'and can you tell me why that would be a tragedy, son?'

'Well,' says the boy, 'because it wouldn't be an accident, and it certainly wouldn't be a great loss.'

Nuisance call

It's two o'clock in the morning and a husband and wife are asleep, when suddenly the phone rings. The husband picks up the phone and says, 'Hello...? How the hell do I know? What am I, the weather man?' and promptly slams the phone down.

His wife rolls over and asks, 'Who was that?'

The husband replies, 'I don't know. Some bloke who wanted to know if the coast was clear.'

The offended waitress

A man is sitting in a restaurant, waiting to order. A stunning waitress with a plunging neckline shimmies over, her tiny skirt revealing the finest pair of legs. She smiles, her huge breasts vying for freedom from her top. 'Would you like to order, sir?' she asks.

The man spies an opportunity – he's single, she's probably single... what's he got to lose? Gathering himself, he looks up from the menu: 'How's about a quickie?'

Enraged by his insolence, the waitress flies off the handle, smacking the man in the face and screaming insults before storming off to see the manager. Having witnessed the entire event, a nearby diner leans across to the man and proffers some advice. 'Don't mind me, but I think it's pronounced "Quiche."'

The fireman's code

Called out to a fire at a fashionable apartment block, a fireman arrives to find flames pouring out of an upstairs window, and a woman screaming. Donning protective gear, he climbs the ladder, enters the flat... and spies a curvy brunette in a see-through nightie.

'Amazing,' says the fireman, 'you're the third pregnant girl I've rescued this week.'

'Hey,' shouts the girl, indignantly, 'I'm not pregnant.'

'Yeah,' the fireman smiles, 'but you're not rescued yet either.'

At the nudist camp

A family are on holiday at a nudist camp. Walking around, the little boy looks at all the different-sized dicks on display. He asks his dad, 'Why are those men's willies all different sizes?'

His dad replies, 'Well, if you have a small dick, you are unintelligent; but if you have a big one you're brainy.'

Later on the dad asks his son, 'Where's your mother?'

'She's speaking to that man over there,' says the little angel, 'and he's getting smarter all the time.'

The sex fence

A young boy went into a chemist's and asked for his first packet of johnnies. He was understandably nervous. The chemist, who was a woman in her sixties, asked, 'What size?'

The boy didn't know. So the woman asked him to go out the back and size up. Round the back of the chemist's was a fence with three different-sized holes in it. As the boy put his knob in the first hole, the old woman surreptitiously ran round to the other side of the fence and started to suck away.

The boy jumped back in amazement, then put his old fella in the second hole. Once again, the woman started to go at it like a sex-crazed dog. Again the boy jumped back.

He then put it in the third hole, and this time the woman bent over so he could poke her.

At this point he ran back to the front of the shop, where the old slag was waiting, panting. 'W-w-well,' she said, 'what size were you?' The boy replied, 'To hell with the johnnies – how much do you want for that fence?'

What's the last thing...

...to go through a fly's head when it hits a windscreen?
Its arse.

The blonde speeder

A traffic cop pulls alongside a speeding car on the motorway. Glancing at the car, he's astounded to see that the blonde behind the wheel is knitting. Not only that, the woman is obviously oblivious to his flashing lights and siren – and so he cranks down his window and turns on his loudhailer.

'Pull over!' he shouts at the top of his voice.

'Nah,' the blonde yells back, 'it's going to be a scarf!'

Legless boozer

An Irishman's been drinking at a pub all night. When he stands up to leave he falls flat on his face. He tries to stand again, with the same result. So he figures he'll crawl outside and get some fresh air, and maybe that will sober him up. Once outside he stands up... and falls flat on his face.

So he decides to crawl down the four streets to his home. When he arrives at the door he stands up, and duly falls flat on his face again. He crawls through the door into his bedroom. When he reaches his bed, he tries one last time to get erect. This time he manages to pull himself upright, but he quickly falls right into bed and is sound asleep as soon as his head hits the pillow.

He awakens the next morning to find his wife standing over him, shouting, 'So you've been out drinking again!'

'What makes you say that?' says the Irishman, putting on an innocent look.

'The pub called,' his wife says. 'You left your wheelchair there again.'

Irish in space!

An Irishman and an American are arguing about who went into space first. The American is adamant that Uncle Sam was the first to put a man on the moon.

'What bollocks,' replies the Irishman, 'and anyhow, I hear that soon we'll be sending an Irish astronaut to the sun!'

The American can't believe his ears. 'Don't be so ridiculous,' he laughs, 'the fool would burn to death!'

'You great eejit,' replies the Irishman. 'We're not all stupid bastards... we're going to send him up at night.'

Rough justice

A judge is passing sentence on a prisoner and asks him, 'Have you anything to say in your defence?'

To which the prisoner says, 'Fuck all, Your Honour.'

Shocked, the judge turns to the counsel for the defence and asks, 'What did he say?'

'Fuck all, Your Honour,' answers the barrister.

'That's funny,' says the judge. 'I could have sworn I saw his lips move.'

The two experts

An off-duty doctor is walking by the side of a canal when he sees a man drowning in the murky waters. The man keeps going under, and is obviously taking in a lot of water. The doctor reaches out and manages to get a hold on the bloke and drags his upper body out of the canal, then turns him on his front, sits astride the body and starts pumping water out. There are gallons of shitty water spewing out of his mouth, plus tin cans, weeds, used condoms and loads of other crap. Suddenly, a second man turns up.

'You don't want to do that mate,' he says.

'Listen,' says the doc, 'I'm a doctor. Don't try and tell me how to do my job.'

'Well, I'm an engineer,' says the second bloke. 'And if you don't take that bloke's arse out of the canal you're going to pump it dry.'

Special marking

A gay man visits a tattoo shop, has a good look at all the designs then finally plumps for a car to be tattooed onto his cock. 'Certainly, chum,' says the tattooist, 'what sort of car would you like?'

The man thinks for a moment. 'Best make it a 4x4 – it's going to have to go through a lot of shit.'

Canine in trouble

Two friends are chatting. 'My mum's got a new dog,' says Dave.

'What's it called?' asks Bob.

'Minton,' continues Dave. 'He's a lovely dog, but he's got this weird habit of eating shuttlecocks.'

'Shuttlecocks, eh,' laughs Bob. 'And he's called Minton? Weird. Have you tried to stop him eating them?'

'Oh yeah, but it's just no good,' explains Dave. 'I told him off last night. Pointed my finger at the bugger and shouted "bad Minton!"'

The Lottery winner

A man runs home and kicks in the front door, yelling, 'Pack your bags honey, I've just won the Lottery!'

'Oh, that's wonderful!' his wife says. 'Should I pack for the beach or the mountains?'

'I don't care,' he replies. 'Just get the fuck out!'

Jacko dilemma

Michael Jackson's wife gives birth to a beautiful baby boy, but Jacko's a little concerned. 'I just have to ask, doc,' he says, taking his exhausted wife by the hand, 'how long before we can have sex?'

'Well, Mike,' says the doc,

'I think you'd better leave it until he's at least walking...'

New wife shocked

A young couple arrive at their hotel for the first night of their honeymoon – and immediately, they're frantically undressing each other. But when the husband removes his socks to reveal mangled, twisted toes, his wife has to stifle a scream.

'I had tolio as a child,' he replies, by way of explanation.

'Don't you mean polio?' his bride asks.

'No, tolio. The disease only affected my toes.'

Satisfied, his wife continues undressing – only to gasp again when she spies his lumpy and deformed legs.

'Oh,' says her husband, seeing her alarm. 'As a child, I also had kneasles.'

'You mean measles?' she replies.

'No, kneasles – a very rare illness affecting the knees.'

Smiling sympathetically, she continues undressing – until finally, her husband has stripped down to his underpants. Slowly, he pulls them down his legs – and his wife yelps again. 'Let me guess,' she says. 'Smallcox?'

The randy parrot

A farmer and his wife are given a parrot by a relative. The male parrot soon sneaks out and screws the next door neighbour's turkeys. The neighbour knocks on the door and explains what the parrot has been doing.

The owners of the parrot tell it if it doesn't stop they'll shave its head. But that night the parrot, overcome with desire, sneaks out and screws the neighbour's turkeys once again. So the next morning the man ties the bird down and shaves its head.

The following day is the farmer's daughter's wedding, and to please the relative who gave them the parrot they sit the randy bird on a piano. As a further punishment, they tell it that it has to greet all the guests and tell them where to sit in the church.

For an hour, the parrot does just fine. 'Groom's side to the left, bride's side to the right,' it squawks, until two bald guys walk in, when it screeches, 'You two turkey-fuckers up on the piano with me!'

East country logic

A man was on holiday in Norfolk when he found he needed a new gas canister for his caravan, so he approached a local in the street and asked, 'Excuse me, do you know if there's a B&Q in Norwich?'

'No,' replied the bumpkin, 'But there are two Es in Leeds.'

The pastor's wife

A large, burly man visits the local pastor's home and asks to see the minister's wife, a woman well known for her charitable impulses. 'Madam,' he says in a broken voice, 'I wish to draw your attention to the terrible plight of a poor family in this parish. The father is dead, the mother is too ill to work and the nine children are starving. They are about to be turned into the cold, empty streets unless someone pays their rent, which amounts to £400.'

'How terrible!' exclaims the preacher's wife.

'May I ask who you are?'

The sympathetic visitor dabs his handkerchief to his eyes. 'Yes,' he sobs, 'I'm the landlord.'

Perverted by language

Two men are driving down the road when a police car pulls them over. 'Do you know you were doing 50 in a 30 area?' says the copper.

'Short back and sides please,' says the driver, 'with a little off the top.'

The policeman's naturally a little puzzled by this, but soldiers on. 'Can I see your licence, sir?'

To which the driver replies, 'A number one blended in up the back and nothing off the top please.'

The policeman is getting angry by this time, and tells the driver, 'If you don't co-operate I'll have to take you down the station!'

'A shampoo, please,' the driver responds.

The policeman is by now very angry, and asks the passenger what's wrong with his mate. The man in the passenger seat replies, 'Sorry, officer. My mate only speaks hairdo.'

Boozer gets frisky

A drunk walked into a bar, looked around and approached a young lady. Without so much as an introduction, he placed his hand up her skirt and began fondling her. The woman jumped up and began screaming her head off. 'Oh Christ! I'm so sorry,' said the man, clearly embarrassed, 'I thought you were my wife – you look exactly like her.'

'Why you drunken, worthless, insufferable heap of shit,' screamed the woman, utterly incensed, 'keep away from me!'

'My God,' said the man, 'you sound just like her, too...'

Starter's orders

Two guys are in a bar. One says to the other, 'How's your sex life, buddy?'

'Not so good,' the second bloke says. 'Every time me and the missus have sex, she loses interest half-way through. It's very frustrating.'

The first pauses, then says, 'Yeah, I know what you mean. I used to have the same problem, but I found a cure. I hid a starter pistol under the bed. When she started to run out of steam, I simply fired the starter pistol. It gave her such a fright that she got all excited. She couldn't get enough!

I wish I'd done it years ago.'

Stunned but desperate, the other guy vows to try it that night. The next day they are back in the bar again. The first guy says, 'How did you get on with the starter pistol?'

His irate pal says, 'Don't talk to me about starter pistols! Last night we were having a little 69. As usual, she lost interest half-way through, so I fired the starter pistol just like you said.'

'So what happened?'

'She bit my cock, shat in my face, and a man came out of the closet with his hands up!'

The sandwich-haters

An Englishman, an Irishman and a Scotsman are working on a building site, and they always sit at the top of their crane to eat their lunches together. The Englishman opens his lunchbox and looks at his sandwiches. 'Cheese and fucking pickle,' he mutters. 'If I get cheese and pickle again tomorrow I'm going to jump off this crane.'

Next, the Scotsman opens his lunchbox and unwraps his sandwiches. 'Ham!' he raves. 'If the wife gives me ham again tomorrow, I'm going to jump off this crane!'

Finally, the Irishman opens up his lunchbox. He too looks at his sandwiches in disgust. 'Fucking jam again,' he cusses. 'If I get jam again tomorrow, I'm going to jump off this crane.'

The following day the three men are again at the top of the

crane for their lunch. The Englishman opens up his lunchbox and is met with cheese and pickle sandwiches. As promised, he jumps off the crane. Next the Scotsman opens up his lunchbox, and he's got ham again. He jumps off. Lastly, the Irishman peers inside the lunchbox at his sandwiches. Jam. Without hesitation, he plunges off.

The three are buried together a few days later, where their wives get to talking. 'I honestly didn't realise he no longer liked cheese and pickle,' says the Englishman's wife.

'My husband has always liked ham sandwiches.

I just can't understand it,' says the Scotsman's wife.

'I'm at my wits end,' says the Irishman's wife.'My husband always made his own sandwiches.'

Nun happy to please

A priest is transferred to a small convent. After meeting the Mother Superior and being shown the buildings, he decides to take a stroll into town and have a look around. Before long, a woman approaches him and whispers, 'Hello, Father – how about a blow job for £20?'

The priest ignores her and continues about his business, but as he trundles along another three women make him the very same offer. Bewildered, he returns to the convent, where Mother Superior asks how he enjoyed his trip.

'Oh fine,' he replies, 'but I just want to know one thing – what's a blow job?'

Mother Superior draws nearer and whispers, 'Twenty quid, same as in town...'

Private takes praise

Pete joins the army. At the end of the first day his commanding officer is outraged. 'Son, I did not see you in camouflage lesson today, you sack of shit!'

'Sir,' shouts Pete, 'thank you very much, sir!'

The outraged punter

A man walks into a garage and tells the salesman he's in the market for a new car. 'But there are no prices showing,' he frowns. 'How much is the blue Escort, for instance?'

'Hmm,' says the salesman, scratching his head.

'That'll cost you two 20ft-long triangular coins and a pink note with a fluffy kitten on it.'

'I'm not paying that!' cries the punter. 'That's silly money.'

A Scotsman, an Englishman and an Irishman...

...are sentenced to spend 15 years in solitary confinement. The judge, feeling sorry for the men, decides to allow each to take with him whatever he wants.

The Scotsman says, 'I'd like to take a woman with me.' The victim of his own logic, the judge reluctantly agrees, and the Scotsman takes his wife and heads off to solitary.

The Englishman says, 'I'd like to take a telephone with me.' The judge agrees, and off goes the Englishman with his telephone.

The Irishman pulls out a hand-held calculator and furiously punches the buttons for a few minutes. He then announces, 'I'd like to take 3,000 cartons of cigarettes with me.' The judge agrees, and off goes the Irishman with his fags.

After 15 years they open the Scotsman's cell, and out he comes with his woman and 15 children. 'That wasnae so bad,' he says.

The Englishman emerges and announces he is now a multimillionaire, having set up a successful business by telephone.

The Irishman then emerges, trembling like a leaf. 'Anybody got a light?' he asks.

Vegetable lover

A man is driving home late one night, feeling very randy. As he passes a pumpkin patch, his mind starts to wander. He thinks to himself, pumpkins are soft and squishy inside... There's no-one around for miles, so he pulls over to the side of the road, picks out a nice juicy-looking pumpkin, cuts the appropriate size hole in it and begins to pump away.

After a while he really starts getting into it, which means he doesn't notice a police car pulling up. The cop walks over and says, 'Excuse me, sir, but do you realise that you are screwing a pumpkin?'

The man looks at the cop in complete horror, thinks fast and says, 'A pumpkin? Shit – is it midnight already?'

The virgins' wedding night

Two virgins are due to be married in three weeks' time. However, the man has a serious problem: he can never get an erection. So he goes to see his doctor and tells him the problem.

'I'll give you some pills,' says the sympathetic medic. 'If you don't get any results, come back to me.'

A week later and no wood, so the man returns to the doctor. 'Try these instead,' says the quack. 'They're extra-strength. If nothing happens, come back and see me again.'

On the morning of the wedding, the bloke is back in the surgery. 'Doctor, you've got to help me – nothing's happened.' So the doctor takes a splint, ties the man's dick in it and wraps some clingfilm round the whole apparatus. Satisfied, the man goes off to get married.

When the couple are alone in their honeymoon suite, the wife says, 'I'll just go and put on something more comfy.'

When she re-emerges, she's wearing nothing but black leather boots and satin gloves. 'See these tits?' she whispers. 'Never been touched by any human being. See this pussy? Never had anyone near it.'

Not wanting to be outdone, the man points to his dick in the splint and clingfilm and says, 'How about this! Still in its wrapping!'

Two women bet

A blonde and a brunette are watching the 10 o'clock news. The lead story is about a man standing on top of a building, about to jump off. The brunette says to the blonde, 'I bet you a tenner that man jumps.'

The blonde says, 'You're on!'

Sure enough, the guy jumps off the building . So the blonde turns to the brunette and says, 'Well I guess that's £10 I owe you.'

The brunette turns to her, laughing. 'It's okay – I actually saw the six o'clock news and I knew that he jumped.'

'I saw the six o'clock news as well,' says the blonde, 'but I didn't think he'd do it twice.'

A little too literal

Being massively overweight, a blonde asks her doctor for a suitable diet. 'Okay,' he says, 'I'd recommend you eat regularly for two days, then skip a day. Repeat this procedure for two weeks and the next time I see you, you'll have lost at least five pounds.'

Happy, the blonde goes away – only to return a fortnight later having lost at least 30 pounds. 'That's amazing!' cries the doctor. 'So you followed my instructions?'

The blonde nods. 'I'll tell you, though, I thought I was going to drop dead that third day.'

'From hunger, you mean?' asks the doctor.

'No,' she says. 'From skipping.'

New sport on TV

The Olympic committee has just announced that Origami is to be introduced in Athens, 2004. Unfortunately it will only be available on paper view.

The truth about sex changes

A man is sitting in the bar when a good-looking woman sits down next to him. 'Hi, Bob,' she says.

'Do I know you?' Bob replies.

'You sure do, Bob, it's Frank, your best friend.'

'My God, Frank – is that really you?'

'Sure is. I went to Sweden and got a sex change!'

'Wow, that's amazing – the make-up and new hair sure had me fooled! Tell me something, does it hurt when they cut your penis off?'

'Yeah,' says Frank, 'that hurts. But not nearly as much as when they stick that metal tube into your head and suck half your brains out.'

The hillbilly wedding

A hillbilly gets married, and on his wedding night his new bride explains that she's a virgin, at which point the groom runs screaming from the bedroom back home to his father. When his dad asks what went wrong, the man repeats what his new bride told him.

'You're quite right to come home, son,' says the old man. If she ain't good enough for her own family, she sure ain't good enough for ours.'

Reincarnated

A woman goes to a seance. 'Is there anybody there?' asks the medium.

'Yes,' a small voice replies.

'Is that you, Bert?' asks the woman.

'Yes,' he replies.

'Are you all right?'

'Lovely,' the voice replies.

'What's it like where you are?' asks the wife.

'It's great,' he replies, 'today I went swimming and did a bit of fishing.'

'Oh,' said his widow, 'you never did any of that while you were alive.'

'No,' the voice says, 'well, I'm a duck now.'

The celibacy test

Three young candidates for the priesthood have spent years at a seminary, until one day they're told by the monsignor that just one last hurdle lies between them and their vocation: the celibacy test. The monsignor leads them into a windowless room where he tells them to undress, then ties a small bell to each man's dick. Standing back, he claps his hands, and in waltzes a beautiful young woman wearing nothing but a belly-dancer costume.

She begins to dance sensually around the first candidate. Ting-a-ling. 'Oh Patrick,' says the monsignor, 'I'm so disappointed in your lack of control. Run along now and take a long, cold shower, and pray about your carnal weakness.'

The chastened candidate leaves. The woman proceeds to the second candidate, weaving seductively while peeling off layers of veils. As the last veil drops... ting-a-ling. 'Giuseppe, Giuseppe,' sighs the monsignor. 'You too are unable to withstand your carnal desires. Off you go: take a long, cold shower and pray for forgiveness.'

The dancer continues dancing in front of the final candidate. Nothing. She writhes her by now naked body up and down against the young priestly candidate. No response. Finally, she quits.

'Sergio, my son, I am truly proud of you,' says the monsignor. 'Only you have the true strength of character needed to become a priest. Now go and join your weaker brethren in the showers.' Ting-a-ling.

Q: 'Doctor, Doctor, my hair keeps falling out. What can you give me to keep it in?'

A: 'A shoebox. Next.'

The four dogs

Four men were bragging about how smart their dogs were. The first man was an engineer, the second man an accountant, the third a chemist and the fourth worked for the local authorities. First, the engineer called to his dog, 'T-Square, do your stuff!'

T-square dutifully trotted over to a desk, took out some paper and a pen and promptly drew a circle, a square and a triangle. Everyone agreed that was pretty smart.

Then the accountant called to his dog: 'Slide Rule, do your stuff!' Slide Rule went out into the kitchen and returned with a dozen biscuits. He divided them into four equal piles of three biscuits each.

Everyone agreed that was good, but the chemist said his dog could do better. 'Measure!' he barked. 'Do your stuff!' So Measure got up, padded over to the fridge, took out a pint of milk, got a 10-ounce glass from the cupboard and poured exactly eight ounces in without spilling a drop.

The local authority worker got to his feet. 'Coffee Break,' he said, 'do your stuff!' So Coffee Break jumped to his feet, ate the cookies, drank the milk, dumped on the paper, sexually assaulted the other three dogs, claimed he'd injured his back while doing so, filed a grievance report for unsafe working conditions, put in for Worker's Compensation and went home on sick leave.

The smart poacher

Late one evening, a man is leaving a lake with two buckets of fish when he's stopped by a gamekeeper. 'Excuse me, sir,' says the keeper, 'but I presume you have a licence to catch those fish?'

The man smiles. 'No,
I haven't. But these are my pet fish.'

'Pet fish?' the gamekeeper replies incredulously.

'Yes, sir. Every night I take them to the lake and let them swim around for a while. When I whistle, they jump back into their buckets and I take them home.'

The gamekeeper frowns. 'My arse!' he scoffs. 'This I've got to see.'

'Okay,' says the man, raising an eyebrow, and with that he turns back to the lake and pours the fish into the murky depths. For several minutes the pair watch the surface until the gamekeeper gets annoyed. 'Well?' he cries, 'when are you going to call them back?'

'Call who back?' the man asks innocently.

'The fish, of course.'

'Fish?' says the man, 'what fish?'

The careful monkey

A man walks into a pub with his pet monkey on his shoulder and orders a pint. While he's drinking, the monkey jumps onto the bar and starts cavorting. First it grabs some peanuts and eats them, then it grabs some sliced limes and stuffs them in his gob, and finally it jumps onto the pool table, grabs the cue ball, sticks it in his mouth and swallows it whole.

Enraged, the barman screams at the man, 'Did you see what your bloody monkey just did? He ate my cue ball!'

'That doesn't surprise me,' replies the punter. 'The little bastard eats everything in sight. I'll pay for the cue ball and other stuff.' And he settles the bill and leaves.

Two weeks later he's back, once more with the monkey in tow. He orders a drink, and within minutes the monkey is running amok – until it finds a stray maraschino cherry on the bar. The monkey grabs the cherry, sticks it up his arse, pulls it out and eats it.

The bartender's disgusted. 'Did you see what your monkey did now?' he shouts. 'He stuck a cherry up his brown eye, then pulled it out and ate it!'

'That doesn't surprise me,' replies the punter. 'He still eats everything in sight, but ever since that damn cue ball he measures it first.'

Outsmarted

Hoping for an easy bust, a traffic copper stations himself outside a popular local pub and waits. As everyone floods out at closing time, he spots his quarry – a man so obviously bombed that he can barely walk. He stumbles around the car park for a few minutes, looking for his car. After trying his keys in five others, he finally finds his own vehicle – whereupon he sits for ten minutes as the other patrons leave, blinking slowly. Slowly, he turns his lights on, then off, wipers on then off, then starts to pull forward into the grass. Finally, alone in the car park, he pulls out onto the road and drives away.

Instantly, the policeman turns on the blue lights, pulls over the man and makes him blow into a breathalyser. However, the readout is 0.00.

'I don't understand,' babbles the officer. 'The equipment must be faulty.'

'I doubt it,' grins the man. 'Tonight, I'm the Designated Decoy.'

Front bottom dentistry

A little girl and a little boy are playing in the garden. All of a sudden the little boy drags the girl into the shed and says, 'If you show me yours I'll show you mine.'

So the little girl takes off her little flowery dress and slides down her little knickers. At that moment the boy's mother comes into the shed and discovers them. Furious at what her son is doing, she sends the girl home crying and banishes the boy to his room to think about what he's done. 'Don't come down till you can behave,' she tells him.

A few hours later the boy comes down to see his mother, who by this time has realised that she must talk to her son about the incident. 'You must never, ever touch girls down there again,' she tells him. The little boy is confused by this and asks why, so his mother says, 'Well, they have teeth down there and they'll bite you!'

Terrified, the boy runs up to his room to count his fingers.

Soon the little boy becomes a big boy, getting the odd snog here and there but never anything more, as he's terrified of those teeth. It gets to his wedding night, and there he is in bed with his new wife, who by now is thinking she's never going to get a shag. Sure enough, her husband just kisses her and turns over to go to sleep. 'Is that it then?' she asks. 'What about the rest of it?'

'I can't,' the man says, 'I'm too scared.'

Thinking this sweet, his wife says, 'Look – you have nothing to worry about. I'll show you what to do.'

But he's still scared, so she asks him why. Upon hearing about the teeth story she can hardly stop herself laughing, but to reassure her new husband she says, 'I'll prove it to you: women do not have teeth in their fannies. Here – have a look.' And she parts her legs so he can see.

He gasps, and says, 'With gums like that I'm not surprised.'

Lawyer unsure

A man visits his lawyer to help settle his divorce proceedings. 'But it says here she's divorcing you because you threw a trifle at her,' says the solicitor.

'Yes,' says the man, downcast. 'Now she's claiming custardy.'

The musical octopus

A bloke walks into a bar, sits down and says to the bartender, 'Pint of beer, please, and a glass of water for the octopus.'

The bartender looks over and sure enough he has an octopus with him. 'No animals allowed in here,' he says. 'And that includes octopuses.'

'This is a special octopus,' says the punter. 'It can play any musical instrument.'

'Right,' says the bartender. 'If your octopus can go over there and play that piano, I'll give you both the beer and the water for free.'

So the octopus wanders over and plays the piano perfectly. Another customer comes over with a flute and says, 'I bet you a tenner that your octopus can't play this flute.' So the octopus picks it up and plays it perfectly, and the man hands over the money.

Next a Scotsman walks over with some bagpipes and dares the octopus to play them. The animal seems puzzled, and simply looks at the instrument. 'Go on!' shouts the man. 'Play the bloody things!'

'Look, mate,' says the octopus. 'As soon as I can work out how to take its pyjamas off, I'm taking it home and fucking it.'

Medical breakthrough

After a game of tennis Sam's arm was hurting, so he set off for the doctor's. 'Don't do that,' said his mate. 'You'll have to spend an hour in the waiting room breathing in other people's germs. There's a computer at the chemist that can diagnose anything quicker and cheaper than a GP – just feed it a sample of your urine, and the computer will diagnose your problem and tell you what to do about it. And it only costs a tenner.'

So Sam pissed in a jar, trooped down to the chemist's and paid the £10. The computer blooped, lights flashed, and after a brief pause out popped a small slip of paper. 'YOU HAVE TENNIS ELBOW,' it said. 'SOAK YOUR ARM IN WARM SALT WATER. AVOID HEAVY LABOUR. IT WILL BE BETTER IN TWO WEEKS.'

Later that evening, thinking how amazing this new technology was and how it would change medical science forever, Sam wondered if the machine could be fooled. So he mixed together some tap water, a stool sample from his dog and urine samples from his wife and daughter. To top it off, he cracked one off into the concoction. Then he went back to the chemist's, poured in the sample and deposited a tenner.

The machine again made the usual noise and printed out the following analysis, 'YOUR TAP WATER IS TOO HARD – GET A WATER SOFTENER. YOUR DOG HAS WORMS – GIVE HIM WORM PILLS. YOUR DAUGHTER IS USING COCAINE – PUT HER IN REHAB. YOUR WIFE IS PREGNANT WITH TWINS; THEY ARE NOT YOURS – GET A LAWYER. AND IF YOU DON'T STOP JERKING OFF, YOUR ELBOW WILL NEVER GET BETTER.'

Talking clock

A drunk is proudly showing off his new flat to a couple of friends late one night, and leads the way to his bedroom, where there's a huge brass gong.

'What's that for?' asks one of the guests.

'That's the talking clock,' replies the man. 'Listen...'

With that, he gives it a big whack with a hammer.

'For pity's sake!' screams a voice from next door, 'it's ten past three in the morning!'

Teenie thug corrected

It's the day after Bonfire Night and little Tommy arrives at school looking miserable. The teacher calms the class down and says, 'Tommy, I hear you were in a bit of trouble last night, weren't you?'

'Yes, miss,' replies Tommy. 'I was caught putting bangers up cats' arses.'

The teacher corrects the young lad, 'Rectum Tommy, rectum.'

'Rectum, miss? I blew their bloody heads off!'

The Scotch challenge

George Michael walks into a bar and says to the bartender, 'I want you to give me 12-year-old Scotch, and don't try to fool me because I can tell the difference.' The bartender is sceptical and decides to try to trick George with a glass of five-year-old. The leather-clad crooner takes a sip, scowls and says, 'Bartender, this crap is five-year-old Scotch. I told you I want 12-year-old.'

The bartender tries once more with eight-year-old Scotch. George takes a sip, grimaces and says, 'Bartender, I don't want this eight-year-old filth. Give me 12-year-old Scotch!'

Admitting defeat, the bartender dusts off the 12-year-old Scotch from the back of the bar. George takes a sip and sighs, 'Ah... now that's the real thing.'

A disgusting, grimy, stinking drunk has been watching all this with great interest. He stumbles over and sets a glass down in front of George and says, 'Pal – I'm impressed by what you can do. Try this one on me.'

George Michael takes a sip... and immediately spits out the liquid, crying, 'Yechhh! This stuff tastes like piss!'

The drunk's eyes light up. 'Aye!' he says. 'Now how old am I?'

Cross-dressing car

A motorist goes to his mechanic and says, 'I think my car may be a transvestite.'

'Are you having me on?' says the grease-monkey.

'No, straight up,' says the motorist. 'It keeps slipping into the wrong gear.'

Statues come to life

There were two statues in the park – one of a boy and one of a girl. One day an angel fluttered by and clicked its fingers. The statues came to life. 'I am the angel of the statues,' said the heavenly vision. 'I can bring you to life for only 15 minutes, but you're free to do anything you would do if you were human.'

The statues looked at each other. 'There's something we've been wanting to do for ages. Can we really do anything?'

'Yes, anything. But you only have 15 minutes.'

Not wanting to waste any more time, the boy grabbed the girl by the hand, they both jumped into a nearby bush, and there was a lot of giggling, thrashing and happy squealing. Finally they emerged, sweaty but very happy, and climbed onto their pedestals. The angel clicked its fingers and they both turned back into stone.

They looked no different, except they had smirks on their faces. The angel flew off into the distance.

A few minutes later, the angel returned and clicked its fingers again. The statues looked a bit surprised, and the angel said, 'I'm not really allowed to do this, but you looked so happy, I thought I'd come back and give you another 15 minutes of life. Remember, you can do whatever you want.'

'Excellent! Let's do it again!' said the boy statue.

'Why don't we do it the other way round, this time?' replied the girl statue. 'You hold the pigeon down and I'll crap on its head.'

The fussy whale

A male whale and a female whale are swimming off the coast of Japan when they notice a whaling ship. The male whale recognises it as the same ship that had harpooned his father many years earlier. Thirsting for revenge, he says to the female whale, 'Let's both swim under the ship and blow out of our air-holes at the same time. It should cause the thing to turn over and sink.'

They try it and, sure enough, the ship turns over and quickly sinks.

Soon, however, the whales realise that the sailors have jumped overboard and are swimming to the safety of the shore. The male is enraged by the possibility of blubber-lovers getting away and tells the female, 'Let's swim after the bastards and gobble them up before they reach the shore.'

Racing after the struggling swabbies, he realises the female is reluctant to follow him. 'Look,' she explains, 'I went along with the blow job, but I absolutely refuse to swallow the seamen.'

Did you hear about the man...

...who wouldn't pay for an exorcism?

He got re-possessed.

Girl kind to pet

A little girl walks into a pet shop and approaches the counter. 'Excuthe me, mithter,' she asks in the sweetest little lisp, 'do you keep wittle wabbith?'

Smiling, the shopkeeper gets down on his knees, so that he's on her level. 'Well,' he asks, 'do you want a wittle white wabby? Or a soft and fuwwy black wabby? Or one like that cute wittle brown wabby over there?'

The little girl leans forward herself. 'Hmm,' she says in a quiet voice, 'I don't fink my pyfon weally giveth a toth.'

The flavoured johnnies

A chap is in the pub with his wife. After the man goes for a slash, he comes back bursting with excitement. 'You'll never guess what they've got in there!' he tells his missus. 'Condoms – fancy ones! They've got all different flavours – banana, strawberry, chocolate! They've even got piña colada and whisky flavours!'

'Nip back in and get a packet,' says the wife, 'and we'll try them out later.'

Back home later that night, the couple retire to bed with their new toys. 'Let's play a game,' says the husband. 'I'll turn out the lights, put on a condom and you have to guess the flavour.'

'Okay,' says his wife, and the lights go out. 'Cheese and onion!' she exclaims 30 seconds later.

'Wait till I get it on first!' says hubbie.

Sticky seat

A man was decorating his bathroom, and had just applied the last coat of varnish to the toilet seat. He left the room for a minute to get a mug of cocoa, but when he came back he found his wife stuck to the seat. So he unscrewed the seat and took his wife – still attached – to the hospital.

After an hour the couple finally got to see the doctor. 'What seems to be the problem?' asked the medic, and the man turned his wife around and lifted her skirt up.

After several minutes of the doctor looking at and feeling his wife's arse, the worried man said, 'So?'

The doc straightened up. 'It's beautiful,' he said, 'but why did you get it framed?'

The three sisters' hot dates

Three sisters are sat in their bedroom discussing what they're going to do that night. While deciding, they hear a knock at the front door. Their dad answers it, to find a lad standing there.

'Hiya,' says the youth. 'My name's Lance – I've come to pick up Flance to take her to the dance. Any chance?'

'Sure,' says the dad, and with this Flance leaves for the dance with Lance.

A short while later there's another knock at the door. Again the dad answers. It's another lad. 'Hello, sir,' he says, 'I'm Joe, I've come to pick up Flo to take her to the show. Can she go?' The dad nods his okay, and away goes Flo to the show.

The one girl left on her own feels a bit left out, when finally there's another knock at the door. Again the dad answers. 'Wotcher,' says the young man on the doorstep. 'My name's Tucker...'

'You can piss off!' shouts the dad as he slams the door shut.

Welcome to Australia

An English emigrant steps off the plane in Australia, clutching his citizenship papers and eagerly awaiting his first meeting with a genuine Aussie. But no sooner has he left the airport than he's appalled to see a young man humping a kangaroo. Shocked but undeterred, he continues his journey – but is again flabbergasted to see another man banging away at yet another kangaroo.

He's stunned and sickened, so heads for the nearest bar. There on the steps is a crusty, old, one-legged Australian, jerking himself off. 'What the hell is wrong with you people?' shouts the immigrant. 'I've just seen two men shagging kangaroos, and now I find you rubbing off outside the local boozer!'

'Come on, mate,' says the oldster. 'You don't expect me to catch a kangaroo with only one leg, do you?'

Irishman abroad

An Irishman had been in Germany looking for work, and on returning to the old country his drinking buddies pressed him for stories about his trip into the big, wide world.

'I stepped off the boat in Hamburg,' said the Irishman, 'and there was this big redhead waving to me as I walked ashore. "Hey, Irish!" she shouted, "how would you like to come with me for the time of your life?" I thought, lovely girl, why not? And yes, I had the time of my life! Next morning she brought me breakfast in bed, a bloody feast I had. But I was starting work that day, so I put on my coat and set off down the stairs. This girl called after me, "Hey, Irish! How about some Marks?" So I gave her nine out of ten.'

Romeo rejected

A pub regular starts to notice that, every evening, a very attractive woman comes in around 8pm and sits at the end of the bar, always alone. After two weeks of seeing her there, he makes his move.

'No thank you,' she rebuffs him politely. 'You see, this may sound rather odd in this day and age, but I'm keeping myself pure until I meet the man I love.'

'That must be rather difficult,' replies the man.

'Oh, I don't mind too much,' she says, nodding, 'but it seems to have upset my husband.'

Sex life spiced up

A couple had been married for six years, and were having trouble with their sex life: all the husband wanted to do was watch the football on telly. So the wife went to the psychiatrist. He asked her if she had tried aphrodisiacs and she said, 'Yes, I've tried everything.'

He then asked her if she'd tried crotchless knickers. She hadn't, so she went out and bought some. Back home, she put them on underneath a very short mini-skirt.

As usual, the husband was sitting watching the football. She walked in and sat down opposite him, and folded her legs. He looked up and frowned. She then unfolded her legs very slowly and widely, a number of times. The husband didn't flinch.

So she thought, 'Bugger it,' and spread them. The husband looked over in horror and said, 'Are those crotchless knickers you're wearing?'

'Yes,' she purred. 'Why?'

'Thank Christ for that,' said the husband. 'I thought it was a rip in the new sofa.'

Spuds you misunderstand

A man strolls into his local grocer's and says, 'Three pounds of potatoes, please.'

'No, no, no,' replies the owner, shaking his head, 'it's kilos nowadays, mate...'

'Oh,' apologises the man, 'three pounds of kilos, please.'

Late night caller

Late one evening, a man is watching television when his phone rings. 'Hello?' he answers.

'Is that 77777?' sounds a desperate voice on the other end of the phone.

'Er, yes, it is,' replies the man, puzzled.

'Thank God!' cries the caller, relieved. 'Can you ring 999 for me? I've got my finger stuck in the number seven.'

Drunk drivers

Bill and Dave are walking home after a night on the sauce. They've no money and are staggering all over the place when they find themselves outside a bus depot. Bill has a brainwave, 'Go and steal us a bus so we can drive home – I'll stay on the lookout.'

Dave agrees and breaks into the garage. He's gone nearly 20 minutes before Bill catches sight of him again.

'What the hell are you doing, Dave?' he shouts. 'Get a move on!'

'But I can't find a number three anywhere...' says Dave.

'You idiot,' shouts Bill, stunned by his friend's stupidity, 'steal a number 11! We'll get off at the Arndale and walk the rest of the way!'

The parrot's pedigree

A woman goes into a pet shop intending to buy a parrot, not realising how expensive the things are. Once inside the shop she begins looking around and discovers that she can't afford any of the multicoloured birds on offer, so she goes up to the owner and asks him if he has anything cheaper. He takes her out back and shows her the dirtiest, ugliest-looking parrot she has ever seen, explaining that it was donated by the local brothel. Desperate for some feathered companionship, she buys it and takes it home.

Later that day her daughter pays her a visit. The parrot, which had been silent to that point, suddenly pipes up, 'New whore house! New whore!'

Embarrassed, the mother explains to her daughter why the parrot said this. An hour later the woman's next door neighbour drops in for a cuppa, and once again the parrot jumps into life. 'New whore house!' the evil creature squawks. 'New whore!' Once again, the woman is left to make her awkward explanation.

Later that night the woman's husband comes home from work. The parrot looks at him for a minute, then screeches, 'How's it going, John?'

Miracle birth

A woman is dating a surgeon and, before long, she becomes pregnant. She doesn't want an abortion, so the doc says he'll come up with a plan. Nine months later, just as the woman is due to give birth, a priest goes into the hospital for a prostate gland infection. The doctor says to the woman, 'I know what we'll do. After I've operated on the priest, I'll give the baby to him and tell him it was a miracle.'

So the surgeon delivers the baby then operates on the priest. After the op he goes in to the man of God and tells him, 'Father, you're not going to believe this.'

'What?' asks the priest, 'what happened?'

'You gave birth to a child!'

'But that's impossible!' says the priest.

'I did the operation myself,' insists the doctor, 'it's a miracle. Here's your baby.'

Fifteen years go by, and the priest realises it's time to tell his son the truth. So he sits the boy down and says, 'Son, I have something to tell you. I'm not your father.'

The son says, 'What do you mean, you're not my father?'

'I'm actually your mother,' the priest replies. 'The archbishop is your father.'

Thirsty playwright

William Shakespeare walks into a pub and asks the barman for a pint of lager. 'On your way, son,' says the barman. 'I'm not serving you.'

Perplexed, Mr Shakespeare repeats his request, only to evoke a similar response. 'Look, pal,' says Shakespeare. 'I've nothing against you or your pub – all I want is a pint of ale.

Now be a good lad and get on with it, eh?'

The barman, getting shirty now, looks Will up and down and, with considerable anger in his voice, asks the famous gent to leave. Shakespeare looks forlorn. 'Why?' he says. 'What have I done?'

The barman grips him by the collar and whispers in his ear, 'You're Bard!'

Woman drops baby

A house catches fire, and there's a woman trapped on the top floor with her baby. She's leaning out the window screaming for help when the firefighters arrive. One of the firemen runs over and shouts to her, 'Throw me your baby!'

'No!' screams the woman. 'You'll drop him!'

The fireman insists. 'It's okay,' he tells her. 'I was a Premiership goalkeeper for ten years. I'll catch him.'

So the woman relents, tossing her baby down. And the fireman catches it, bounces it twice and kicks it over a wall.

Q: What do you call a woman who's lost 95 per cent of her intelligence?

A : Divorced.

Lord seeks graft

Looking for work, Jesus goes to the local Job Centre. 'Okay, Mr Christ,' says the assistant, after typing in his details, 'there are two jobs that come up for your spec. One is a carpenter in Jerusalem at £2,000 per week; the other a carpenter in Aberdeen at £200 a week.'

And lo, the Son of God did speak, 'I'll take the one in Aberdeen, cheers.'

The assistant is surprised. 'Why? You'd get far more money in the other job.'

'I know,' Jesus spake thus. 'But the last time I worked in Jerusalem I got hammered with tax.'

The English copper

An English policeman starts his first day of work in Ireland. Being new on the job he wants to look good in front of his fellow workers. While he is sitting in a lay-by looking for speeders, he spots a Ferrari driving past. 'Right,' he thinks, 'the perfect opportunity to impress my colleagues.'

So he sets off, sirens blazing, and stops the driver, intending to provoke the man so he can arrest him. 'Could you step out of the car, sir.' The Irishman behind the wheel obliges. 'Right sir,' says the cop, 'I'm going to draw this circle of chalk on the ground. You must stay in it at all times.'

'All right, officer,' says the Irishman.

Then, with the Irishman standing in the circle, the cop walks over to the car, gets out his truncheon and breaks the car's headlight. He then turns around, and to his surprise sees that the Irishman is still standing in the circle, looking completely calm. So the cop turns back around and smashes the windscreen. Once again he spins round – but the Irishman has a smirk on his face!

Not believing his eyes, the policeman smashes the windows. Once again he turns, to find the Irishman pissing himself. Now he gets out a penknife and slashes all four tyres. When he looks up, the Irishman is actually rolling around on the road in fits of hysterics.

'What's so funny, Paddy?' says the cop. 'I just smashed up your new Ferrari!'

'I know,' says the Irishman. 'But what you didn't see was that when you turned around I stepped out of the circle!'

What's the biggest drawback...
...in the circus?

An elephant's foreskin.

Fisherman gives wife ultimatum

Waking one sunny morning, a man turns to his wife and tells her they're going fishing for the day. 'Oh no – I'm not wasting a lovely day like this,' replies his wife. 'Besides, you know how much I hate fishing.'

'Okay,' answers the man, 'you have three choices: me, you and the dog go fishing; you give me a blow job; or you take it up the tradesman's. I'm off to the shed for ten minutes, and I want your decision when I get back.'

A few minutes later he returns. 'I've decided on the blow job,' his wife says. 'Good,' he says, losing no time in dropping his trousers.

But just as she kneels down to perform the act, the wife notices a strange smell. 'But your crotch reeks of shit!' she cries.

'Yeah,' says her husband, nonchalantly. 'The dog didn't want to go fishing either.'

Brooms to be

Two brooms are standing in a closet. Before long they're chatting away – within a week, they're married. On the big day the bride broom looks stunning in her white dress; the groom broom suave in his suit. The ceremony is wonderful, and soon everyone is seated at dinner. The bride broom leans across and whispers to her husband, 'I've a surprise... I think we're going to have a little broom!'

'That's impossible,' shouts the angry broom, 'we haven't even swept together!'

What's green...

...and eats balls?

Gonorrhoea.

Fragrance misplaced

Two blondes walk into the perfume section of a department store and pick up a sample bottle. The first blonde sprays it on her wrist and smells it. 'That's quite nice,' she coos. 'What's it called?'

'It says "Viens à moi" on the label,' replies her friend.

'Viens à moi?' says the first bonde, 'what the hell does that mean?'

At this stage the assistant offers some help. 'Viens à moi, ladies, is French for "come to me".'

The first blonde takes another sniff, 'Here, Kerry,' she says offering her arm to her mate. 'It doesn't smell like come to me. Does that smell like come to you?'

It is easier for a camel...

A teacher, a dustman and a lawyer find themselves waiting outside the Pearly Gates. Eventually Saint Peter emerges and informs them that in order to get into Heaven, they'll each have to answer one question. Peter turns first to the teacher. 'What was the name of the ship that crashed into the iceberg? They just made a movie about it.'

The teacher answers quickly, 'That would be the Titanic.' Saint Peter lets him through the gate.

He then turns to the dustman and says: 'How many people died on the ship?' Fortunately for him, the trash-collector had just seen the movie. '1,228,' he answers.

'That's right! You may enter.' Peter then turns to the lawyer. 'Name them.'

The decorating nuns

Two nuns are ordered to paint a room in the convent, and Mother Superior's last instruction is that they must not get one drop of paint on their new habits. After conferring about this, the two nuns decide to lock the door of the room, strip off and paint in the nude.

In the middle of the project there comes a knock at the door. 'Who is it?' calls one of the nuns.

'Blind man,' replies a voice from the other side of the door.

The two nuns look at each other, shrug and, deciding that no harm can come from letting a blind man into the room, they open the door.

'Nice tits,' says the man. 'Where do you want these blinds?'

Unauthorised withdrawal

A bloke in a balaclava bursts into a sperm bank, armed with a shotgun. 'Open the safe!' he yells at the terrified girl at reception.

'But we're not a real bank,' she stammers. 'We don't have any money. This is a sperm bank.'

'Don't argue – open the safe or I'll blow your head off!' screams the guy with the gun. The terrified woman obliges. Once she's opened the safe door, the guy says, 'Take out one of the bottles and drink it!'

'But it's full of spunk!' the poor girl replies.

'Don't argue! Just drink it!' says the gunman. So she prises the cap off one of the bottles and gulps it down.

'Take another one out and drink that too!' demands the gunman. She does as she's told. Suddenly the man pulls off his balaclava and, to the receptionist's amazement, it's her husband.

'There,' he says, 'it's not that bloody difficult, is it?'

Pre-natal dilemma

A woman is six months pregnant with her first child, and is visiting her obstetrician for a check-up. Just as the examination is finishing, she turns to the doctor, 'Um, this is sort of awkward... my husband wants me to ask you...'

'Really, don't worry, I get this question all the time,' says the doctor, placing a reassuring hand on her shoulder. 'Sex is absolutely fine until late in the pregnancy.'

'Er... no,' continues the woman. 'He wants to know if I can still mow the lawn.'

Disappointing opening

The first day at the London sperm bank was pretty unsuccessful. Only two blokes made appointments. One came on the bus and the other missed the tube.

Sheep love

A researcher is conducting a survey into sheep shagging. First of all he visits a Cornish farmer. 'So, Cornish farmer, how do you shag your sheep?' he asks.

'Well, I take the hind legs of the sheep and put them down my wellies, and take the front legs of the sheep and put them over a wall,' the yokel replies.

'That's very interesting,' says the researcher, and he gets on a train to the Midlands. 'So, Midlands farmer, how do you shag your sheep?' he asks.

'Well, I take the hind legs of the sheep and put them down my wellies and take the front legs of the sheep and put them over a wall,' replies the old scrote.

'That's very interesting,' says the researcher. 'That's how they do it in Cornwall too.' And he gets on a plane to Aberdeen.

'So, Aberdeenshire farmer, how do you shag your sheep?'

'Well, I take the hind legs of the sheep and put them down my wellies, and take the front legs of the sheep and put them over my shoulders.'

'Over your shoulders?' quizzes the researcher. 'Don't you put them over a wall like everyone else?'

'What?' says the Scottish farmer. 'And miss out on all the kissing?'

Smart thinking

A married man was having an affair with his secretary. Not for the first time, their passions overcame them at work and they took off for her house, where they made passionate love all afternoon. Exhausted from the wild sex, they then fell asleep, awakening around eight in the evening. As the man threw on his clothes he told the woman to take his shoes outside and rub them through the grass and dirt. Mystified, she nonetheless complied.

He then slipped into his shoes and drove home. 'Where have you been?' demanded his wife when he entered the house.

'Darling, I can't lie to you,' said the man. 'I've been having an affair with my secretary and we've been screwing like rabbits all day.'

The wife glanced down at his shoes and said, 'You lying bastard! You've been playing golf again!'

The stray earring

A mechanic is at work one day when he notices that his fellow grease-monkey is wearing an earring. This man knows his co-worker to be a conservative fellow, and is curious about this sudden change in fashion sense.

'Tom, I didn't know you were into earrings,' he says.

'Oh, sure,' replies Tom sheepishly.

'Really? How long have you been wearing one?' asks the mechanic.

'Ever since my wife found it in our bed.'

At the playschool

As a class project, a playschool teacher asks her pupils what, out of all the materials in the world, they would like to be made of. Quickly, one little boy's arm shoots up. 'I would be made out of gold, miss,' he squeaks. 'Then I could scratch my arm and use a few flakes of gold to buy a new car.'

Another young cherub pipes up. 'Miss, miss!' he cries. 'I'd be made of platinum. It's worth more than gold, and a few flakes could buy two cars.'

'And what about you, Johnny?' asks the teacher of the little boy at the back.

'Simple, miss,' replies Johnny. 'Pubic hair.'

'Why on Earth would you want to be made out of that?' asks the teacher, aghast. 'Well, my older sister's only got a little,' the youngster replies. 'But you should see the number of cars outside our house.'

Q: What did the leper say to the prostitute?

A: You can keep the tip.

The escaped gorillas

Three gorillas escape from the zoo, and the director decides to hire a professional hunter to recapture them. The hunter accepts and goes to assess the situation. 'I should be able to get them back for you,' he says, 'All I need is a dozen helpers with nets, a couple of vans, my dog and my shotgun.'

Having acquired the equipment, the hunter and the zoo director head off into a nearby forest, where they quickly locate the gorillas up three separate trees. The hunter makes his way up to the first tree and gives it a good shake. The unfortunate gorilla falls to the floor, where the hunter's dog toddles up to it and bites off his knackers before the helpers drag him off into the van.

The same thing happens to the second gorilla.

The third is reluctant to come down, however, so the hunter decides to climb up the tree and coax it down with a banana. The zoo director calls up to him, 'If it attacks you, shall I shoot it with the shotgun?'

'No!' the hunter shouts down, 'but if I fall out of this tree, shoot the fucking dog!'

Nice bird

A man is talking to a woman at the bar, when he looks at her and asks, 'Have you ever had a magpie on your left wrist?'

'No,' the lady replies.

'Okay. Have you ever had a parrot on your right wrist?' the man continues.

'No,' the lady replies.

The man then gets the woman to poke out her tongue. 'Well,' he says, 'it looks like you've had a cockatoo on there.'

The bottle opener

One day, after striking gold in Alaska, a lonesome miner came down from the mountains and walked into a saloon in the nearest town. 'I'm lookin' fer the meanest, roughest, toughest whore in the Yukon!' he growled to the bartender.

'Well, we got her!' barked the barkeep. 'She's upstairs – second room on the right.'

The miner handed the bartender a gold nugget to pay for the whore and two beers. He grabbed the bottles, stomped up the stairs, kicked open the second door on the right and yelled, 'I'm lookin' for the meanest, roughest, toughest whore in the Yukon!'

The woman inside the room looked at the miner and said, 'Well, you found her!' She then stripped naked, bent over and grabbed both ankles.

'How'd ya know I like to do it in that position?' asked the miner.

'I didn't,' replied the whore, 'but I thought ya might like to open them beers before we get started.'

Atishoo!

A man and a woman are riding next to each other in first class. The man sneezes, pulls out his wang and wipes the tip off. The woman can't believe what she just saw and decides she is hallucinating.

A few minutes pass. The man sneezes again. He pulls out his wang and wipes the tip off. The woman is seething – she can't believe such an uncouth person exists.

A few minutes pass. The man sneezes yet again. He takes his wang out and wipes the tip off. The woman has finally had enough. She turns to the man and says, 'Three times you've sneezed, and three times you've removed your penis from your pants to wipe it off! What the hell kind of degenerate are you?'

'I'm so sorry to have disturbed you, ma'am,' the man apologises. 'The fact is that I have a very rare condition. When I sneeze, I have an orgasm.'

The woman looks aghast. 'I'm so sorry! What are you taking for it?'

'Pepper.'

The naked rescuer

A young couple go out for a drive one evening. While bombing down the road the man says to the girl, 'If I go at 100 miles an hour, will you take off your clothes?' She agrees and he begins to speed up. When the speedometer hits a ton she starts to strip. When she gets all her clothes off he is so busy staring at her that he drives off the road and flips the car.

The girl is thrown clear without a scratch, but her clothes and her boyfriend are trapped in the car. 'Go get help!' he pleads.

'I can't,' she replies, 'I'm naked.'

He points to his shoe that was thrown from the car and says, 'Cover your snatch with that and go get help.'

So she takes his shoe, covers herself up and runs to the petrol station down the road. When she arrives she's frantic, and yells to the attendant, 'Help me! My boyfriend's stuck!'

The attendant looks down at the shoe covering her crotch and replies, 'I'm sorry, miss. He's too far in.'

The dead cat

An old maid wanted to travel by bus to the pet cemetery with the remains of her cat. As she boarded the bus, she whispered to the driver, 'I have a dead pussy.'

The driver pointed to the woman in the seat behind him. 'Sit next to my wife,' he said. 'You two have a lot in common.'

One-armed combat

Bruised and battered, Paddy hobbles into his local pub on a crutch with one arm in a cast. 'My God!' the barman says. 'What happened to you?

'I got in a tiff with Riley,' groans Paddy.

'Riley? He's just a wee fellow,' cries the surprised barkeep. 'He must have had something in his hand.'

'Aye, that he did,' Kelly grimaces. 'A shovel, it was.'

'Dear Lord,' nods the landlord. 'Didn't you have anything in your hand?'

'Aye, I did – Mrs Riley's left tit,' nods Paddy. 'A beautiful thing it was, too. But not much use in a fight.'

Battle of the sexes

If your wife comes out of the kitchen to shout at you, what have you usually done wrong?

Made her chain too long.

Stone misread

Two tramps walk past a church and start to read the gravestones. The first tramp says, 'Bloody hell – this bloke was 182!'

'Oh yeah?' says the other. 'What was his name?'

'Miles, from London.'

The wall-walker

A bloke strolls into a pub and walks up the wall, across the ceiling, back down the other wall then over to the bar, where he orders two whiskies. He drinks them, walks up the wall, across the ceiling, back down the other wall and out the door.

'That's strange,' said a punter to the barman.

'I know,' the barman replies. 'He normally orders a pint.'

Blowing smoke

Three young kids are smoking behind the barn. 'My dad can blow smoke through his nose,' says the first boy.

'That's nothing,' says the second. 'Mine can blow smoke through his ears.'

'You think that's good,' says the third. 'Mine can blow smoke through his arse. And I've seen the nicotine stains in his pants to prove it.'

Heads it's 'yes'...

Arriving for her university entrance exam, a blonde is overjoyed to find the questions all have Yes/No answers. Staring at the question paper for five minutes, she realises she still hasn't a clue. So, in a fit of inspiration, she takes a coin out of her purse and starts flipping it – marking a 'Yes' for heads and 'No' for tails.

Within half an hour she's finished – but she still spends the last few minutes desperately throwing the coin, sweating and muttering. Alarmed, the examiner wanders over and asks what's wrong. 'I want to be thorough,' she cries. 'So I'm rechecking my answers.'

Constructive dismissal

A man walks into the dole office and asks to sign on. 'What was your previous job?' asks the clerk.

'I worked in a butcher's shop,' replies the fella.

'And why did you leave?'

'I was sacked for putting my knob in the meat grinder,' comes the reply.

The clerk ponders this for a bit and says, 'Oh, right... what happened, by the way?'

'She got sacked as well.'

Plum in the mouth

Three young women are discussing their boyfriends over coffee. 'It's funny,' says the first, 'Pete's balls are always cold as ice when I'm sucking his cock...'

'Weird,' replies the second girl, 'it's the same with my Richard...'

They turn to their friend, 'What about you? When you blow your man, are his balls cold?'

'Eugh, that's disgusting,' spits the girl. 'I never put his pee-pee in my mouth!'

'You're crazy,' laugh her friends. 'A good blow job is the best way to keep a man! Try it!'

The next morning they meet at the café, and the blow job novice is sporting a nasty shiner. 'Yep... the bastard hit me last night while I was sucking him off,' she sniffs.

'What for?' ask her friends.

'I don't know,' replies the girl. 'All I did was tell him how strange it was that his balls were so warm, seeing as Pete and Richard's are always so cold...'

What does a blonde's...

...right leg say to her left leg?

Nothing – they've never met.

Love in Scotland

A young Scottish lad and lassie are holding hands and gazing out over the loch. After a few minutes, the girl says to the boy, 'A penny for your thoughts, Angus.'

'I was thinkin'... perhaps it's time we had a wee cuddle.'

Blushing, the girl leans over and cuddles him.

After a while, the girl says, 'Another penny for your thoughts, Angus.'

'I was thinkin'... perhaps it's aboot time for a wee kiss.' She leans over and pecks him lightly on the cheek.

There's another silence before the girl pipes up, 'Another penny for your thoughts, Angus.'

'I was thinkin'... perhaps it's aboot time ah poot ma hand on your leg.'

Shyly, she puts his hand on her knee. At this point, she sees his brows knitting. 'Angus,' she cries, 'another penny for your thoughts!'

'Well, now,' he frowns, 'ma thoughts are more serious this time.'

'Really?' whispers the girl, biting her lip in anticipation of the ultimate request.

'Aye,' he says, 'isn't it aboot time ye paid me them first three pennies?'

Why is pubic hair...

...curly?

If it were straight it would poke your eyes out.

The waiting game

A policeman is on night patrol near a local well-known Lovers' Lane, when he sees a car. The light is on and inside he can see a couple – a young man in the driver's seat reading a computer magazine, and a girl in the back seat calmly knitting. Suspicious, he wanders over to the driver's window and knocks. 'Yes, officer?' says the young man, obligingly winding down the window, 'can I help?'

'What do you think you're doing?' the policeman barks.

'What does it look like?' answers the young man, 'I'm reading this magazine.'

The copper points at the girl in the back seat. 'And what is she doing?' he mutters.

The young man glances over his shoulder. 'I think,' he says, 'she's knitting a scarf.'

Confused, the officer asks, 'How old are you, young man?'

'I'm 19,' he replies.

'And how old is she?' asks the officer, glancing at the young lady.

The young man looks at his watch. 'Well,' he says after a thoughtful pause, 'in about 12 minutes she'll be 16.'

Dissatisfied customer

A woman walked into a sex shop and asked for a vibrator. The shop assistant gestured with his index finger and said, 'Come this way.' The woman replied,

'If I could come that way, I wouldn't need a bloody vibrator.'

Down boy

A man took his Rottweiler to the vet. 'My dog's cross-eyed,' he told the doc. 'Is there anything you can do for him?'

'Well,' said the vet, 'let's see.' So he picked the dog up by its ears and had a good look at its eyes. 'Sorry,' said the vet, 'I'm going to have to put him down.'

'Just because he's cross-eyed!' exclaimed the man.

'No,' said the vet. 'Because he's bloody heavy.'

A horse walks into a bar...

...and asks for a pint. The barman thinks, 'Hmm – I can rip off this horse without him realising,' so charges £13 for the pint.

Serving the nag with his drink the barman says, 'We don't get many horses in this pub.'

'I'm not surprised,' the horse replies, 'the price you charge for a bloody pint.'

Drunk takes a leak

A man is gently drinking himself into a stupor. After burping loudly, he turns groggily to the bartender. 'Hey mate,' he slurs, 'where's your toilet?'

With more than a little disdain, the bartender replies, 'Go down the hall and it's on your right.'

Nodding dumbly, the man slides off his stool and stumbles off down the corridor. Within minutes, the other pub patrons jump at the sound of an ear-splitting scream. A few minutes of confusion go by, when suddenly another pained yell echoes around the bar. Locating the source of the noise, the barman decides to investigate, and runs into the pub toilets.

'What's all the screaming about in here?' he shouts at the drunk. 'You're scaring all my customers away.'

'I'm sorry,' he burbles, opening the cubicle door, 'but I'm sitting on the toilet, and every time I go to flush it, something comes up and squeezes the hell out of my balls.'

The bartender shakes his head sadly. 'No wonder,' he grimaces. 'You're sitting on a mop bucket.'

The engineer goes to Heaven

An engineer dies and reports to the Pearly Gates. Saint Peter checks his dossier and says, 'Ah, I see you're an engineer – you're in the wrong place.' So the engineer reports to the Gates of Hell and is let in.

Pretty soon, however, the engineer gets dissatisfied with the level of comfort in Hell, and starts designing some improvements. Soon they've got air conditioning and flush toilets and escalators, and the engineer is a pretty popular guy.

One day, God calls Satan up on the telephone and says with a sneer, 'So, how's it going down there in Hell?'

'Hey, things are going great!' says the Devil. 'We've got air conditioning and flush toilets and escalators! There's no telling what this engineer is going to come up with next...'

God replies, 'What? You've got an engineer? That's a mistake – he should never have got down there. Send him back up.'

'No way,' says Satan. 'I like having an engineer on the staff, and I'm keeping him.'

'Send him back up here or I'll sue!' says God.

Satan laughs uproariously and answers, 'Yeah, right. And just where are you going to get a lawyer?'

Fairy developments

Snow White walks into her local chemist to pick up some photos she left for developing. Sadly, due to a technical glitch, the assistant informs her that her photos have been delayed, and that he's unable to give her a time when she can pick them up. With a look of despair, Snow White bursts into song, 'Some day my prints will come...'

Codger orders ice-cream

Cedric and Bill, two old men suffering from Alzheimer's, are out walking one day when Cedric sees an ice-cream van at the end of a road. 'Bill, go get me a 99,' says Cedric, 'a 99.'

'I'll never remember that,' replies Bill.

'Just think, "99, 99, 99,"' says Cedric.

So off trots Bill toward the ice-cream van, saying, '99, 99, 99,' when Cedric calls him back. 'Bill, get me some chopped nuts on that.'

'Chopped whats on what?' replies poor Bill, looking confused.

'Just remember, "99, chopped nuts,"' says Cedric.

Again Bill wanders off, repeating Cedric's order over and over again. But no sooner has he walked a few steps when Cedric cries out, 'Strawberry sauce as well!'

Bill stops and turns around, 'I'll never remember that.'

'Look, Bill, remember 99, chopped nuts, strawberry sauce,' Cedric patiently explains.

Off Bill wanders, saying, '99, nuts, strawberry sauce; 99, nuts, strawberry sauce; 99, nuts, strawberry sauce...'

Half an hour later, Bill comes back with a bag of chips. 'What do you call that!' shrieks Cedric.

'Bag of chips,' says Bill.

'I can see that!' screams the other codger. 'Where's my fucking pie!'

At the barber's

A man walks into a barber's at lunchtime and asks how long it'll be before he can get his hair cut. The barber looks round at his shop full of hirsute customers and replies, 'Two hours.' The man leaves the shop.

Lunchtime the next day and he's back again, asking how long it'll be before he can get his hair cut. Once again the place is rammed, so the barber replies, 'Two hours.' The man walks out.

The next day, same time, he's back for a third time, and once again the answer is two hours.

He walks out – but this time the barber asks a friend to follow him and see where he goes. Twenty minutes pass and the friend returns, grim-faced.

'Well,' asks the barber, 'where does he go?'

'Your house.'

Mountie misunderstanding

An eccentric English colonel met a Canadian Mountie in a bar and expressed an interest in joining Canada's finest. The Mountie explained that there was a traditional initiation ceremony and invited the colonel over to Vancouver the following week.

Once there, the Mounties explained that the initiation involved drinking a whole bottle of Canadian Club whisky, then venturing into the nearby forest to shoot a grizzly bear, before finishing off by making love to an Inuit girl.

The Colonel accepted and, after downing the bottle of Canadian Club, he staggered off in the direction of the forest. An hour later he returned, his clothes torn, battered and bruised and covered in blood.

'Okay,' he said, 'where's this Inuit girl I've got to shoot?'

One-upmanship

Four businessmen are playing golf. At the first hole, the first man says, 'I'm so important that my company has bought me this nuclear-powered mobile phone so I can keep in touch all over the world.'

At the second hole, the next man says, 'I'm so important to my company that they have sewn my mobile phone to the palm of my hand.'

At the third hole, the third man starts mumbling away to himself. 'Who are you talking to?' ask the other three, to which he replies, 'I'm so important to my company that they've inserted a miniature mobile phone in my lip.'

They get to the next hole, when all of a sudden the fourth man makes a dash for the bushes. The others wait for ten minutes before going to check if he's alright. They peep through the bushes and find him squatting with his trousers around his ankles. 'Oh, sorry,' they apologise.

'It's okay,' the fourth man replies, 'I'm just expecting a fax.'

Honeymoon etiquette

A nervous young bride became irritated by her husband's lusty advances on their wedding night, and reprimanded him severely.

'I demand proper manners in bed,' she declared, 'just as I do at the dinner table.'

Amused by his wife's formality, the groom smoothed his rumpled hair and climbed quietly between the sheets. 'Is that better?' he asked, with a hint of a smile.

'Yes,' replied the girl, 'much better.'

'Very good, darling,' the husband whispered. 'Now would you be so kind as to pass your tits.'

Prankster not amused

Paul Daniels is doing tricks on live TV, but he runs out of 'magic' with five minutes to go, so he asks if anyone in the audience has any tricks. A guy puts his hand up and Paul invites him onto the stage. Paul then asks him what he needs for the trick. The bloke replies, 'Your assistant – the lovely Debbie – and a table.'

Paul is slightly confused but gets the table and Debbie anyway. The guy then bends Debbie over the table and starts rodding her from behind. Paul, slightly concerned about the situation, says, 'What are you doing? This isn't a trick.'

'I know,' replies the bloke, 'but it's fucking magic.'

Satan gets stumped

One beautiful Sunday morning, the tiny town of Smithvale wakes up and goes to church. Before the service starts, most of the congregation have seated themselves. They're all nattering to their neighbours when – shazam! – Satan himself appears at the altar in a flash of flame.

Naturally the church erupts in chaos, with people fleeing left, right and centre – except for Bill Scroggs. Beelzebub is confused. He walks up to Bill and says, 'Don't you know who I am?'

Bill replies, 'Aye, I do.'

Bewildered, Satan asks, 'So you aren't afraid of me, then?'

'No I'm not,' says Bill calmly.

By now, Satan's melon is twisted beyond all recognition. 'Why the hell not?' the Dark Overlord enquires.

'Because I've been married to your sister for 25 years,' Bill replies.

Blighted by verse

Tony Blair is being shown around a hospital. Towards the end of his visit, he strolls into a ward whose patients appear to have no obvious sign of injury. He greets the first patient and the chap replies, 'Fair fa' your honest, sonsie face, Great chieftain o' the puddin-race! Aboon them a' ye tak your place, Painch, tripe, or thairm: Weel are ye wordy of a grace, As lang's my arm.'

Baffled, Tony simply effects his usual big stupid grin and moves on to the next patient, who instantly pipes up, 'Wee, sleekit, cowrin', tim'rous beastie, O, what a panic's in thy breastie! Thou need na start awa sae hasty, Wi' bickering brattle!

I wad be laith to rin an' chase thee, Wi' murd'ring pattle!'

Tony turns to the doctor. 'Forgive me, are we in the mental ward?' he asks.

'No,' replies the doctor, 'Burns unit.'

How old am I?

An old man took pride in his appearance, and didn't look anywhere near his actual age of 74. He walked into a pub one afternoon and ordered a pint. When the barman gave the man his pint, the old man said, 'Guess how old I am!'

The barman thought for a while and said, '50?'

The old man laughed. 'I'm 74,' he said proudly.

'Surely not,' said the barman, 'you don't look a day over 50.'

Feeling extremely happy the man drank his pint and wandered off towards the chemist. In the chemist, he did the same thing. 'Tell me,' he said to the woman behind the counter, 'how old do you think I am?'

The woman thought, and said eventually, '50?'

'No!' laughed the man.

'I'm 74!'

'Wow!' exclaimed the woman. 'You look great.'

The man paid for his goods and left. Later, while he was standing at the bus stop, an old woman approached and stood next to him.

'Tell me,' he said again. 'How old do you think I am?'

'Oh, I'm good at these games,' said the woman. 'But what you'll have to do is get your willy out.'

The man looked around, and couldn't see anyone else, so he pulled down his trousers and got his willy out. The woman grabbed it and began to rub. This went on for about five minutes until she said, 'Right – now let me guess.' She pondered for a while, then said, '74!'

Amazed, the man questioned her, 'How on Earth did you know that?'

'I was standing behind you in the chemist's,' she said.

Police arrested two kids yesterday...

...one was drinking battery acid, the other was eating fireworks. They charged one and let the other one off.

The two hikers

After hiking through the woods for hours, two women come to a stream. Unable to cross, they decide to look for a narrower part – and soon they come across an old bridge spanning the water. Deciding that the bridge is safe, the two women proceed to walk over it. Halfway across, one woman stops. 'You know,' she says, 'I've always wanted to be like a bloke and piss off a bridge.'

'Well I don't see anyone around,' replies her friend. 'Now's your chance.'

So the first woman pulls down her hiking shorts and backs over to the side of the bridge. But just as she begins to urinate, she looks over her shoulder.

'Holy shit!' she exclaims, 'I just pissed on a canoe!'

Alarmed, the second woman peeks at the stream. 'That wasn't a canoe,' she says. 'That was your reflection.'

The Good Samaritan

Bob goes into the public restroom and sees a man standing next to the urinal. The man has no arms. As Bob's standing there, taking care of business, he wonders to himself how the poor wretch is going to take a leak. Bob finishes and starts to leave when the man asks Bob to help him out. Being a kind soul, Bob says, 'Okay, sure.'

'Can you unzip my zipper?' asks the man.

'Okay,' says Bob.

'Can you pull it out for me?' asks the man.

'Uh, yeah, okay,' says Bob. So he pulls it out. It's covered in all kinds of mould and bumps, with hair clumps, rashes, moles, scabs and scars, and it reeks something awful. Then the guy asks Bob to point it for him, and Bob points it for him. Bob then shakes it, puts it back in and zips up the man's flies for him.

'Thanks, I really appreciate it,' the man tells Bob.

'No problem,' says Bob,

'I hope you don't mind me asking, but what's wrong with your penis?'

The guy pulls his arms out of his shirt. 'I don't know,' he says, 'but I sure as hell ain't touching it.'

A sergeant major...

...stomps into a brothel, 'I am here for a woman!' he shouts. He is immediately escorted upstairs to the best girl, where he disrobes and booms, 'Woman, I've been in the army 30 years and I'm a master of my mind and body! DICK! 'TEN-HUT!'

Immediately, his penis is fully erect.

'Sweet mama! How did you do that?' asks the prostitute.

'Been in the army 30 years,' shouts the sarge, 'and I'm a master of my mind and body! DICK! AT EASE!' And with that, his penis goes limp. The prostitute is amazed and requests another demonstration.

'Wilco,' he hollers, 'been in the army 30 years and I'm a master of my mind and body! DICK! 'TEN-HUT!'

Again, his cock stands proud. 'DICK! AT EASE!' he booms, but when he glances down, he's still hard as a rock.

'Apparently you didn't HEAR me soldier! DICK! AT EASE!'

Still nothing happens. 'I'm giving you one last chance,' he fumes, 'DICK! AT EASE!'

But nothing happens, so he grabs his penis and starts tugging furiously. 'What the Hell's going on?' asks the prostitute.

'Stand back, ma'am!' he shouts. 'For disobeying a direct order, this soldier's getting a dishonourable discharge!'

Wild West medicine

There were two church-going women gossiping in front of a store when a cowboy rode up. He tied up in front of the saloon, walked around behind his horse and slapped his mouth full on its rectum.

One of the stunned women cried, 'That's disgusting, why did you do that?'

'I've got chapped lips,' replied the cowpoke.

Confused, the woman continued, 'Does that make them feel better?'

'No,' said the cowboy, 'but it sure as hell stops me from licking them.'

The dead man's dick

A coroner is working late at the hospital, and as he's preparing Mr Smith for the crematorium he makes an amazing discovery: Smith had the longest cock he's ever seen. After surveying it in awe for a few minutes, the man comes to a decision. 'I'm sorry Mr Smith,' he says to the corpse, 'but I can't send you off to be cremated with such a tremendous cock.'

And with that, the coroner takes his scalpel and quickly removes the dead man's spam javelin. Rushing over to the genito-urinary department, he asks his surgeon pal to perform a penis transplant on him. Upon waking from the operation, the coroner stuffs his tuberous prize into his briefs and goes home.

His wife opens the door, and immediately asks where he's been. 'Honey! Don't worry!' he says, opening his fly, 'I have something wonderful to show you.'

'Oh my God!' she screams, 'Smith's dead!'

Camel talk

A mother and baby camel are talking one day when the baby camel asks, 'Mum – why have I got these huge three-toed feet?'

The mother replies, 'Well, son, when we trek across the desert your toes will help you to stay on top of the soft sand.'

'Okay,' says the lad. A few minutes later the son asks, 'Mum, why have I got these great long eyelashes?'

'They're there to keep the sand out of your eyes on the trips through the desert.'

'Thanks, Mom,' replies the li'l camel.

After a short while, the son returns and asks, 'Mum, why have I got these great big humps on my back?'

The mother, now a little impatient with the boy, replies, 'They're there to help us store water for our long treks across the desert, so we can go without drinking for long periods.'

'That's great, Mum,' says the baby camel, thinking for a minute. 'So what are we doing in Whipsnade?'

Dinner's ready!

A sex-starved housewife decided she'd gone without for too long, so she stripped naked and waited upstairs for her husband to return. As soon as he shut the door behind him, she came out of hiding and slid down the banister. Shocked, her husband asked, 'What are you doing, woman?'

To which she replied, 'Warming up your dinner.'

Mice in love

There were two mice named Josephine and Earnest. They were in love and used to visit one another every day to have a coffee. They lived a long way apart so it was a big trek every afternoon. One day it was Josephine's turn to visit Earnest, and she was merrily trotting along, humming a little song to herself. She was running a little late so she decided to use the shortcut across the field. She was a little way in when she heard a faint noise in the distance.

She paused and listened. 'Whirrrrrrrr chunka chunka whirrrrrrrr chunka chunka.'

The noise was getting progressively louder. She thought to

herself, 'That's strange...' and she continued on her way, a bit faster this time.

Before long the noise was overbearing. The ground started to vibrate. She stopped running and looked around just in time to see sharp blades coming down on top of her. She screamed, but her screams were lost in the piercing noise. She was picked up, tossed around, scraped, cut and beaten, until she was just a quivering pulp. Only then was it over.

She crawled bleeding to Earnest's house and dragged herself to the door. Earnest rushed out and held her in his arms. 'Darling,' said her mouse lover. 'What happened to you?'

'Earnest,' she whispered, 'it was awful. I've been reaped.'

Three strikes you're out

A farmer just got married and was going home on his wagon pulled by a team of horses. When one of the horses stumbled, he said, 'That's once.'

Then it stumbled again. He said, 'That's twice.'

Later, it stumbled a third time. This time, he didn't say anything, just pulled out a shotgun and shot the horse dead.

His wife cried out and started to yell at him. The farmer turned to her and said, 'That's once.'

The bus driver and the baby

A woman got on a bus, holding a baby. 'Hot damn!' exclaimed the driver. 'That's the ugliest baby I've ever seen!' In a huff, the woman slammed her fare down and tramped to the rear of the bus, where she sat, fuming.

The man seated next to her sensed she was agitated and asked what was wrong.

'The bus driver insulted me!' explained the woman.

The man sympathised. 'He's a public servant,' he said. 'He shouldn't say things to insult the passengers.'

'You're right!' said the woman. 'I think I'll go back up there and give him a piece of my mind!'

'That's a good idea,' the man said. 'Let me hold your monkey.'

Paging Dr Freud

A man goes to a psychiatrist. 'Doc,' he says, 'I keep having these alternating recurring dreams. First I'm a marquee; then I'm a wigwam; then I'm a marquee; then I'm a wigwam again. It's driving me crazy. What's wrong with me?'

'It's very simple,' the doctor replies. 'You're two tents.'

What do women get...

...that's long and hard when they marry a Greek?

A surname.

No betting man

A chap walks into a butcher's and asks for a pound of mince. 'No problem, mate,' says the butcher. 'In fact

I will give you £1,000 if you can reach the meat hanging above your head.'

'A thousand pounds, you say...' The guy thinks about it then says, 'Sorry, I'm not even going to try.'

'Why the hell not? This is a great offer!' says the butcher.

'Sorry Mr Butcher, but the steaks are just too high.'

Complimentary check-up

A middle-aged woman is at home, merrily jumping up and down on her bed and squealing with delight. Her husband arrives home from work, walks in and is astounded at what he sees. 'Do you have any idea how ridiculous you look?' he shouts. 'What the hell's the matter with you?'

'I just came from the doctor,' replies his wife. 'He says I have the breasts of an 18-year-old!'

'Oh really,' says her husband, 'and what did the old coot say about your 40-year-old arse?'

'Strangely enough,' replies his wife, 'your name never came up...'

The crossword fanatics

Two blokes are sitting in a pub having a pint. One of them is doing the crossword. 'Eight letters,' he reads out, 'centre of female pleasure.'

'Clitoris,' says the other.

'Do you know how to spell that?' asks the crossword fan.

'No,' replies the other. 'You should have asked me last night – it was on the tip of my tongue.'

Pre-paid plan

A guy goes to a brothel. He selects a girl, pays her £200 up front and gets undressed. She's about to take off her sheer blue negligée, when the fire alarm rings.

She runs out of the room, with his £200 still in her hand. He quickly grabs his clothes and runs out after her. He's searching the building, but the smoke gets too heavy, so he runs outside looking for her.

By this time, the firemen are there. He sees one of them and asks, 'Did you see a beautiful blonde, in a sheer blue negligée, with £200 in her hand?'

The fireman says, 'No!'

The guy then says, 'Well if you see her, screw her. It's paid for.'

Proud father

A man has six children and is very proud of his achievement. He is so proud of himself that he starts calling his wife 'Mother of Six' in spite of her objections.

One night they go to a party. The man decides that it's time to go home, and wants to find out if his wife is ready to leave as well.

He shouts at the top of his voice, 'Shall we go home now Mother of Six?'

His wife, finally fed up with her husband, shouts back, 'Any time you're ready, Father of Four!'

A materialist lawyer?

There was a lawyer who drove his shiny new Merc to work one day. He parked it in front of the company where he worked to show it off to all his lawyer colleagues. As he got out, a lorry hit the door and ripped it right off.

The driver stopped and ran to the lawyer saying 'Are you alright, are you alright?'

The lawyer, now furious, started to scream and berate the driver. 'What the hell do you think you are doing? This is my brand new Mercedes... You know,

I am a lawyer and I am going to sue you for all you are worth!'

Then a policeman ran up to the scene and said to the lawyer, 'Calm down! You lawyers are so materialistic it's disgusting! Don't you know, when that lorry ripped your door off, it took your arm with it?'

The lawyer looked down and saw his left arm missing and said, 'Oh God... my Rolex!'

The squaddie's bonus

Upon returning from the Falklands War, General Thompson calls his three toughest fighters to his office for a debrief. 'Gentlemen, I want you to know your efforts were appreciated,' the General begins. 'So the top brass have decided to let each of you choose two parts of your body to be measured, then be given £100 for each inch between those points. Fair?' The men nod slowly – before the first, a Commando, steps up. 'Sah!' he shouts, 'I choose the top of me head to me toes, sah!'

Nodding, the General pulls out his tape measure. 'Very good,' he barks. 'That's 70 inches... which comes to £7,000.'

An expert sniper is next up. 'Sah! I'm going for the tip of one hand to the other, sah!' he shouts.

'Even better,' replies the General, measuring his outstretched arms. 'That's 72 inches, which comes to £7,200.'

Finally, an explosives expert in the infantry steps forward. 'Sah!' he shouts, 'I'll go for the tip of my dick to my balls, sah!'

The General frowns. 'That's a strange request, soldier,' he

mutters, 'but drop your trousers.' He bends down, tape measure in hand, but quickly stands up again. 'My God, soldier!' he cries. 'Where are your balls?'

The soldier smiles. 'Falkland Islands, sah.'

Sex gift

Adam was talking to his friend at the bar, and he said, 'I don't know what to get my wife for her birthday – she has everything, and besides, she can afford to buy anything she wants, so I'm stuck.'

His friend said, 'I have an idea! Why don't you make up a certificate saying she can have 60 minutes of great sex, any way she wants it. She'll probably be thrilled.' Adam decided to take his friend's advice.

The next day at the bar his friend said, 'Well? Did you take my suggestion?'

'Yes, I did,' Adam replied.

'Did she like it?'

'Oh yes! She jumped up, thanked me, kissed me on the forehead and ran out the door, yelling, "I'll be back in an hour!"'

Bad reception

A blonde went to an electronics store and asked, 'How much is this TV?'

The salesman said, 'Sorry, we don't sell to blondes.'

The next day she came back as a brunette. She asked the salesman how much the TV was. He said, 'Sorry, we don't sell to blondes.'

The next day she came back as a redhead and asked the salesman how much the TV was. He said, 'Sorry we don't sell to blondes.'

She replied, 'I came in here as a brunette and a redhead. How do you know I am a blonde?'

'Because that is not a TV, it's a microwave.'

My what a lovely cucumber

A beautiful woman loved to garden, but couldn't seem to get her tomatoes to turn red. One day while taking a stroll she came upon a neighbour who had the most beautiful garden full of huge red tomatoes. The woman asked the gentleman, 'What do you do to get your tomatoes red?'

The gentleman responded, 'Well, twice a day I stand in front of my tomato garden and expose myself, and my tomatoes turn red from blushing so much.'

The woman was so impressed, she decided to try doing the same thing to her tomato garden to see if it would work. So twice a day for two weeks she exposed herself to her garden hoping for the best.

One day the gentleman was passing by and asked the woman, 'By the way, how did you make out? Did your tomatoes turn red?'

'No,' she replied, 'but my cucumbers are enormous.'

Overheard ... in a London cab

A butter boy: A driver who has only recently earned the right to call himself a 'cabbie'.

The gasworks: The place you and I would normally call the Houses of Parliament.

Mush: An owner/driver.

A bilk: One of the minority who spoil things for everyone by running off without paying.

A legal: Tight-fisted type who finds tipping impossible.

Droshki: Sounds foreign and exotic, but really it's just a black cab.

Hair dryer: Jocular description for the hated hand-held radar speed device.

Bowler hat: A city gent.

The Oil Rig: The Lloyd's Building in the City of London.

The Wedding Cake: London's Queen Victoria memorial.

Icory: Heaven knows why, but it's the taxi meter.

Scab: Even more reprehensible than a 'bilk', this lowly creature is a mini-cab driver.

A roader: A long job.

A shit: A short job.

A wrong'un: Similar to a 'shit' – especially unwelcome from fares at airports.

Overheard ... in the Army

X'd: Annoyed. From 'cross'. Hence 'Triple X'd' – even crosser.
On scotches: Walking. Lord only knows why.
Comics: Not the Beano, not Morecambe and Wise, but maps.
Muzzy: As a newt.
Twang your wire: Solitary sexual entertainment.
A wet weekend: Sex (on leave) with a partner who is menstruating.
Snafu: Yankee WWII acronym – 'Situation normal, all fucked up'.
Load of reg: Bollocks. From 'regimental', or a stickler for discipline.
Honey: Unappetizing combination of shit and piss, familiar to latrine cleaners.
To have a shellfish on the beach: To have a crab scuttle across your loins.
Gum-bumper: A sergeant prone to shouting, whose gums, presumably, bump together constantly.
On a 48: Forty-eight hours of weekend leave.
Film for your brownie: Izal and Andrex – a double bill of great 'films'.

Overheard ... in Australia

Apple-islander: A resident of Tasmania.
Banana bender: A resident of Queensland.
Bludger: A lazy person.
Comfort station: A toilet, fittingly.
Crow-eater: A resident of Southern Australia.
Dag: Pieces of dried sheep shit. Also a handy insult.
Floater: A dish consisting of a meat pie immersed in soup.
Franger: A condom.
'G'day, Blue': A perverse but standard greeting applied to anyone who possess red or ginger hair.
Manchester: Not just a city, but also a pile of laundry.
One-pot screamer: A man who can't hold his drink.
Sand-groper: A resident of Western Australia.
Slygrogging: The practice of drinking after hours.
Thongs: Not a piece of dodgy groin-wear popular with the lead singer from Cameo, but a pair of flip-flops.
Underground mutton: A plate of rabbit.

Overheard … the boys in blue

Black rats: Bubonic plague carriers. Also, traffic police.

'We had him across the pavement': We caught chummy in the act of stealing.

'In the bin': In prison.

Dippers: Funfare-themed term for pickpockets.

Toms: Ladies of the night.

Blaggers: Armed chummy.

Woodentops: Constables on the beat; a kids' TV programme in the Fifties.

Probbys: Probationary policemen and women.

Plonk: Derogatory term for a female officer. Nothing whatsoever to do with cheap wine.

Guv'nor: An Inspector. Used to very good effect by Carter in The Sweeney.

A producer: Not a Mel Brooks film, but the order to show all driving documents at your local cop shop.

Old sweat: An ageing, run-down police constable.

Polacc: An accident involving a police car and a member of the general public.

To bag someone: A breathalyser test.

Stick/peg: Truncheon.

To stick someone: To hit them with the aforementioned wooden implement.

Overheard … at the racecourse

Carpet: Rug-like description of 3/1 odds.

Connections: People closely involved with the horse, especially the owner and the trainer.

Ear'ole: Odds of 6/4.

Faces: People with inside information. Nothing to do with Rod Stewart.

Headquarters: Newmarket.

Jolly: Cheery nom de plume of the favourite.

Layers: The bookmakers.

Monkey: £500 in real money.
Pony: £25.
Rag: A horse with little chance of winning.
Steamer: A heavily backed nag.
Plum: £1,000.
Double carpet: Odds of 33/1.
Canadian plus: Twenty-six bets on five selections.
Heinz plus: Fifty-seven bets on six selections.
Patent: Seven bets on three selections.
Trixie: Four bets on three selections.
Yankee plus: Eleven bets on four selections.

Overheard ... in South Africa

Gentoo: A whore. In the 19th century, a ship called the Gentoo
landed in South Africa. Much to the resident Afrikaners' delight
it was full of prostitutes.

Soutpeil: An English South African who can't decide what country
he is from. Soutpeil translates as 'salt penis', referring to the fact
that the man has one foot in each country, leaving his knob
dangling in the ocean.

Koffie-moffie: Disparaging term for an airline steward.

Witblits: A very strong, clear spirit, brewed at home and made from
grapes which have already been pressed for wine-making.

A chalkdown: What happens when teachers go on strike.

The ore: Nothing to do with gold mines, this is the nickname for
the Johannesburg police force.

Opstoker: A troublemaker.

Esel: Originally a type of donkey, but now applied to anyone
considered to be of limited intelligence. As in 'That Koffie-moffie
spilt beer all over me, the fucking esel.'

Goosie: How Afrikaners refer to their girlfriends when insulting
them. A goosie is a partner who is willing to dole out sexual
favours.

The hairybacks: How the black population often refer to the
notoriously hirsute Afrikaners.

Overheard ... at a London market

The joint: The pitch, where the trader builds his stall each day.

A schnorrer: 'How much is this? How much is that?' asks the schnorrer, before wandering off empty-handed half an hour later because everything is too expensive.

Sore one: A bad day – everybody with a stall has them.

Cavalry: A customer who spends freely on a 'sore one' (qv), thus 'rescuing' the trader.

A dog: Not man's best friend, but a rotter who steals a traders' pitch.

Grass: Asparagus.

Jack and Jill: It's where you find the money, because it's the till.

On the penny: Cheap.

Richard: Confusingly, a young lady. From Richard the Third – bird.

Dlo: Imaginatively pronounced 'dee-lo', it's old stock – 'old' spelt backwards.

Jekyll: Another rhymer, it means 'snide', which in turn also means bad stock. Don't buy it!

Overheard ... at Eton

A wet bob: One who volunteers to spend time afloat, oar in hand, rowing upriver.

Oppidan: A thicko, who's presence can only be explained by rich parents.

Pop: A club of the most popular boys, elected by the previous year's most popular boys.

Div: A lesson.

Half: A term, three in a year.

Slack Bob: A serving, volleying, umpire-berating, tennis-playing pupil.

Chambers: A pause between 'divs' to enjoy a bottle of milk.

Dame: Also known as Matron, she's the Hattie Jacques-dimensioned boil-lancer and cough medicine dispenser everyone tries to avoid.

M'tutor: Not an African city, but your housemaster.

Tap: The school pub.

Tardy book: Contains the names of all those boys to be punished by caning, lines or public tweaking for various offences.

In the bill: When you're up to your neck in trouble.

Mess: A group of students with whom you take tea.

New tit: Not a third breast, but a new boy.

Overheard ... behind bars

Lamp: One who scoffs at personal hygiene. From paraffin lamp – tramp.

Crib/Peter/Home: They're all your bed.

White Windsor: A lowly type, from the prison issue soap – the quality lag buys his own.

In for touching a dog's arse: TDA – taking cars and driving them away.

Screw: A warder, but that's 'Guv' to you, Sonny Jim.

Kitting: Passing bad cheques.

Joey: In some jails a grass, in others an illicit smuggled package.

On the out: The condition of not being behind bars.

Civvies: Filter-tipped smoking products.

A cell spin: When the authorities rearrange your furniture, in search of things you shouldn't be in possession of.

Having a pop: Leave before you're supposed to.

In patches: Wearing the stripes awarded to someone who's had a pop and failed.

Nitto!: Careful, everyone. Warders!

Turtle: Shy chap who rarely strays from his cell.

Overheard ... cowboys

Airin' the paunch: Getting rid of a few excess calories by vomiting.

Axle grease: Butter for your sarnie.

Bar dog: Moustachioed bartender.

Bean master: The cook, also known as the dough wrangler.

Brown gargle: Good coffee.

Belly wash: Bad coffee.

Black-eyed Susan: A six-gun.

Bob wire: Cowboy's attempt at saying barbed wire.

Can openers: Spurs.

Hair case: Hat.

Neck oil: Whiskey.

Necktie party: Not a posh do, but a public hanging.

Prairie oyster: A fried calf's testicle.

Sand: Courage, as in grit.

Top waddy: Highly-skilled, Wayne-esque cowboy.

Whistleberries: Beans.

Overheard ... in the Navy

Figmo: Acronym indicating annoyance at imminent departure. Stands for, 'Fuck it, got my orders.'

Black gang: The chaps in the engine room, from days when coal was the navy's fuel of choice.

A banjo: Not a five-stringed instrument, but a bit of a ruck.

Elastoplasts: Used to be known as sawbones, but not any more. They're the medics.

Laced: To indulge in a tot too many from the grog barrel.

Shit on a shingle: A popular breakfast dish, involving minced beef atop toast.

Monty: Gay. From Montego Bay.

Keel: An officer may express dissatisfaction with his men by administering a kick up the keel.

Pompey: Portsmouth.

Guz: Devonport.

Samantha Fox: Not the stacked 1980s pin-up, but the clap, or pox, with which her surname unfortunately rhymes.

A full house: Painful combination of gonorrhea and syphilis. At the same time.

Boards: The officers, from those things they wear on their shoulders.

HMS Pepperpot: HMS Penelope, which has been hit so many times she's riddled with holes.